WHO WE ARE

WHO WE ARE

On Being
(*and Not Being*)
a Jewish American Writer

edited by

DEREK RUBIN

 Schocken Books, New York

All rights reserved under International and Pan-American
Copyright Conventions. Published in the United States by
Schocken Books, a division of Random House, Inc., New York,
and simultaneously in Canada by Random House of Canada
Limited, Toronto. Distributed by Pantheon Books, a division of
Random House, Inc., New York.

Schocken and colophon are registered trademarks of Random
House, Inc.

Owing to space limitations, additional copyright information
follows Permissions Acknowledgments.

Library of Congress Cataloging-in-Publication Data

Who we are : on being (and not being) a Jewish American writer /
edited with an introduction by Derek Rubin.
p.   cm.
ISBN 0-8052-4239-2
1. Jewish authors—United States—Biography.   2. Jews—
United States—Intellectual life.   I. Rubin, Derek, 1954–

PS129.W46 2005
810.9'8924—dc22   2004059044

Printed in the United States of America

First Edition

9 8 7 6 5 4 3 2 1

To Marijke

CONTENTS

Contents

DEREK RUBIN

Introduction

A large library could easily be filled with books and articles on the work of the great Jewish American luminaries, such as Saul Bellow, Cynthia Ozick, E. L. Doctorow, and Philip Roth. And in recent years the body of criticism on subsequent generations of Jewish American writers has been growing rapidly. Recurrent questions in much of this critical work are: What is it that makes this fiction Jewish? How is it that Jewish writers who emerged after the Second World War spoke to the imagination of so many American readers at large and became so central to American literature? Is there a future for Jewish American literature after the great postwar writers? And what is the place of Jewish writing in contemporary multicultural America? Given the contentiousness of these tangled issues, it's not surprising that critics and scholars have felt the need to have their say. What is surprisingly lacking, and long overdue, however, is a substantial and representative collection of essays *by* fiction writers themselves that sheds light on what it means to *them* to be Jewish and a writer in America. This book aims to fill that gap by bringing these writers out on stage and giving them a voice in this debate.

Over the years a number of Jewish American writers have written essays reflecting on the state of Jewish writing in America or on their own personal experiences as writers. However, most of these remain uncollected, and even the few that have been published in one-author collections remain dispersed and available only to a select readership. This anthology brings together essays by twenty-nine major Jewish American fiction writers. Approximately half of the essays were written especially for this book. A number of those that were previously published have been thoroughly revised and updated by their authors for publication in this volume.

Although by no means exhaustive, this anthology presents essays by a wide range of writers who represent the rich diversity of Jewish American fiction in the second half of the twentieth century. The lives of the contributors, whose essays are arranged chronologically by date of birth, span much of the last century. The anthology opens with Saul Bellow's self-deprecatory account of his unbridled literary ambition as a young writer starting out in Chicago in the 1930s and ends with Yael Goldstein's discussion of how the Bible stories she learned at the Orthodox schools she attended in the 1980s and 1990s shaped her as a writer. Geographically the essays range from Hollywood, where Leslie Epstein describes growing up in an affluent assimilated environment, to the Bronx, where Grace Paley reminisces about growing up on a street full of children. The religious spectrum of American Jewry is also represented here: at one end we have Pearl Abraham, who offers a vivid description of her rebellion against her Hasidic background, and at the other we find Robert

Cohen, who humorously traces his ill-defined sense of Jewishness back to his upbringing as a "suburban Reform kid, New Jersey division."

Yet, in spite of these authors' generational, geographical, and religious diversity, placed side by side in a single volume their essays speak to each other in fascinating and often unexpected ways. As a means of locating themselves on the literary map, several writers refer to the same famous claims about Jewish American writing that have been advanced by other writers and critics over the years. Some of the authors actually refer to fellow writers who appear in this anthology. They describe reading each other's work and walking in each other's footsteps. Binnie Kirshenbaum uses Brenda Patimkin in Philip Roth's *Goodbye, Columbus*, which was published in the same year she was born, as her point of reference in exploring her journey from affluent suburbia to the life of a writer in New York City; Jonathan Wilson describes vividly the impact of *Portnoy's Complaint* on his own development as a writer—to cite just two examples among many.

Other writers in the anthology measure their aspirations and positions as Jewish writers in America today against their predecessors. Allegra Goodman rejects what she takes to be the facile self-deprecatory stance toward their Jewishness of writers like Saul Bellow and Philip Roth, who have become institutionalized, mainstream *American* writers, and have thereby been cut off from their ethnic roots. Rather, she believes that at the risk of seeming parochial, Jewish writers of her generation "must recapture the spiritual and the religious dimension of Judaism" in their fiction. Jonathan Rosen, on the other hand, started out as a writer aspiring to emulate his Jewish American forerunners—like Bellow, whom he particularly admired—by continuing their great literary journey outward into America. He soon found, however, that the country had changed and that in the age of multiculturalism one discovered America by exploring one's own ethnic, religious, or cultural particularity. And Robert Cohen, in yet another response to the plight of the younger generation of Jewish American writers, describes how, desperately trying to define himself as a writer in relation to his predecessors (Jewish, American, or a combination thereof, with the added complication of his having an international array of other literary heroes), he came to wonder whether his very need—and inability—to do so might not be what being "post-acculturated" meant.

In addition to sharing common points of reference, the writers in this anthology also respond in competing and complementary ways to a set of shared concerns, highlighting continuities and discontinuities in their views on what constitutes Jewish American literature and in their perception of themselves and others as Jews writing in America. The definitions of Jewish literature offered by the authors in this anthology are rich and diverse. There are those who look to their hybrid experience as Jews in America to define the "Jewishness" of their fiction. Chaim Potok, for example, describes how growing up in the Bronx in the 1930s and 1940s he was exposed to what he calls "core-to-core culture confrontations" between aspects of his Orthodox Jewish background and Western secular humanism. Living between these two worlds led to his artistic and literary creativity and to his explorations of such confrontations in his fictional characters. Max Apple, who grew up in a Yiddish-speaking home, also points to the advantages of living between worlds. He portrays himself as a hybrid inhabited by two complementary identities whom he refers to as Max and Mottele. Through an engaging dialectic between Max, the American, and Mottele, the son of Eastern European immigrants, he describes how his hybridity renders him less dogmatic and more open to new experiences than people who live in one culture or one world. He refers to such people as "ones." As Mottele puts it, "They see one thing; they know one thing. How hard is it for one to be right? One is always right."

Hybrid experience does not, however, characterize only the postimmigrant generation. Living in the margins or between worlds takes many shapes and forms among the younger writers in this anthology. Robert Cohen's tangled, divided sense of self as an acculturated Jew and as an American figured prominently in his struggle to turn himself into a writer and yielded what he conceived as his "Jewish" novel, *The Here and Now*. Tova Mirvis's status as both insider and outsider in the Orthodox Jewish community plays a constitutive role in her novels. Lev Raphael, who grew up with an acute sense of not belonging because he was both gay and the child of Holocaust survivors, discusses the way his writing helped him to reconcile himself to his being different and to the worlds he lived in— the Jewish community and American society at large. Jonathan Wilson recounts how he emigrated from England because he believed that in America, where the Jews were at home, he could become a Jewish writer; in time, however, he discovered that he remains a partial outsider—not as a Jew but as an American writer of British origin. And another immigrant writer, Lara Vapnyar, went from being an outsider in Russia because she was Jewish to not belonging fully in the United States because she was Russian. Vapnyar describes poignantly her subsequent discovery that only in her writing can she feel fully at home—as a Russian, a Jew, and an American.

As Wilson's and Vapnyar's essays suggest, outsidership and insidership are tricky concepts that often overlap and designate intertwined experiences. To Erica Jong, becoming a writer was a means of giving herself class in a WASP-dominated world to which she, being Jewish, could never belong. Yet she realizes that without this very longing she would never have felt the edginess that drives her to write. Moreover, this rootlessness that makes her long for roots, she says, is in itself a quintessential American quality shared by writers and nonwriters, Jews and non-Jews alike. Pearl Abraham describes a similar paradoxical journey. With a strong streak of individualism and an attraction to novels and learning, she did not belong fully in the Hasidic world of her youth. Yet later, when she pursued the ideal of becoming a writer—which to her signified becoming an American—she discovered that she had in fact attained an authentic, antiestablishment Hasidic ideal, only this time dressed in American garb.

Other writers focus less on the American experience per se and more on their own relationship to Jewish history. Leslie Epstein defines Jewish literature as a response to a history of persecution. Thane Rosenbaum, the son of Holocaust survivors, argues that Jewish literature is an attempt to reimagine the tragic endings in Jewish history. He and two other children of survivors, Melvin Jules Bukiet and Art Spiegelman, describe their work as being fueled by the hopeless need to come to grips with their parents' horrifying past, which cast a dark shadow over their lives but to which they would never have access except partially through the imagination. And Johanna Kaplan traces what defines her in the deepest sense as a

Jew and as a writer to the formative family myths of her great-grandfathers—the lofty-minded rabbi of czarist Russia renowned for his good deeds, and the cantonist kidnapped as a child by the Russian government and forcibly baptized. These, together with a profound attraction to the Jewish history of suffering, gave her the phantom characters who one day would inhabit her stories.

For other writers, language and traditional Jewish storytelling play an important role in the definition of Jewish literature. Grace Paley writes about finding her Jewish voice amidst multiple literary influences ranging from Mother Goose and the King James Bible, which she read as a child, to W. H. Auden, with whom she studied poetry as a young adult. She finally managed to clear her Jewish throat, as she puts it, when she sought to give a truthful voice to her characters, which were mostly Jewish and drawn from the New York world she inhabited. Nessa Rapoport and Dara Horn suggest that all Jewish literature is a commentary on the Bible, the essential narrative of the Jewish experience. In their own writing they each attempt to use the language of the ancient religious texts so as to join, as Jewish writers in America, the long history of Jewish religious commentary. And Yael Goldstein dubs herself a "writerly Jew"—one whose Jewishness is defined by the grand Bible stories she knows so intimately because she grew up among them in an Orthodox environment. As a writer, she says, she constantly measures her fiction against these tales narrated in the elevated voice of God that filled her childhood.

If these authors embrace the idea of being identified as Jewish writers, the label remains problematic for many others in this anthology. Saul Bellow scorns the epithet as a senseless badge of tribal pride; he says that he may be considered a Jewish American writer "in much the same way one might be called a Samoan astronomer or an Eskimo cellist or a Zulu Gainsborough expert." To him, becoming a writer meant inventing himself not as a Jew but as an interpreter of *American* urban experience. Cynthia Ozick views the term "Jewish writer," when applied to fiction, as an oxymoron. The Jewish American novel, she argues, is a contradiction in terms because Jewish books are by definition didactic and ethical, whereas novels are premised on the freedom of the unfettered imagination. She rejects the sociological label of "ethnic writer" as restrictive. "No writer should be a moral champion or a representative of 'identity,' " she writes.

In a defense against criticism of his early fiction for its being self-hating and anti-Semitic, Philip Roth, like Ozick, argues that he is not trying to write a sociological study, but to reveal how people think and feel. He claims that he writes about human beings who are essentially Jewish, but he is not making a statement about Jews. E. L. Doctorow and other, younger, writers, such as Rachel Kadish, similarly view the notion of ethnic literatures or ethnic writers as restrictive and reductive. All literature, Doctorow writes, is fundamentally secular and universal. Voicing a view shared by other writers in the anthology, he argues that although one's religious, ethnic, and national background affects what one writes about, *real* writers are unaffiliated individuals concerned with the drama of humanity.

And yet, in spite of their skepticism about being perceived by others or viewing themselves as Jewish writers, some of these writers still subscribe to—and sometimes refer explicitly to—Isaac Bashevis Singer's dictum that every writer must have an address. Ozick views herself as a Jewish writer in the sense that her fiction embodies her connection to the Jewish literary tradition and to Jewish history, in particular the Holocaust. Allegra Goodman, although wary of being pigeonholed, welcomes the label of Jewish writer insofar as it suggests that she writes for fellow Jews in America, who constitute an important community of readers of her work. Rachel Kadish, who reserves the freedom to draw on diverse sources in her fiction, among them her Jewish background, views Singer's proverbial address as just that, an address: "Not destiny, not a cage." Binnie Kirshenbaum, who describes her journey from her suburban, assimilationist background to the "warm embrace" of the Jewish past, takes Singer's dictum to mean that every writer must have "a place where the soul resides." But, she says, her being Jewish, like her being a woman and a New Yorker, constitutes just one aspect of her multifaceted identity. Tova Mirvis, who grew up in an Orthodox community in Memphis, Tennessee, is also happy to consider herself a Jewish writer, just as she is also a Southern writer and a woman writer. And Rebecca Goldstein—who describes herself as five-ninths a Jewish writer because five of the nine stories in her collection *Strange Attractors* are "Jewish"—explores why it is she chooses to write Jewish fiction among the many choices she has.

In looking to the future, several writers in this anthology respond—whether explicitly or implicitly—to Irving Howe's controversial prediction that, as the immigrant experience recedes into the past and a younger generation of Jewish writers emerges, fully acculturated and well integrated into American suburban and middle- and upper-middle-class urban life, so Jewish literature will cease to exist as a rich, distinct presence in the American literary landscape. Alan Lelchuk subscribes to Howe's thesis—at least up to a point—when he says that, now that American Jews are fully integrated into American life, Jewish literature as ethnic literature is dead. Jewish literature will survive, he suggests, only in the most general sense insofar as it is able to draw on the timeless qualities of what he calls the Jewish sensibility. Steve Stern, on the other hand, believes that Jewish American literature does have a future. He offers himself as an example: growing up in a Reform environment that, as he says, could quite easily have been Methodist, he was an unlikely candidate for a place in the Jewish American canon—yet he eventually found himself returning imaginatively to the past to re-create shtetl life in his hometown of Memphis, Tennessee. Jonathan Rosen argues that "there is romance and urgency to life in every generation and . . . every generation has its own story to tell." He describes how his subject as a writer became the irreconcilable tension between the world of "easy prosperity" that he belonged to as a fourth-generation American on his mother's side and that of darkness and tragedy that he inherited from his immigrant father, who lost his parents and many of his family members in the Holocaust.

Reading this anthology, one indeed wonders whether the Jewish immigrant experience is in actual fact a thing of the past. More than anything it is perhaps a rite of passage binding many of the writers represented here. There are those, like Saul Bellow, Grace Paley, and E. L. Doctorow, whose parents or grandparents came to America at the turn of the twentieth century as part of the great wave of Jewish immigration from Eastern Europe. Others, such as Jonathan Wilson and Lara Vapnyar, immigrated more recently themselves. Still others have made what Jonathan Rosen calls the metaphorical journey to the Jewish past by embracing Jewish history or Judaism in their lives and through their writing. One might even extend the metaphor and argue that one of the great attractions of being washed up on the shores of Jewish American literature is that with each new generation of writers, we as readers discover new fictional landscapes and new possibilities for imagining the Jewish experience.

WHO WE ARE

SAUL BELLOW

Starting Out in Chicago

What was it, in the thirties, that drew an adolescent in Chicago to the writing of books? How did a young American of the Depression period decide that he was, of all things, a literary artist? I use the pretentious term literary artist simply to emphasize the contrast between such an ambition and the external facts. A colossal industrial and business center, knocked flat by unemployment, its factories and even its schools closing, decided to hold a World's Fair on the shore of Lake Michigan, with towers, high rides, exhibits, Chinese rickshaws, a midget village in which there was a midget wedding every day and other lively attractions, including whores and con men and fan dancers. There was a bit of gaiety, there was quite a lot of amoebic dysentery. Prosperity did not come back. Several millions of dollars were invested in vain by businessmen and politicians. If they could be quixotic, there was no reason why college students shouldn't be impractical too. And what was the most impractical of choices in somber, heavy, growling, lowbrow Chicago? Why it was to be the representative of

3

beauty, the interpreter of the human heart, the hero of ingenuity, playfulness, personal freedom, generosity, and love. I cannot even now say that this was a bad sort of crackpot to be.

The difference between that time and this is that in the thirties crackpots were not subsidized by their families. They had to go it alone for several years. Or at least until the New Deal (thanks largely to Harry Hopkins) recognized that a great government could *buy* the solution of any problem and opened WPA projects in many parts of the country. I think it possible that Hopkins and Roosevelt, seeing how much trouble unhappy intellectuals had made in Russia, Germany, and Italy between 1905 and 1935, thought it a bargain to pay people twenty-three dollars a week for painting post-office murals and editing guidebooks. This plan succeeded admirably. If I am not mistaken, America continued to follow the Hopkins hint in postwar Europe and perhaps in Vietnam.

I know, for instance, that John Cheever has been conducting creative writing courses at Sing Sing. Writers and criminals have often found that they had much in common. And correctional officials seem to understand, thanks to the psychology courses they take in the universities, that it is excellent therapy to write books and that it may soften the hearts of criminals to record their experiences. Politicians, too, when they fall from power or retire, become writers or university professors. Thus Hubert Humphrey and Dean Rusk became lecturers, Eugene McCarthy became a poet, and an altogether different sort of politician, Spiro Agnew, a novelist. Interviewed not long ago in *The New York Times*, Mr. Agnew said that, having suffered greatly, he felt the need to do something creative to recover his spirits, and was setting to work writing a novel because he was not yet strong enough to do serious mental work.

But I started out to recall what it was like to set one-self up to be a writer in the Midwest during the thirties. For I thought of myself as a Midwesterner and not a Jew. I am often described as a Jewish writer; in much the same way one might be called a Samoan astronomer or an Eskimo cellist or a Zulu Gainsborough expert. There is some oddity about it. I am a Jew, and I have written some books. I have tried to fit my soul into the Jewish-writer category, but it does not feel comfortably accommodated there. I wonder, now and then, whether Philip Roth and Bernard Malamud and I have not become the Hart Schaffner and Marx of our trade. We have made it in the field of culture as Bernard Baruch made it on a park bench, as Polly Adler made it in prostitution, as Two Gun Cohen, the personal bodyguard of Sun Yat-Sen, made it in China. My joke is not broad enough to cover the con-tempt I feel for the opportunists, wise guys, and career types who impose such labels and trade upon them. In a century so disastrous to Jews, one hesitates to criticize those who believe that they are making the world safer by publicizing Jewish achievements. I myself doubt that this publicity is effective.

I did not go to the public library to read the Talmud but the novels and poems of Sherwood Anderson, Theodore Dreiser, Edgar Lee Masters, and Vachel Lind-say. These were people who had resisted the material weight of American society and who proved—what was not immediately obvious—that the life lived in great man-ufacturing, shipping, and banking centers, with their slaughter stink, their great slums, prisons, hospitals, and schools, was also a human life. It appeared to me that this one thing, so intimately known that not only nerves, senses, mind, but also my very bones wanted to put it into words, might contain elements that not even Dreiser, whom I admired most, had yet reached. I felt that I was born to be a performing and interpretive creature, that I was meant to take part in a peculiar, exalted game. For there are good grounds to consider this, together with other forms of civilized behavior and ceremony, a game. At its noblest this game is played, under discipline, before God himself—so Plato said, and others as well. The game can be an offering, a celebration, an act of praise, an acknowledgment also of one's weaknesses and limitations. I couldn't have put it in this manner then. All that appeared then was a blind, obstinate impulse expressing itself in bursts of foolishness. I loved great things. I thought I had a right to think of that exalted game. I was also extremely proud, ornery, and stupid.

I was, in 1937, a very young, married man who had quickly lost his first job and who lived with his in-laws. His affectionate, loyal, and pretty wife insisted that he must be given a chance to write something. Having anyone pay attention to my writing wasn't a real possibility. I am as often bemused as amused at the attention my books have since received. Neglect would have been frightful, but attention has its disadvantages. The career of a critic, when I am feeling mean about it, I sometimes compare to that of a deaf man who tunes pianos. In a more benevolent mood I agree with my late father that people must be encouraged to make as honest a living as they can. For this reason I don't object to becoming a topic. When I visited Japan, I saw that there were prayer-and-fortune-telling papers sold for a penny at each temple. The buyers rolled up these long strips of paper and tied them by threads to bushes and low trees. From the twigs there dangled hundreds of tightly furled papers. I sometimes compare myself to one of these temple trees.

So I sat at a bridge table in a back bedroom of the apartment while all rational, serious, dutiful people were at their jobs or trying to find jobs, writing something. My table faced three cement steps that rose from the cellar into the brick gloom of a passageway. Only my mother-in-law was at home. A widow, then in her seventies, she wore a heavy white braid down her back. She had been a modern woman and a socialist and suffragette in the old country. She was attractive in a fragile, steely way. You felt Sophie's strength of will in all things. She kept a neat house. The very plants, the ashtrays, the pedestals, the doilies, the chairs, revealed her mastery. Each object had its military place. Her apartment could easily have been transferred to West Point.

Lunch occurred at half past twelve. The cooking was good. We ate together in the kitchen. The meal was followed by an interval of stone. My mother-in-law took a nap. I went into the street. Ravenswood was utterly empty. I walked about with something like a large stone in my belly. I often turned into Lawrence Avenue and stood on the bridge looking into the drainage canal. If I had been a dog I would have howled. Even a soft howl would have helped. But I was not here to howl. I was here to interpret the world (its American version) as brilliantly as possible. Still I would have been far happier selling newspapers at Union Station or practicing my shots in a poolroom. But I had a discipline to learn at the bridge table in the bedroom.

No wonder a writer of great talent and fine intelligence like John Cheever volunteers to help the convicts with their stories. He knows how it feels to be locked in. Maybe he thinks the prisoners, being already locked in, may as well learn the discipline. It is the most intolerable of privations for people whose social instincts are so highly developed that they want to write novels to be confined in rooms. Nuns fret not, perhaps, but writers do. Bernanos, the French religious novelist, said that his soul could not bear to be cut off from its kind, and that was why he did his work in cafés. Cafés indeed! I would have kissed the floor of a café. There were no cafés in Chicago. There were greasy-spoon cafeterias, one-arm joints, taverns. I never yet heard of a writer who brought his manuscripts into a tavern. I have always taken an interest in the fact that Schiller liked to smell apples when he was writing, that someone else kept his feet in a tub of water. The only person whose arrangements seemed to me worth imitating was the mystic and guru Gurdjieff. Gurdjieff, when he had work to do, set forth from headquarters in Fontainebleau with his disciples in several limousines. They carried hampers with caviar, cold fowl, champagne, cheese, and fruit. At a signal from the master the cars would stop. They would picnic in a meadow, and then, with all his followers around him, Gurdjieff did his writing. This, if it can be arranged, seems to me worth doing.

I am glad to say that I can't remember what I was writing in Ravenswood. It must have been terrible. The writing itself, however, was of no importance. The important thing was that American society and S. Bellow came face to face. I had to learn that by cutting myself off from American life in order to perform an alien task, I risked cutting myself off from everything that could nourish me. But this was the case only if you granted the monopoly of nutrients to this business-industrial, vital, brutal, proletarian, and middle-class city that was itself involved in a tremendous struggle. It was not even aggressively hostile, saying, "Lead my kind of life or die." Not at all. It simply had no interest in your sort of game.

Quite often, in the Hudson belonging to J.J., my brother-in-law, my mother-in-law and I drove to the cemetery. There we tended her husband's grave. Her trembling but somehow powerful, spotty hand pulled weeds. I made trips with a Mason jar to the faucet and made water splotches about the nasturtiums and sweet williams. Death, I thought, Chicago-style, might not be such a bad racket after all. At least you didn't have to drive down Harlem Avenue in rush hour back to the house with its West Point arrangements, with its pages of bad manuscript on the bridge table, and the silent dinner of soup and stew and strudel. After which you and your wife, washing dishes, enjoyed the first agreeable hours of the day.

J.J., my brother-in-law, born Jascha in the old country, practiced law in the Loop. He was a Republican, member of the American Legion, a golfer, a bowler; he drove his conservative car conservatively, took the *Saturday Evening Post*; he wore a Herbert Hoover starched collar, trousers short in the ankle, and a hard straw hat in summer. He spoke in a pure Hoosier twang, not like a Booth Tarkington gentleman but like a real Tippecanoe country dirt farmer. All this Americanism was imposed on an exquisitely oriental face, dark, with curved nose and Turkish cheekbones. Naturally a warm-hearted man, he frowned upon me. He thought I was doing something foreign.

There was an observable parallel between us. As I was making a writer of myself, this exotic man was transforming his dark oriental traits and becoming an American from Indiana. He spoke of Aaron Slick from Punkin' Crick, of Elmer Dub: "Ah kin read writin', but ah can't read readin'." He had served in the Army—my wife wore his 1917 overcoat (too small for me), and J.J. told old, really old, La Salle Street Republican sex jokes about Woodrow Wilson and Edith Bolling. It was common in that generation and the next to tailor one's appearance and style to what were, after all, journalistic, publicity creations, and products of caricature. The queer hunger of immigrants and their immediate descendants for true Americanism has yet to be described. It may be made to sound like fun, but I find it hard to think of anyone who underwent the process with joy. Those incompetents who lacked mimetic talent and were pure buffoons were better off—I remember a cousin, Arkady, from the old country who declared that his new name was now, and henceforth, Lake Erie. A most poetic name, he thought. In my own generation there were those immigrants who copied even the unhappiness of the Protestant majority, embracing its miseries, battling against Mom; reluctant, after work, to board the suburban train, drinking downtown, drinking on the club car, being handed down drunk to the wife and her waiting station-wagon like good Americans. These people martyred themselves in the enactment of roles that proved them genuine—just as madly wretched in marriage as Abe Lincoln and Mary Todd. Cousin Arkady, a clown who sold dehydrated applesauce on the road, giving dry applesauce demonstrations to housewives in small-town department stores, was spared the worst of it. He simply became "Archie," and made no further effort to prove himself a real American.

The point of this brief account, as I see it, is to evoke that mixture of imagination and stupidity with which people met the American Experience, that murky, heavy, burdensome, chaotic thing. I see that my own error, shared with many others, was to seek sanctuary in what corners of culture one could find in this country, there to enjoy my high thoughts and to perfect myself in the symbolic discipline of an art. I can't help feeling that I overdid it. One didn't need as much sanctuary as all that.

If I had to name the one force in America that opposes the symbolic discipline of poetry today as much as brutal philistinism did before World War II, I would say the Great Noise. The enemy is noise. By noise I mean not simply the noise of technology, the noise of money or advertising and promotion, the noise of the media, the noise of miseducation, but the terrible excitement and distraction generated by the crises of modern life. Mind, I don't say that philistinism is gone. It is not. It has found many disguises, some highly artistic and peculiarly insidious. But the noise of life is the great threat. Contributing to it are real and unreal issues, ideologies, rationalizations, errors, delusions, nonsituations that look real, nonquestions demanding consideration, opinions, analyses in the press, on the air, expertise, inside dope, factional disagreement, official rhetoric, information—in short, the sounds of the public sphere, the din of politics, the turbulence and agitation that set in about 1914 and have now reached an intolerable volume. Nadezhda Mandelstam, writing of poets in the Soviet Union, says of the Russian noise: "Nowhere else I believe were people so much deafened as they were here by the din of life—One after another poets fell silent because they could no longer hear their own voices." She adds: "The noise drowned out thought and, in the case of millions, conscience as well."

William Wordsworth, nearly two hundred years ago, expressed his concern over the effects of modern turbulence on poetry. He was right, too. But in the language of my youth—"He didn't know the half of it."

GRACE PALEY

Clearing My Jewish Throat

In the United States writers are often invited by colleges, community centers, churches, synagogues to read from their work or give literary talks or argue political positions on panels. This is a normal way to make a living, to supplement inadequate midlist or no-list royalties.

A couple of months ago my friend, the novelist Jay Cantor, and I were invited to read at the Hebrew Union College in Boston. There were lots of Jews in the audience plus a scattering of whatever else there is. We were applauded generously. As is the custom, listeners then asked questions. These questions, as usual, were not too dissimilar, but because they were asked by different people, they were particular to the questioner and deserved specific answers. I like this kind of audience participation. Some writers don't.

After a short discussion, I noticed a man with a face somewhere between gloomy and grouchy. He raised his hand and called out, "What's so Jewish about what you people do? Are there even Jews in those stories? I never saw Jews like that."

Of course we were offended. Jay pointed out the class and Jewish disposition of so many characters in his novel *Great Neck*, the different politics of the generations. The man and his face were unmoved. I finally said, "Well if you don't see anything Jewish in these stories, I guess you don't. So that's that." He walked out probably happy to be misunderstood by fools.

I wondered then and still do, what did he really want?

•••

In 1959 three volumes of short stories were published to reviews that cheered the authors. They were then told by their publishers that they'd have to write a novel. Short stories were not a popular genre. (The collections, *Tell Me a Riddle*, *Goodbye, Columbus*, and *The Little Disturbances of Man*, are still in print some forty-five years later, still read at homes, libraries, schools.) Obediently Tillie Olsen and I made an honest effort. She labored at Yonondio for years, starting and stopping as life permitted, and it was finally published. I tried for about two years and a hundred pages to make a novel, saw that it was not good, and have written short stories and poems ever since. Philip Roth, equally obedient, was successful, writing the big books so truthfully and well that the Jews were angry at him for at least fifteen years before they became extremely proud. In any event we were all Jews. Of course we hoped that Americans, the regular kind, were listening too.

Saul Bellow, already at the Jewish literary helm, had been steering into American waters for a number of years, singing out certain directions—*Dangling Man*, *The Victim*, *The Adventures of Augie March*, *Seize the Day*. Then Bernard Malamud, more mysterious and simpler, added a darker tone.

...

But how did I become a Jewish writer—if that's the capitalized adjective to describe my work, or maybe only a description of me. It's not because I read Jewish writers as a child, not because Yiddish literature, even in translation, educated my ear. (And there was a wonderful Yiddish literature being written in the twenties and thirties, some of which my grandmother may have known.)

What then? First there was Mother Goose, a major influence for more writers than admit it. It was the first old English American tune that I heard. Soon there was *Hiawatha* by Longfellow, for which I had a fine Indian headdress, then the novels of childhood, which came from the public library. The library allowed me four big books every two weeks. If at supper I mentioned liking one of them a lot, my aunt or sister would probably buy the book for me—books like *Hans Brinker* or *Heidi*. And as those nice childhood years passed, Thomas Wolfe's *Look Homeward, Angel* appeared. My best friend Evie and I read pages of it aloud to one another. We had stolen it from her seventeen-year-old sister. But by then I was beginning to read and hear poetry again. Those high school classes were the only ones I could bear. The poems! The Poems! We read Shelley, Keats, Coleridge, Wordsworth—not yet Blake or Donne or even Whitman. It was also rumored that our English teacher's boyfriend was in the Abraham Lincoln Brigade fighting in Spain for the Spanish Republic. This, for some reason, gave me an even greater understanding of early nineteenth-century Romantic poetry.

At last I began to have a couple of serious literary agemates, and we talked mostly about Joyce, sometimes Proust, Gertrude Stein. It was many years later that I read

Peretz, Agnon, and even Isaac Babel. When I did read them I felt at home, but by then I had been writing stories for a couple of years.

By the time I was seventeen anyway, I cared about the poets themselves. These poets, except for Muriel Rukeyser, a Manhattan person, were quite far from the Bronx—Robinson Jeffers, who said he'd "rather kill a man than a hawk," then Yeats the Irishman, and W. H. Auden, who had just come to the United States. I liked him best, his poetry and his politics. He was teaching a class at the New School. I was working as a second-class typist about ten blocks away, having either quit school or been asked to leave (I've never been sure). But I had great happiness as I walked every Thursday to that class. There were probably about a hundred other students, maybe more. These were lectures. I could hardly understand his Cambridgese. It didn't matter. The presence of the poet was almost enough. One day he invited us to show him our work. I did. I dared. He asked me if I used words like "subaltern" frequently. He pointed out in my poems a couple of first-class British English expressions. "Well, sometimes we say that," I said. I understood that he thought I ought to try writing in American. But I couldn't, despite the fact, the audible fact, that I spoke a pure Bronx, New York American English.

•••

It took me years to clear my Jewish throat. This did not happen until I began to write stories—in my midthirties. The people in my stories were often opinionated, sometimes took over all the telling. These women and children, the men also, were mostly New Yorkers, occasionally Irish or Black, frequently two or three generations of Jews.

They were invented family, neighbors, friends with whom I might have taught school, done lots of politics, local and global, probably worked with them in the mother trade with pleasure, anxiety, innocence, communal exhaustion. I had to let them speak and I noticed that when they were telling the truth, any truth, they spoke well, or at least interestingly. I had gone to school for years to poetry so I understood a little about form.

I had been living among Jews most of my life. Not so singly as my noticeably smart father and noticeably honorable mother. They hardly knew any non-Jews and were often quite shy if they met one. (Like my husband for instance.) Of course I had lived in the mid-twentieth-century Manhattan, New York working world and there were some strangers in it, but still, mostly Jews. This was true about my life, until I began to live in Vermont, about fifteen years ago, and there I sought out the Jewish community, not my own urban community, but present and essential.

As far as literature is concerned, I've mentioned Mother Goose and W. H. Auden, but said nothing yet about Torah—well, actually the King James Version of our own Old Testament (and their new one). This great book was referred to from time to time in our strictly atheistic household. I seem to have always known Genesis. (Had any one of our short extended family read me those Bible stories? Grandmother, two aunts, sister, brother?) Of course we celebrated Passover, my father reading the Hebrew of his Russian bar mitzvah at top speed, slowing down in English to remind us of our responsibility to the stranger because we were strangers so often. I have not forgotten and have told it to my children yearly as we were admonished to do. I will talk about luck in the next few paragraphs but it seems to me that one of the sweetest pieces of luck for American Jewish writers of the last half century is the plain fact that the King James Bible version of the Old Testament, a piece of stunning English literature, is about us—our history (often inaccurate), our bossy (often ridiculous) rules and laws, our songs and psalms (always beautiful), our prophets (nearly always right). What a literary inheritance!

•••

Finally, it appears that many of us are lucky to have been Jewish writers in the last fifty or sixty energetic perceptive years. Of course, for about twenty years it was wonderful to have been a male Jewish writer. But with the cheering intervention of the women's movement, it became lucky to be a female Jewish writer as well.

I use the word "luck" in the same way I used it as a child—that is, I was lucky to live in the Bronx on a street as full of children as there are stars in an eighth of an inch of the nighttime sky. (I thought that one night, looking up.) That is the kind of luck which has to do with the year in which you were born and the day your family, outrunning the Russian pogroms and outsmarting or outdreaming the Germans, said, "We stop here, now, in this great city New York."

Meanwhile (basic luck) my parents talked and talked in Russian and Yiddish—and English—encouraging me to listen to their old words, never trying at secrecy like some of my friends' families. This enabled me to grow up, singing or speaking a couple of strong foreign tunes into English, this extraordinary, hospitable language, which, having given the children of Eastern European Jews such good talking space, is now making room for the Spanish language in its many accents and dialects. And young Asians as well. The women have not had to wait quite so long for the men to speak first as we did.

But listen—from Russia again, another Russia, but with their hard *r*s and no-holds-barred consonants— young people like Gary Shteyngart and Lara Vapnyar have appeared. And a young Israeli woman, Naama Goldstein, decides to write in English and sings into our welcoming English a caustic Hebrew melody.

CYNTHIA OZICK

Tradition and (or Versus) the Jewish Writer

What is a Jewish book? A narrow definition—but also conceptually the widest—would chiefly include the Torah and the Talmud (the Hebrew Bible and the ocean of ethically transformative commentaries), and all other texts that strive to unriddle the Job-like vagaries of the human heart while urging it toward the moral life. A Jewish book is liturgy, ethics, philosophy, ontology. A Jewish book speaks of the attempt to create a world in the image of God while never presuming to image God. A Jewish book, whether it is Maimonides' *Guide for the Perplexed*, written in the twelfth century, or Joseph Soloveitchik's *The Lonely Man of Faith*, written in the twentieth, derives ultimately from the radical commandment in Leviticus, "Love thy neighbor as thyself," and from the still more radical imperative of the Sh'ma, the Unitary Credo.

A Jewish book is didactic. It is dedicated to the promotion of virtue attained through study. It summons obligation. It presupposes a Creator and His handiwork. Is what we nowadays call "the Jewish American novel" likely to be a Jewish book? I think not; indeed, I hope not. If a novel's salient aim is virtue, I want to throw it against the wall. To be a Jew is to be a good citizen, to be responsible, to be charitable, to respond to society's needs. To be a novelist is to be the opposite—to seize unrestraint and freedom, even demonic freedom, imagination with its reins cut loose. The term "Jewish writer" ought to be an oxymoron. That may be why novelists born Jewish, yet drawn wholly to the wild side—Norman Mailer, for instance—are not altogether wrong when they decline to be counted among Jewish writers.

What we want from novels is not what we want from the transcendent liturgies of the synagogue. The light a genuine novel gives out is struck off by the nightmare calculations of art: story, language (language especially), irony, comedy, the crooked lanes of desire and deceit.

The late Irving Howe defined the American Jewish novel (it had not yet become the Jewish American novel) exclusively by its subject matter. And the Jewish novel's only viable subject matter, he insisted, was the great crisis of immigration and its aftermath; when that was played out, as it inevitably would be, the hands of Jewish writers would hang empty. But the complexities of immigration and the conflicts between older and newer generations are hardly confined to Jews, and Willa Cather's immigrant Bohemians had already made claim to that territory; so Howe's self-imploding definition was mistaken from the start.

Still, he was right to predict an absence of Jewish subject matter in America. The profoundly Jewish themes of our time are to be found in Europe (the effect of the mass murder of one-third of the world's Jewish population) and in the restitution of historic Jewish sovereignty in Israel (the twentieth century's most revolutionary event, which only Philip Roth has had the wit to touch on). All other subject matter in the so-called Jewish American novel is, well, American, written in the American language, telling American stories.

Multiculturalism, aka diversity, likes to manufacture "ethnic" fiction. (Ethnic: a sociologist's invention producing fake and demeaning splintering. The word is Greek in origin, and refers to pagans—i.e., to persons neither Jewish nor Christian.) In recent decades, almost all anthologies of fiction, in order to be "inclusive," have occasionally harvested weak prose. This practice, steeped in societal goodwill, results in ill will toward literature. Background, however individuated, is not the same as literature. The living Jewish luminaries of American literature today are Saul Bellow and Philip Roth; no Jewish writer of their generation or the next matches them. Yet their engine and their genius have been toward the making of literature, not the expression of background. If background is powerfully there, it is because, as Isaac Bashevis Singer shrewdly put it, every writer needs to have an address. Isaac Babel had his ebullient Odessa gangsters, but also his stories of pogrom. Sholem Aleichem's shtetl terrors are masked as comedy, Singer's as demonology. Kafka's dread—the Jewish dread of the denial of the right to exist—wears the counterfeit name of justice.

But address means more than geography; it means being addressed by a literary tradition inherent in one's language, meaning the particular history secreted in the very syllables of language. Why else do we speak of Chekhov, Dostoyevsky, Tolstoy as Russian writers, and of Jane Austen and Dickens and George Eliot as English writers, and of Jorge Luis Borges and Gabriel García Márquez as South American writers, and so on? There is an element of instinctive coloration in being Russian, English, Argentinian, Colombian, that emerges in the hidden turns of a work of literature. And what is true of national perception and nuance is true of religious perception and nuance (even if one has given up religious identity).

In this sense—and with conscious respect for the obvious differences in stature and renown—I am a Jewish writer as John Updike is a Christian writer, or as V. S. Naipaul is a Hindu writer, or as Salman Rushdie is a Muslim writer. I have been enchanted by Jewish fable (the golem tale, for instance) or struck to the marrow by Jewish historical catastrophe (as in the little book called *The Shawl*). It is self-evident that any writer's subject matter will emerge from that writer's preoccupations, and it goes without saying that all writers are saturated, to one degree or another, in origins, in history. And for everyone alive in the century we have left behind, the cataclysm of murder and atrocity that we call the Holocaust is inescapable and indelible, and inevitably marks—stains—our moral nature; it is an event that excludes no one.

And yet no writer should be expected to be a moral champion or a representative of "identity." That way lies tract and sermon and polemic, or, worse yet, syrup. When a thesis or a framework—any kind of prescriptiveness or tendentiousness—is imposed on the writing of fiction, imagination flies out the door, and with it the freedom and volatility and irresponsibility that imagination both confers and commands. I have never set out to be anything other than a writer of stories. It disturbs me when, as sometimes happens, I am mistaken for a champion of identity within the spectrum of the currently fashionable multicultural line, with its emphasis on collectivities. "Tradition," to be sure, suggests a collectivity, and invokes a kind of principled awareness; it carries with it a shade of teacherliness, of obligation. Tradition is useful to the writer only insofar as the writer is unconscious of its use; only insofar as it is invisible and inaudible; only insofar as the writer breathes it in with the air; only insofar as principled awareness and teacherliness are absent; only insofar as the writer is deaf to the pressure of the collectivity. What could be more treacherous to the genuine nature of the literary impulse than to mistake the writer for a communal leader, or for the sober avatar of a glorious heritage? No writer is trustworthy or steady enough for that. The aims of imaginative writers are the aims of fiction. Not of community service or communal expectation.

As a writer I feel responsible only to the comely shape of a sentence, and to the unfettered imagination, which sometimes leads to wild places via wild routes. At the same time I reserve my respect for writers who do not remain ignorant of history (a condition equal to autolobotomy), who do not choose to run after trivia, who recognize that ideas are emotions, and that emotions are ideas; and that this is what we mean when we speak of the insights of art.

CHAIM POTOK

Culture Confrontation in Urban America: A Writer's Beginnings

The Bronx of the thirties and forties was my Mississippi River Valley. Yes, I saw poverty and despair, and I remember to this day the ashen pallor on my father's face that night in the late thirties when he told us we would have to go on welfare. And, yes, the streets were on occasion dark with gang violence and with the hate that had made the sea journey from the anti-Semitic underbelly of Europe. But there were books and classes and teachers; there were friends with whom I invented street games limited only by the boundaries of the imagination. And alone, on a concrete and asphalt Mississippi, I journeyed repeatedly through the crowded sidewalks and paved-over backyards, the hallways of the brick apartment houses, the hushed public libraries, dark movie houses, candy stores, grocery stores, Chinese laundries, Italian shoe-repair shops, the neighborhoods of Irish, Italians, blacks, Poles—journeys impelled by eager curiosity and a hunger to discover my sense of self, my place in the tumult of the world. I was an urban sailor on the raft of my own two feet.

I had little quarrel with my Jewish world. I was deep inside it, with a child's slowly increasing awareness of his own culture's richness and shortcomings. But beyond the tiny Hannibal of our apartment, there was an echoing world that I longed to embrace; it streamed in upon me, its books, movies, music, appealing not only to the mind but also to the senses. Faintly redolent of potential corruptions of the flesh, dark with the specter of conquest by assimilation, it seemed to hold out at the same time the promise of wordly wisdom, of tolerance, of reward for merit and achievement, and—the most precious promise of all—the creations of the great minds of man.

I was one of millions, millions, making that concrete Mississippi journey. We were the children and grandchildren of the last great tribal migration of our species on this planet, the east-west wandering of the frightened, the persecuted, the hungry, the poor, the seekers after new wealth and power—the movement around the turn of the century from Europe that inundated this land. The immigrant generation crashed into urban America. Often I think that our parents and grandparents, watching the world of urban America work its beguiling charms upon us, must have wondered if they had acted wisely in leaving their land, desolate and oppressive as it no doubt had been. To lose a child to an alien culture is to suffer a lifetime of anguish and pain.

Wandering through the urban world of my early years, I encountered almost everywhere the umbrella civilization in which all of us live today, the culture we call Western secular humanism. It is Western because it functions pretty much only on this side of our planet; the Eastern side is off on a tack all its own. It is secular because it makes no fundamental appeal to the supernatural; it is committed to the notion that man will either make it alone or he will not make it at all. No gods, no God, no comforting Truths and Absolutes; only stumbling, fumbling man, provisional truths, and an indifferent cosmos in which man, though a trifling speck in the totality of things, commits himself to life and dreams and to pumping meaning into the universe. It is humanist because of its concept of the individual, the self, not as a member of a community, but as a separate entity hungering to fulfill his or her own potentialities the one time around each of us has on this planet.

I encountered many of the cultures embedded beneath this umbrella civilization, varieties of Judaism and Christianity, ethnic groups, interest groups. I saw how each of these subcultures rubs up against the other and also against the umbrella civilization. In the world of urban America these rub-ups are intense, grating, relentless. Ideally, the umbrella acts as a protective cover that keeps all the subgroups in check and prevents any of them from becoming so powerful that it can threaten the existence of the others. The umbrella is tenuous, fragile. When it fails—and it fails too often—there are riots in the streets, as there were in my teens when the city grew dark with the rage of one of its suffering peoples.

In the libraries of urban America I learned that a culture is the still mysterious creation on the part of members of our species who have somehow clustered together— whether for reasons of geography, tribal loyalty, cataclysm, and the like—and have worked out their own unique responses to the questions we normally conceal from ourselves during the busy day, the four-o'clock-in-the-morning questions that sometimes snap us awake in the night. We lie in the darkness and listen to the questions swarm around us. What is all this really about? Does anything that I do mean anything? How can I ever hope to comprehend this awesome universe in which I live? I barely understand myself, how can I ever understand another human being? What is this narrow river of light I wander upon between the darkness from which I came and the darkness toward which I am inexorably headed? Cultures work out hard responses to these questions, responses which adherents are at times asked to defend with their lives. Often different sets of responses collide—as a result of armies in the field, merchants at fairs, scholars in libraries, or a youngster's urban wanderings. The collision generates questions and tension: Why are my answers better than those of another culture? Sometimes the tension gets out of hand, and there is bloodshed. Sometimes it results in creativity—books, music, art—and gold is given us to mine forever. Sumerians and Akkadians, Israelites and Canaanites, Judaism and Hellenism, Christianity and Rome, Islam and ancient Greek thought, Christianity and Judaism—and ancient Greek thought: these collisions of great thought systems and styles of life were culture confrontations.

I learned as I grew up that culture confrontation has been one of the ongoing dynamics of our species for the five thousand years that we can track ourselves through writing. Today, in the Western world, the dynamic is umbrella and subculture in confrontation. The rhythm of confrontation has accelerated in this century. The culture highways are wide open. The traffic is dense, especially in cities. The word "civilization"—it cannot hurt to remind ourselves—comes from the Latin *civitas*, which means city or city-state.

Those who made that urban journey confronted

other cultures in a variety of ways. Let me briefly describe one such confrontation—my own.

In the Jewish tradition, writing stories occupies no point of any significance in the hierarchy of values by which one measures achievement. Scholarship—especially Talmudic scholarship—is the measure of an individual. Fiction, even serious fiction—as far as the religious Jewish tradition is concerned—is at best a frivolity, at worst a menace.

When I was about fourteen or fifteen years old, I read *Brideshead Revisited* by Evelyn Waugh. That was the first serious adult novel I ever read. In high school English classes in those days you read works like *Treasure Island* and *Ivanhoe*. I was overwhelmed by that book. Somehow Evelyn Waugh reached across the chasm that separated my tight New York Jewish world from that of the upper-class British Catholics in his book. I remember finishing the book and marveling at the power of this kind of creativity. We each have our own beginnings with the hot madness called writing fiction.

From that time on, I not only read works of literature for enjoyment but also studied them with Talmudic intensity in order to teach myself how to create worlds out of words on paper. During the mornings in my school I studied the sacred subjects of my religious tradition; during the afternoons I studied the secular subjects of our umbrella civilization; at night and during weekends I read and wrote fiction. The great writers who created modern literature became my teachers.

The years went by.

In time I discovered that I had entered a tradition—modern literature. Fundamental to that tradition was a certain way of thinking the world; and basic to that was the binocular vision of the iconoclast, the individual who grows up inside inherited systems of value and, while growing, begins to recoil from the games, masks, and hypocrisies he sees all around him. About three hundred years ago, on this side of the planet, certain writers began to use one of the oldest instrumentalities of communication known to our species—storytelling—as a means of exploring the taut lines of relationship between individuals on the one hand and societies on the other, the small or large coherent worlds with which those individuals had entered into tension. Individual and society in polarization—that is one of the mighty rivers in the geography of modern literature. Sometimes the world of that individual is tiny and benign, as in Jane Austen; sometimes it is cruel and sentimental, as in Dickens; sometimes it is stagnant and decadent, as in James Joyce and Thomas Mann; sometimes it is icy and brutal, as in the early Hemingway. That is what I saw in the novels I read during my high school and college years in the teeming urban world of New York.

It was not difficult for me to realize that nothing was sacred to the serious novelist; nothing was so sacrosanct an inheritance from the past that it could not be opened up and poked into by the pen of the novelist. Someone born into an ancient tradition enters the world with baggage on his shoulders. If, in your growing up, no one messed up your particular world in an irreversible way— parents and teachers brought patience and love to your problems—you might come out of your subculture appreciating its richness, its echoing history, and eager to cope with its shortcomings. And if, at the same time, you have stumbled upon modern literature during the years of your growing loyalty to your private past, you find by the time you are nineteen or twenty years old that you have become a battleground for a culture confrontation of a certain kind. I call it a core-to-core culture confrontation. From the heart of your subculture, trained in its best schools, able to maneuver through its system of thought, its language, its way of structuring the world, you have come upon literature, an element from the core of the umbrella civilization in which all of us live today. Literature is a core endeavor of Western secular man; it is one of the ways Western secular man gives configuration to his experience—through the faculty of the imagination and a certain aesthetic form. In the history of our species, core-to-core culture confrontations have often resulted in explosions of creativity. An encounter with soaring alien ideas often sets us soaring toward new ideas of our own; or we enter into a process of selective affinity, finding in the alien thought system elements with which we feel the need to fuse. Few experiences are more extraordinary in the history of our species than that sort of culture confrontation in which one culture will spark another into seminal creativity.

I do not intend to write a novel about my encounter with the novel. But some who grew up with me might have encountered other elements from the core of Western secular humanism. And that is what my work has been about so far. In *The Chosen*, Danny Saunders encounters Freudian psychoanalytic theory; in *The Promise*, Reuven Malter encounters text criticism; in *My Name Is Asher Lev*, a young man encounters Western art; in *In the Beginning*, David Lurie encounters modern Bible scholarship. All these disciplines are located in the core of Western culture. And all my people are located in the core of their subculture.

...

You can grow up along the periphery of your subculture and enter the rich heart of Western secular humanism—say, by going to a university, the generating plant of Western secular civilization. You will experience a periphery-to-core culture confrontation. Saul Bellow's *Herzog* is about such a culture confrontation: Herzog at the heart of Western secular humanism experiencing the crises of our world and his life through his peripheral emotive connection to his subculture, his memories of an ethnic past.

You can grow up along the periphery of your subculture and experience only the periphery of Western civilization. That is a periphery-to-periphery culture confrontation. The early stories of Philip Roth are accounts of that kind of collision of cultures. Almost always, that sort of culture confrontation gives rise to cultural aberrations, awkward misunderstandings, bizarre fusions.

At the core of a culture is its worldview, its literature, art, and music, its special ways of thinking the world. The more difficult it becomes to move inside an alien culture, the closer you are to its core. Peripheries of culture—street language, foods, clothes, fad music, superstitions—are almost always the easiest elements to understand, imitate, absorb.

I am writing about a particular subculture, about people and events that were of special concern to me as I grew up and began my own Mississippi journey into this world. The compression of urban existence, the living mix of peoples and cultures in my Bronx world, made possible for me a rich variety of culture confrontations. I chose to write about core-to-core confrontation because that is the world I know best.

What happens when two ultimate commitments—one from your subculture, the other from the umbrella culture—meet in you and you love them both and they are antithetical one to the other? There is a dimension of Greek tragedy in this collision of two equally valid systems of values. How do you maneuver? How do you talk on the phone, go to school, ride a train, cross a street, attend class, relate to others, talk to your parents and friends, go out on a date, read texts? What are your dreams? What are your loves, your hates? I am writing about the feelings involved in the experience of core-to-core culture confrontation.

Urban wanderings that result in core-culture confrontations often shape a certain kind of individual. I call that individual a *Zwischenmensch*, a between-person. Such an individual will cross the boundaries of his or her own culture and embrace life-enhancing elements from alien worlds. I remember the pink-faced, bald-headed Italian shoemaker who sang in his tenor voice as he pounded away at my torn shoes. He taught me the word "opera." That was the birth of that passion for me. I always listened carefully from then on to the classical radio station. Can you conceive of how distant the tumultuous world of opera is from the mind-centered ambience of Talmudic disputation?

Late one spring day a seedy-looking man wandered into my parochial school. He was an artist, he said, and was willing to teach a summer course in art for a pittance. It would keep the children off the street, he said; give them something to do. He was in his late forties, a tired man reeking of tobacco, his eyes watery, the cuffs of his shirtsleeves frayed, his jacket and trousers creased. He looked weary, worn. Inexplicably, he was taken on. There were sixteen of us in that class. I was about ten years old. He watched me move colors across a canvas board one day and took me aside. "How old are you, kid?" he asked. "Who've you studied with?" That was my first step into the world of Western art. In my childhood, what Joyce was to Jesuits, painting was to Talmud.

To be a Zwischenmensch is to feel at home everywhere and nowhere simultaneously, to be regarded with suspicion by those along the banks as they watch you float by on your raft.

My Mississippi has no Delta ending. It runs on and on. We are most human when we communicate creatively across the Hannibals we make for ourselves. Yes, the raft is frail. Anything made and experienced by man seems frail—anything. Each new day of sun and sky is frail, frail. Still we remember the journeys begun a long time ago on the cement rivers of urban America. Different cities boil within each of us. There is so much we hate—the dirt, the poverty, the prejudice; there is so much we love—the one or two friendships that somehow crossed boundaries, the libraries where we joined ourselves to the dreams of others, the places where we composed dreams of our own, the museums where we learned how to defeat time, certain streets, alleys, staircases, apartment-house roofs, certain radio stations we would listen to deep into the night, certain newspapers we read as if they were a testament to the ages. We remember the terrors and joys of our early urban wanderings. We write, and continue the journey.

E. L. DOCTOROW

Deism

M y parents were first-generation Americans born in New York City. It was their parents who as young people as yet unmarried arrived separately not at Ellis Island but at Castle Garden in the 1880s, having emigrated from White Russia, now called Belarus. My father's father, Isaac Doctorow, was twenty when he arrived in 1885. He had come over in despair of the life that faced him in Russia, the ever-present murderous whimsy of the pogromists of the time and, more closely and stultifyingly, the rabbinically run village life that demanded fealty to what seemed to him arbitrary ancient proscriptions to induce catatonia, and which offered absolutely no practical means of answering to the poverty and slavery and degradation delivered by the Russian world outside the shtetl. Normative Judaism was neither life nor hope for my grandfather, it was praying your way to death.

At any rate, when he was settled in New York, ensconced on the Lower East Side and apprenticed to a printer, he immediately enrolled in a class on socialism taught by a well-known legal scholar of the time, Morris

Hillquit, and at the conclusion of the course was rewarded as class valedictorian with the gift of an unabridged dictionary.

By the time I was old enough to know him and think about him, he was elderly and living in the Bronx, a gentle, slim, and handsome man with fine white hair. I. Doctorow was the way he signed his name. He was a retired printer, a chess player—we played chess when I visited—and a voracious reader with a library I was always invited to dip into. Books in English, Russian, and Yiddish. Around the time I was studying for my bar mitzvah, he presented me with his copy of Tom Paine's *Age of Reason,* that still deliciously eloquent analysis of the Bible's inconsistencies, contradictions, and fantasies; not for Paine the intricate and imaginative work of midrash. "My own mind is my church," Paine says, announcing his blasphemous Deism.

(It was something of a mysterious coincidence when, 155 years after Paine's death, my wife and I bought a house in New Rochelle, New York, that turned out to stand in what had been the apple orchard behind Paine's home there in the 1800s.)

As we sat playing chess my grandfather Isaac was an island of sweet calm amid the maelstrom of activity going on around him. This maelstrom was my grandmother, Gussie, a tiny sprightly woman who wore her hair in a crown of braid and who unlike her husband was devout in her belief. She had come over from the same village in the Minsk district—they had known each other casually in the old country and had found something more going on between them only when they lived near each other on the Lower East Side. She was living with her widowed mother when he courted her. Gussie Doctorow was rigorous in her observances, kept an impeccably kosher household, and went off to sit upstairs in the synagogue every chance she had. Her great complaint was that, in her lifelong arguments about religion with her nonbelieving husband, he could quote the Bible more accurately than she. And of course, skeptic or not, I. Doctorow came to my bar mitzvah and sat there beaming as I read my passage, which by the way—in the manner of bar mitzvah preparation in the Bronx in those days—I didn't understand a word of, Hebrew being taught by rote for memorization with no concern for what the words meant.

My father, Dave, was the second of Isaac and Gussie's three children, and in the life of my own family, of my own father and mother, this same male-female dynamic prevailed. My mother Rose was a musician like her immigrant father before her. As a girl she played the piano for silent movies to earn money for her lessons. She and my father met as teenagers, and after they married in the 1920s they liked to spend their evenings in Greenwich Village—when it was a bohemian quarter alive with poets actors musicians radicals of every stripe. But as they grew older and as life became harder—this was the Depression and my father was by then the struggling proprietor of a music shop—my mother became active in the sisterhood of the local synagogue, and every Friday night she lit the candles and put her hand over her blue eyes and said the blessing and threw in a few silent prayers for good measure. My father never went near the synagogue. He believed like his father that the problems of Earth must be solved on Earth and that religion must not be used as it had been historically as a means of persuading people to live with the misery of social injustice.

It is my belief that the profound incompatibility of opposing ideas expressed in all the complex love flowing to a child of that family was a necessary condition of the child's creativity. He would mature having combined within himself the secular humanism and the impulse to reverence of the male and female lines of his elders. I think of it as a spiritual sort of alternating current, wherein never at rest I swing constantly back and forth from one pole to the other. This is a serendipitous arc for a writer's mind. It describes the less than comfortable state of freedom. As the son of my fathers, I am nonobservant, a celebrant of the humanism that has no patience for a religious imagination that asks me to abandon my intellect. But as the son of my mothers, I am unable to discard reverence, however unattached to an object, in recognition that a spontaneously felt sense of the sacred engages the whole human being as the intellect alone cannot.

I understand from biblical scholarship that the Ten Commandments have a generic form—they are modeled on the lord-and-vassal treaties of ancient Mesopotamia. They are man-made. But I honor the biblical minds who crafted them to structure civilization on an ethically conceived family life—a life that leads us to live in states of moral consequence that, if not yet, may someday bring us closer to a union with, or a truer perception of, what Einstein, with his scrupulously precise scientific humanistic outlook, could only bring himself to call the Old One.

So how has this all played out? Coming of this conflicted articulate household—moneyless, but filled with books and music—I had the privileged childhood of the undogmatized spirit. From the time I began to read, it never occurred to me to wonder about an author's religious background. When I read Jack London and Mark Twain and Charles Dickens, whatever their religious preference might have been never crossed my mind. Were they Christians? Perhaps in some unconscious way I knew that their background was not Jewish. But in fact they were not Christians either, they were Jack London, Mark Twain, and Charles Dickens. And if you think this was a selective blackout on my part, I'll admit that, however strongly circumstantial the evidence may have been, as a high school student I didn't think of Kafka, I. B. Singer, and Saul Bellow as Jews. I thought of them as Kafka, I. B. Singer, and Saul Bellow. I read them and was inspired by them when I was just starting out. But it was never the case of any sort of ethnic bonding with them—they were too spectacularly themselves. Of course the writer's background, religious tradition, nationality, lived life is crucially directive as to what she writes about whom and where . . . but as a reader I find it quite beside the point that García Márquez is a Catholic from Colombia or Jane Austen is an Anglican from Britain, as instrumental as their cultures may have been in forming them. Dostoyevsky is a fanatically orthodox Christian from Russia. What else could he be? But there is another religion the great ones practice in their art, and it has no name.

Or, to change the metaphor, I wonder if great fiction and great poetry are not, down to their deepest roots, secular. W. H. Auden once said that a writer's politics are more of a danger to him than his cupidity. I would add that the writer's religion is as much a danger to him as his politics. Certainly in this country we worry that if a work is formed by ideas exterior to it, if there is some sort of programmed intention, a set of truths to be illustrated, the work will be compromised and will not be art but polemic. We will have corrupted the occasion and betrayed the calling.

Having cut my teeth on the existentialist fictions of

Camus and Sartre, I tend to think of them, contrarian as they are, as somehow emblematic of the digging in of the heels that is characteristic of all authorship. As an artifact created of its author's self-differentiation, the successful novel must necessarily lack the humility of reverence, the surrendering quality of the religious spirit. True surrender for an author would find all that needs to be written in the sacred text of his religion. This is clearly not something to occur to Proust, for example. Or even the biblically melancholic Bernard Malamud. I would of course say the same of poets. The Israeli poet Yehuda Amichai went down fighting all the way. Dante, right from the heart of Roman Catholicism, builds his own tripartite version of the afterlife, populates Hell with his Florentine enemies, wanders through it with a pagan mentor, and, most shockingly of all, as the critic Harold Bloom has shown us, exalts Beatrice to the point of blasphemy. And the great devoutly religious poet Gerard Manley Hopkins springs from his palpably elastic lines and image-bouncing bursts of inspiration right up out of Christianity into poetry.

All writers worth the name are unaffiliated. The novelist, the poet, will understand the institutions they live within, including their religious traditions, as aggregate historically amended fictions. Appointing themselves as witnesses, they are necessarily independent of all institutions, including the institution of the family—which may be why nothing makes family members more nervous than the discovery that one of them is a writer. They will not quite understand that the writer of the most personalist story, a roman à clef of her own family life or marriage, can be read as protesting the large social structures of the society or the terrible injustice of our brutal ordinary human inadequacy.

However well intentioned, constructive, and generous in spirit it may be to label the work of any group of writers as if their value is first and foremost local, a boon to the neighborhood—as if they are uniformly bound in the cultural context in which they find themselves—to do so runs the risk of portraying them as a chorus, rather than as the soloists, temperamental divas, and unconscionable upstagers that they in fact are. And it seems not to recognize the truth that every author responds to all of the given literature, and that the authorial conversation transcends borders and spans generations.

Of course I understand the hunkering down of all of us into our group loyalties in the past thirty or forty years—there is enough wretchedly catastrophic history behind us to explain why that has happened. I point out that the phrase *political correctness* was revived by the political right to mock or defame the effort, or even to undermine the desire, of ethnic, racial, and gender minorities to articulate their own identities instead of accepting the stereotypical and demeaning identities that history had imposed upon them. In many ways political correctness has been socially constructive. People *should* take pride and satisfaction in who and what they are. The Reconstructionist rabbi Mordecai Kaplan makes the distinction between *separateness* and *otherness*. Ideally, it is not separateness but otherness that is practiced when people affirm their roots while warranting themselves as citizens of the larger community. Nevertheless, with all of this said, I think something peculiar—and politically inert—is going on when I walk into a bookstore and see it sectioned off with shelves devoted to gay and lesbian writers, or African American writers, as if the expected readers for these books can only be gays and lesbians or African

Americans, as if the writers of these books have something to say only to gays and lesbians or African Americans, as if Edmund White and Toni Morrison are consumer products, or as if the genres are primary, the writers secondary—as in Inspirational, or Cooking, or Self-Help.

I question any subcultural division of the literary project, which I see, in the Emersonian manner, as arising from an unmediated exercise of the lonely mind.

The term *assimilation* as used in the sociological sense refers to a gratifying integration into the great American diaspora, but it may mean as well the disappearance of one's ethnic identity and tradition, a devolution of a rich and complex culture, as Jews marry gentiles, for example, and cease to observe the rituals and practices.

But as I apply the term to literature the meaning is reversed. If I speak of literature as assimilation what is assimilated is the larger culture into the specificity of the book's representations. It is America that is being assimilated when a true book, a true poem, enlarges the cast of stubborn humanity. Something has happened, some small thing, a new synaptic recognition has fired, a fresh little nourishing artery has opened into the national mind—or even the global mind.

People of diverse appearances and dictions may rise from book to book. But the crisis of human consciousness is always revealed as universal.

PHILIP ROTH

Writing About Jews

1

Ever since some of my first stories were collected in 1959 in a volume called *Goodbye, Columbus,* my work has been attacked from certain pulpits and in certain periodicals as dangerous, dishonest, and irresponsible. I have read editorials and articles in Jewish community newspapers condemning these stories for ignoring the accomplishments of Jewish life, or, as Rabbi Emanuel Rackman recently told the convention of the Rabbinical Council of America, for creating a "distorted image of the basic values of Orthodox Judaism," and even, he went on, for denying the non-Jewish world the opportunity of appreciating the "overwhelming contribution which Orthodox Jews are making in every avenue of modern endeavor. . . ." Among the letters I receive from readers, there have been a number written by Jews accusing me of being anti-Semitic and "self-hating," or, at least, tasteless; they argue or imply that the sufferings of the Jews throughout history, culminating in the murder of six million by the Nazis, have made certain criticisms of Jewish life insulting and trivial. Furthermore, it is charged that such criticism as I make of Jews—or apparent criticism—is taken by anti-Semites as justification of their attitudes, as "fuel" for their fires, particularly as it is a Jew himself who seemingly admits to habits and behavior that are not exemplary, or even normal and acceptable. When I speak before Jewish audiences, invariably there have been people who have come up to me afterward to ask, "Why don't you leave us alone? Why don't you write about the Gentiles?" "Why must you be so critical?" "Why do you disapprove of us so?"—this last question asked as often with incredulity as with anger; and often by people a good deal older than myself, asked as of an erring child by a loving but misunderstood parent.

It is difficult, if not impossible, to explain to some of the people claiming to have felt my teeth sinking in that in many instances they haven't been bitten at all. Not always, but frequently, what readers have taken to be my disapproval of the lives lived by Jews seems to have to do more with their own moral perspective than with the one they would ascribe to me: at times they see wickedness where I myself had seen energy or courage or spontaneity; they are ashamed of what I see no reason to be ashamed of, and defensive where there is no cause for defense.

Not only do they seem to me often to have cramped and untenable notions of right and wrong, but looking at fiction as they do—in terms of "approval" and "disapproval" of Jews, "positive" and "negative" attitudes toward Jewish life—they are likely not to see what it is that the story is really about.

To give an example. A story I wrote called "Epstein" tells of a sixty-year-old man who has an adulterous affair

with the lady across the street. In the end, Epstein, who is
the hero, is caught—caught by his family, and caught and
struck down by exhaustion, decay, and disappointment,
against all of which he had set out to make a final struggle.
There are Jewish readers, I know, who cannot figure out
why I found it necessary to tell this story about a Jewish
man: don't other people commit adultery too? Why is it
the Jew who must be shown cheating?

But there is more to adultery than cheating: for one
thing, there is the adulterer himself. For all that some
people may experience him as a cheat and nothing else, he
usually experiences himself as something more. And generally speaking, what draws most readers and writers to
literature is this "something more"—all that is beyond
simple moral categorizing. It is not my purpose in writing
a story of an adulterous man to make it clear how right
we all are if we disapprove of the act and are disappointed
in the man. Fiction is not written to affirm the principles
and beliefs that everybody seems to hold, nor does it seek
to guarantee the appropriateness of our feelings. The
world of fiction, in fact, frees us from the circumscriptions
that society places upon feeling; one of the greatnesses
of the art is that it allows both the writer and the reader
to respond to experience in ways not always available in
day-to-day conduct; or, if they are available, they are not
possible, or manageable, or legal, or advisable, or even
necessary to the business of living. We may not even know
that we have such a range of feelings and responses *until*
we have come into contact with the work of fiction. This
does not mean that either reader or writer no longer
brings any judgment to bear upon human action. Rather,
we judge at a different level of our being, for we are judging not only with the aid of new feelings but also without

the necessity of having to act upon judgment. Ceasing for a while to be upright citizens, we drop into another layer of consciousness. And this expansion of moral consciousness, this exploration of moral fantasy, is of considerable value to a man and to society.

I do not care to go at length here into what a good many readers take for granted are the purposes and possibilities of fiction. I do want to make clear, however, to those whose interests may not lead them to speculate much on the subject, a few of the assumptions a writer may hold—assumptions such as lead me to say that I do not write a story to make evident whatever disapproval I may feel for adulterous men. I write a story of a man who is adulterous to reveal the condition of such a man. If the adulterous man is a Jew, then I am revealing the condition of an adulterous man who is a Jew. Why tell that story? Because I seem to be interested in how—and why and when—a man acts counter to what he considers to be his "best self," or what others assume it to be, or would like it to be. The subject is hardly "mine"; it interested readers and writers for a long time before it became my turn to be engaged by it too.

One of my readers, a man in Detroit, was himself not too engaged and suggested in a letter to me that he could not figure out why I was. He posed several questions which I believe, in their very brevity, were intended to disarm me. I quote from his letter without his permission.

The first question: "Is it conceivable for a middle-aged man to neglect business and spend all day with a middle-aged woman?" The answer is yes.

Next he asks: "Is it a Jewish trait?" I take it he is referring to adultery and not facetiously to the neglecting of business. The answer is: "Who said it was?" Anna Karenina commits adultery with Vronsky, with consequences more disastrous than those Epstein brings about. Who thinks to ask, "Is it a Russian trait?" It is a decidedly human possibility. Even though the most famous injunction against it is reported as being issued, for God's own reasons, to the Jews, adultery has been one of the ways by which people of *all* faiths have sought pleasure, or freedom, or vengeance, or power, or love, or humiliation . . .

The next in the gentleman's series of questions to me is: "Why so much *shmutz?*" Is he asking, Why is there dirt in the world? Why is there disappointment? Why is there hardship, ugliness, evil, death? It would be nice to think these were the questions he had in mind when he asks, "Why so much *shmutz?*" But all he is really asking is, "Why so much *shmutz* in that story?" This is what the story adds up to for him. An old man discovers the fires of lust are still burning in him? *Shmutz!* Disgusting! Who wants to hear that kind of stuff! Struck as he is by nothing but the dirty aspects of Epstein's troubles, the gentleman from Detroit concludes that I am narrow-minded.

So do others. Narrow-mindedness, in fact, was the charge that a New York rabbi, David Seligson, was reported in *The New York Times* recently as having brought against me and other Jewish writers who, he told his congregation, dedicated themselves "to the exclusive creation of a melancholy parade of caricatures." Rabbi Seligson also disapproved of *Goodbye, Columbus* because I described in it a "Jewish adulterer . . . and a host of other lopsided schizophrenic personalities." Of course, adultery is not a characteristic symptom of schizophrenia, but that the rabbi should see it this way, as a sign of a diseased personality, indicates to me that we have different notions as to what health is. After all, it may be that *life* produces a melancholy middle-aged businessman like Lou Epstein, who in Dr. Seligson's eyes looks like another in a parade of caricatures. I myself find Epstein's adultery an unlikely solution to his problems, a pathetic, even doomed response, and a comic one too, since it does not even square with the man's own conception of himself and what he wants; but none of this *unlikeliness* leads me to despair of his sanity, or humanity. I suppose it is tantamount to a confession from me of lopsided schizophrenia to admit that the character of Epstein happened to have been conceived with considerable affection and sympathy. As I see it, one of the rabbi's limitations is that he cannot recognize a bear hug when one is being administered right in front of his eyes.

The *Times* report continues: "The rabbi said he could only 'wonder about' gifted writers, 'Jewish by birth, who can see so little in the tremendous saga of Jewish history.' " But I don't imagine the rabbi "wonders" about me any more than I wonder about him: that wondering business is only the voice of wisdom that is supposed to be making itself heard, always willing to be shown the light, if, of course, there is any; but I can't buy it. Pulpit fairmindedness only hides the issue—as it does here in the rabbi's conclusion, quoted by the *Times*: " 'That they [the Jewish writers in question] must be free to write, we would affirm most vehemently; but that they would know their own people and tradition, we would fervently wish.' "

However, the issue is not knowledge of one's "people." At least, it is not a question of who has more historical data at his fingertips, or is more familiar with Jewish tradition, or which of us observes more customs and rituals. It is even possible, needless to say, to "know" a good deal about tradition, and to misunderstand what it is that tradition signifies. The story of Lou Epstein stands or falls not on how much I know about tradition but on how much I know and understand about Lou Epstein. Where the history of the Jewish people comes down in time and place to become the man whom I called Epstein, that is where my knowledge must be sound. But I get the feeling that Rabbi Seligson wants to rule Lou Epstein *out* of Jewish history. I find him too valuable to forget or dismiss, even if he is something of a *grubber yung* and probably more ignorant of history than the rabbi believes me to be.

Epstein is pictured not as a learned rabbi, after all, but as the owner of a small paper-bag company; his wife is not learned either, and neither is his mistress; consequently, a reader should not expect to find in this story knowledge on my part, or the part of the characters, of the *Sayings of the Fathers;* he has every right to expect that I be close to the truth as to what might conceivably be the attitudes of a Jewish man of Epstein's style and history toward marriage, family life, divorce, and fornication. The story is called "Epstein" because Epstein, not the Jews, is the subject; where the story is weak I think I know by this time; but the rabbi will never find out until he comes at the thing in terms of what *it* wants to be about, rather than what he would like it to be about.

Obviously, though, his interest is not in the portrayal of character; what he wants in my fiction is, in his words, a "balanced portrayal of Jews as we know them." I even suspect that something called "balance" is what the rabbi would advertise as the most significant characteristic of Jewish life; what Jewish history comes down to is that at long last we have in our ranks one of everything. But his assumptions about the art of fiction are what I should like to draw particular attention to. In his sermon Rabbi Seligson says of Myron Kaufmann's *Remember Me to God* that it can "hardly be said to be recognizable as a Jewish sociological study." But Mr. Kaufmann, as a novelist, probably had no intention of writing a sociological study, or—for this seems more like what the rabbi really yearns for in the way of reading—a nice positive sampling. *Madame Bovary* is hardly recognizable as a sociological study either, having at its center only a single, dreamy, provincial French-woman, and not one of every other kind of provincial Frenchwoman too; this does not, however, diminish its brilliance as a novel, as an exploration of Madame Bovary herself. Literary works do not take as their subjects characters and events which have impressed a writer primarily by the *frequency* of their appearance. For example, how many Jewish men, as we know them, have come nearly to the brink of plunging a knife into their only son because they believed God had demanded it of them? The story of Abraham and Isaac derives its meaning from something other than its being a familiar, recognizable, everyday occurrence. The test of any literary work is not how broad is its range of representation—for all that breadth may be characteristic of a kind of narrative—but the depth with which the writer reveals whatever he has chosen to represent.

To confuse a "balanced portrayal" with a novel is finally to be led into absurdities. "Dear Fyodor Dostoyevsky—All the students in our school, and most of the teachers, feel that you have been unfair to us. Do you call Raskolnikov a balanced portrayal of students as we know them? Of Russian students? Of poor students? What about those of us who have never murdered anyone, who do our schoolwork every night?" "Dear Mark Twain—None of the slaves on our plantation has ever run away. But what will our owner think when he reads of Nigger

Jim?" "Dear Vladimir Nabokov—The girls in our class . . ." and so on. What fiction does and what the rabbi would like it to do are two entirely different things. The concerns of fiction are not those of a statistician—or of a public-relations firm. The novelist asks himself, "What do people think?"; the PR man asks, "What *will* people think?" But I believe this is what is actually troubling the rabbi when he calls for his "balanced portrayal of Jews": What will people think?

Or, to be exact: What will the goyim think?

2

This was the question raised—and urgently—when another story of mine, "Defender of the Faith," appeared in *The New Yorker* in April 1959. The story is told by Nathan Marx, an army sergeant just rotated back to Missouri from combat duty in Germany, where the war has ended. As soon as he arrives, he is made first sergeant in a training company, and immediately is latched on to by a young recruit who tries to use his attachment to the sergeant to receive kindnesses and favors. The attachment, as he sees it, is that they are both Jews. As the story progresses, what the recruit, Sheldon Grossbart, comes to demand are not mere considerations but privileges to which Marx does not think he is entitled. The story is about one man who uses his own religion, and another's uncertain conscience, for selfish ends; but mostly it is about this other man, the narrator, who, because of the ambiguities of being a member of his religion, is involved in a taxing, if mistaken, conflict of loyalties.

I don't now, however, and didn't while writing, see

Marx's problem as nothing more than "Jewish": confronting the limitations of charity and forgiveness in one's nature—having to draw a line between what is merciful and what is just—trying to distinguish between apparent evil and the real thing, in one's self and others—these are problems for most people, regardless of the level at which they are perceived or dealt with. Yet, though the moral complexities are not exclusively a Jew's, I never for a moment considered that the characters in the story should be anything other than Jews. Someone else might have written a story embodying the same themes, and similar events perhaps, and had at its center Negroes or Irishmen; for me there was no choice. Nor was it a matter of making Grossbart a Jew and Marx a Gentile, or vice versa; telling half the truth would have been much the same here as telling a lie. Most of those jokes beginning "Two Jews were walking down the street" lose a little of their punch if one of the Jews, or both, is disguised as an Englishman or a Republican. Similarly, to have made any serious alteration in the Jewish factuality of "Defender of the Faith," as it began to fill itself out in my imagination, would have so unsprung the tensions I felt in the story that I would no longer have had left a story that I wanted to tell, or one I believed myself able to.

Some of my critics must wish that this had happened, for in going ahead and writing this story about Jews, what else did I do but confirm an anti-Semitic stereotype? But to me the story confirms something different, if no less painful, to its readers. To me Grossbart is not something we can dismiss solely as an anti-Semitic stereotype; he is a Jewish fact. If people of bad intention or weak judgment have converted certain facts of Jewish life into a stereotype of The Jew, that does not mean that such facts are no longer important in our lives, or that they are taboo for the writer of fiction. Literary investigation may even be a way to redeem the facts, to give them the weight and value that they should have in the world, rather than the disproportionate significance they obviously have for some misguided or vicious people.

Sheldon Grossbart, the character I imagined as Marx's antagonist, has his seed in fact. He is not meant to represent The Jew, or Jewry, nor does the story indicate that the writer intends him to be understood that way by the reader. Grossbart is depicted as a single blundering human being, one with force, self-righteousness, cunning, and, on occasion, even a little disarming charm; he is depicted as a man whose lapses of integrity seem to him so necessary to his survival as to convince him that such lapses are actually committed in the name of integrity. He has been able to work out a system whereby his own sense of responsibility can suspend operation, what with the collective guilt of the others having become so immense as to have seriously altered the conditions of trust in the world. He is represented not as the stereotype of The Jew, but as a Jew who acts like the stereotype, offering back to his enemies their vision of him, answering the punishment with the crime. Given the particular kinds of humiliations and persecutions that the nations have practiced on the Jews, it argues for far too much nobility to deny not only that Jews like Grossbart exist but that the temptations to Grossbartism exist in many who perhaps have more grace, or will, or are perhaps only more cowed, than the simple frightened soul that I imagined weeping with fear and disappointment at the end of the story. Grossbart is not The Jew; but he is a fact of Jewish experience and well within the range of its moral possibilities.

And so is his adversary, Marx, who is, after all, the

story's central character, its consciousness and its voice. He is a man who calls himself a Jew more tentatively than does Grossbart; he is not sure what it means—means for *him*—for he is not unintelligent or without conscience; he is dutiful, almost to a point of obsession, and confronted by what are represented to him as the needs of another Jew, he does not for a while know what to do. He moves back and forth from feelings of righteousness to feelings of betrayal, and only at the end, when he truly does betray the trust that Grossbart tries to place in him, does he commit what he has hoped to all along: an act he can believe to be honorable.

Marx does not strike me, nor any of the readers I heard from, as unlikely, incredible, "made up"; the verisimilitude of the characters and their situation was not what was called into question. In fact, an air of convincingness that the story was believed to have, caused a number of people to write to me, and *The New Yorker,* and the Anti-Defamation League, protesting its publication.

Here is one of the letters I received after the story was published:

> Mr. Roth:
> With your one story, "Defender of the Faith," you have done as much harm as all the organized anti-Semitic organizations have done to make people believe that all Jews are cheats, liars, connivers. Your one story makes people—the general public—forget all the great Jews who have lived, all the Jewish boys who served well in the armed services, all the Jews who live honest hard lives the world over. . . .

Here is one received by *The New Yorker:*

> Dear Sir:
> . . . We have discussed this story from every possible angle and we cannot escape the conclusion that it will do irreparable damage to the Jewish people. We feel that this

story presented a distorted picture of the average Jewish soldier and are at a loss to understand why a magazine of your fine reputation should publish such a work which lends fuel to anti-Semitism.

Clichés like "this being Art" will not be acceptable. A reply will be appreciated.

Here is a letter received by the officials of the Anti-Defamation League, who, because of the public response, telephoned to ask if I wanted to talk to them. The strange emphasis of the invitation, I thought, indicated the discomfort they felt at having to pass on messages such as this:

Dear ———,

What is being done to silence this man? Medieval Jews would have known what to do with him. . . .

The first two letters I quoted were written by Jewish laymen, the last by a rabbi and educator in New York City, a man of prominence in the world of Jewish affairs.

The rabbi was later to communicate directly with me. He did not mention that he had already written to the Anti-Defamation League to express regret over the decline of medieval justice, though he was careful to point out at the conclusion of his first letter his reticence in another quarter. I believe I was supposed to take it as an act of mercy: "I have not written to the editorial board of *The New Yorker*," he told me. "I do not want to compound the sin of informing. . . ."

Informing. There was the charge so many of the correspondents had made, even when they did not want to make it openly to me, or to themselves. I had informed on the Jews. I had told the Gentiles what apparently it would otherwise have been possible to keep secret from them:

that the perils of human nature afflict the members of our minority. That I had also informed them it was possible for there to be such a Jew as Nathan Marx did not seem to bother anybody; if I said earlier that Marx did not seem to strike my correspondents as unlikely, it is because he didn't strike them at all. He might as well not have been there. Of the letters that I read, just one mentioned Marx, and only to point out that I was no less blameworthy for portraying the sergeant as a "white Jew," as he was described by my correspondent, a kind of Jewish Uncle Tom.

But even if Marx were that and only that, a white Jew, and Grossbart a black one, did it in any way follow that because I had examined the relationship between them—another concern central to the story which drew barely a comment from my correspondents—that I had then advocated that Jews be denationalized, deported, persecuted, murdered? Well, no. Whatever the rabbi may believe privately, he did not indicate to me that he thought I was an anti-Semite. There was a suggestion, however, and a grave one, that I had acted like a fool. "You have earned the gratitude," he wrote, "of all who sustain their anti-Semitism on such conceptions of Jews as ultimately led to the murder of six million in our time."

Despite the sweep there at the end of the sentence, the charge made is actually up at the front: I "earned the gratitude . . ." But of whom? I would put it less dramatically but maybe more exactly: of those who are predisposed to misread the story—out of bigotry, ignorance, malice, or even innocence. If I did earn their gratitude, it was because they failed to see, even to look for, what I was talking about . . . Such conceptions of Jews as anti-Semites hold, then, and as they were able to confirm by misunderstanding my story, are the same, the rabbi goes on to say, as those which "ultimately led to the murder of six million in our time."

"Ultimately"? Is that not a gross simplification of the history of the Jews and the history of Hitler's Germany? People hold serious grudges against one another, vilify one another, deliberately misunderstand one another, but they do not always, as a consequence, *murder* one another, as the Germans murdered the Jews, and as other Europeans allowed the Jews to be murdered, or even helped the slaughter along. Between prejudice and persecution there is usually, in civilized life, a barrier constructed by the individual's convictions and fears, and the community's laws, ideals, values. What "ultimately" caused this barrier to disappear in Germany cannot be explained only in terms of anti-Semitic misconceptions; surely what must also be understood here is the intolerability of Jewry, on the one hand, and its usefulness, on the other, to the Nazi ideology and dream.

By simplifying the Nazi–Jewish relationship, by making *prejudice* appear to be the primary cause of annihilation, the rabbi is able to make the consequences of publishing "Defender of the Faith" in *The New Yorker* seem very grave indeed. He doesn't appear to be made at all anxious, however, by the consequences of his own position. For what he is suggesting is that some subjects must not be written about, or brought to public attention, because it is possible for them to be misunderstood by people with weak minds or malicious instincts. Thus he consents to put the malicious and weak-minded in a position of determining the level at which open communication on these subjects will take place. This is not fighting anti-Semitism but submitting to it: that is, submitting to a restriction of consciousness as well as communication, because being conscious and being candid are too risky.

In his letter the rabbi calls my attention to that famous madman who shouts "Fire!" in a "crowded theater." He leaves me to complete the analogy myself. By publishing "Defender of the Faith" in *The New Yorker*: (1) I am shouting; (2) I am shouting "Fire!"; (3) there is no fire; (4) all this is happening in the equivalent of a "crowded theater." The crowded theater: there is the risk. I should agree to sacrifice the freedom essential to my vocation, and even to the general well-being of the culture, because—because of what? The "crowded theater" has absolutely no relevance to the situation of the Jew in America today. It is a grandiose delusion. It is not a metaphor describing a cultural condition but a revelation of the nightmarish visions that plague people as demoralized as the rabbi appears to be: rows endless, seats packed, lights out, doors too few and too small, panic and hysteria just under the skin . . . No wonder he says to me finally, "Your story—in Hebrew—in an Israeli magazine or newspaper—would have been judged exclusively from a literary point of view." That is, ship it off to Israel. But please don't tell it here, now.

Why? So that "they" will not commence persecuting Jews again? If the barrier between prejudice and persecution collapsed in Germany, this is hardly reason to contend that no such barrier exists in our country. And if it should ever begin to appear to be crumbling, then we must do what is necessary to strengthen it. But not by putting on a good face; not by refusing to admit to the intricacies and impossibilities of Jewish lives; not by pretending that Jews have existences less in need of, and less deserving of, honest attention than the lives of their neighbors; not by making Jews invisible. The solution is not to convince people to like Jews so as not to want to kill them; it is to let them know that they cannot kill them even if they despise them. And how to let them know? Surely repeating over and over to oneself, "It can happen here," does little to prevent "it" from happening. Moreover, ending persecution involves more than stamping out persecutors. It is necessary, too, to unlearn certain responses to them. All the tolerance of persecution that has seeped into the Jewish character—the adaptability, the patience, the resignation, the silence, the self-denial—must be squeezed out, until the only response there is to any restriction of liberties is "No, I refuse."

The chances are that there will always be some people who will despise Jews, just so long as they continue to call themselves Jews; and, of course, we must keep an eye on them. But if some Jews are dreaming of a time when they will be accepted by Christians as Christians accept one another—if *this* is why certain Jewish writers should be silent—it may be that they are dreaming of a time that cannot be, and of a condition that does not exist this side of one's dreams. Perhaps even the Christians don't accept one another as they are imagined to in that world from which Jews may believe themselves excluded solely because they are Jews. Nor are the Christians going to feel toward Jews what one Jew may feel toward another. The upbringing of the alien does not always alert him to the whole range of human connections which exists between clannish solidarity on the one hand and exclusion or rejection on the other. Like those of most men, the lives of Jews no longer take place in a world that is just *landsmen* and enemies. The cry "Watch out for the goyim!" at times seems more the expression of an unconscious wish than of a warning: Oh that they were out there, so that we could be together in here! A rumor of persecution, a taste of exile, might even bring with it that old world of feelings and habits—something to replace the new world of social accessibility and moral indifference, the world which tempts all our promiscuous instincts, and where one cannot always figure out what a Jew is that a Christian is not.

Jews are people who are not what anti-Semites say they are. That was once a statement out of which a man might begin to construct an identity for himself; now it does not work so well, for it is difficult to act counter to the ways people expect you to act when fewer and fewer people define you by such expectations. The success of the struggle against the defamation of Jewish character in this country has itself made more pressing the need for a Jewish self-consciousness that is relevant to this time and place, where neither defamation nor persecution are what they were elsewhere in the past. For those Jews who choose to continue to call themselves Jews, and find reason to do so, there are courses to follow to prevent it from ever being 1933 again that are more direct, reasonable, and dignified than beginning to act as though it already is 1933—*or as though it always is.* But the death of all those Jews seems to have taught my correspondent, a rabbi and a teacher, little more than to be discreet, to be foxy, to say this but not that. It has taught him nothing other than how to remain a victim in a country where he does not have to live like one if he chooses. How pathetic. And what an insult to the dead. Imagine: sitting in New York in the 1960s and piously summoning up the "six million" to justify one's own timidity.

Timidity—and paranoia. It does not occur to the rabbi that there are Gentiles who will read the story intelligently. The only Gentiles the rabbi can imagine looking into *The New Yorker* are those who hate Jews and those who don't know how to read very well. If there are others,

they can get along without reading about Jews. For to suggest that one translate one's stories into Hebrew and publish them in Israel is to say, in effect: "There is nothing in
our lives we need to tell the Gentiles about, unless it has to
do with how well we manage. Beyond that, it's none of
their business. We are important to no one but ourselves,
which is as it should be (or better be) anyway." But to indicate that moral crisis is something to be hushed up is not,
of course, to take the prophetic line; nor is it a rabbinical
point of view that Jewish life is of no significance to the
rest of mankind.

Even given his own kind of goals, however, the rabbi
is not very farsighted or imaginative. What he fails to see
is that the stereotype as often arises from ignorance as
from malice; deliberately keeping Jews out of the imagination of Gentiles, for fear of the bigots and their stereotyp-
ing minds, is really to invite the invention of stereotypical
ideas. A book like Ralph Ellison's *Invisible Man*, for
instance, seems to me to have helped many whites who are
not anti-Negro, but who do hold Negro stereotypes, to
surrender their simpleminded notions about Negro life. I
doubt, however, that Ellison, describing as he does not
just the squalor Negroes must put up with but certain bes-
tial aspects of his Negro characters as well, has converted
one Alabama redneck or one United States senator over to
the cause of desegregation; nor could the novels of James
Baldwin cause Governor Wallace to conclude anything
more than that Negroes are just as hopeless as he's always
known them to be. As novelists, neither Baldwin nor Ellison are (to quote Mr. Ellison on himself) "cogs in the
machinery of civil rights legislation." Just as there are Jews
who feel that my books do nothing for the Jewish cause, so
there are Negroes, I am told, who feel that Mr. Ellison's

work has done little for the Negro cause and probably has harmed it. But that seems to place the Negro cause somewhat outside the cause of truth and justice. That many blind people are still blind does not mean that Ellison's book gives off no light. Certainly those of us who are willing to be taught, and who needed to be, have been made by *Invisible Man* less stupid than we were about Negro lives, including those lives that a bigot would point to as affirming his own half-baked, inviolable ideas.

3

But it is the treachery of the bigot that the rabbi appears to be worried about and that he presents to me, to himself, and probably to his congregation, as the major cause for concern. Frankly, I think those are just the old words coming out, when the right buttons are pushed. Can he actually believe that on the basis of my story anyone is going to start a pogrom, or keep a Jew out of medical school, or even call some Jewish schoolchild a kike? The rabbi is entombed in his nightmares and fears; but that is not the whole of it. He is also hiding something. Much of this disapproval of "Defender of the Faith" because of its effect upon Gentiles seems to me a cover-up for what is really objected to, what is immediately painful—and that is its direct effect upon certain Jews. "You have hurt a lot of people's feelings because you have revealed something they are ashamed of." That is the letter the rabbi did not write but should have. I would have argued then that there are things of more importance—even to these Jews—than those feelings that have been hurt, but at any rate he would have confronted me with a genuine fact, with something I was actually responsible for, and which my conscience would have had to deal with, as it does.

For the record, all the letters I saw that came in about "Defender of the Faith" were from Jews. Not one of those people whose gratitude the rabbi believes I earned wrote to say, "Thank you," nor was I invited to address any anti-Semitic organizations. When I did begin to receive speaking invitations, they were from Jewish ladies' groups, Jewish community centers, and from all sorts of Jewish organizations, large and small.

And I think this bothers the rabbi too. Some Jews are hurt by my work; but some are interested. At the rabbinical convention I mentioned earlier, Rabbi Emanuel Rackman, a professor of political science at Yeshiva University, reported to his colleagues that certain Jewish writers were "assuming the mantle of self-appointed spokesmen and leaders for Judaism." To support his remark he referred to a symposium held in Israel this last June at which I was present; as far as I know, Rabbi Rackman was not. If he had been there, he would have heard me make it quite clear that I did not want to, did not intend to, and was not able to speak *for* American Jews; I surely did not deny, and no one questioned the fact, that I spoke *to* them, and I hope to others as well. The competition that Rabbi Rackman imagines himself to be engaged in hasn't to do with who will presume to lead the Jews; it is really a matter of who, in addressing them, is going to take them more seriously—strange as that may sound—with who is going to see them as something more than part of the mob in a crowded theater, more than helpless and threatened and in need of reassurance that they are as "balanced" as anyone else. The question really is, who is going to address men and women like men and women, and who like children. If there are Jews who have begun to find the stories the novelists tell more provocative and pertinent than the sermons of some of the rabbis, perhaps it is because there are regions of feeling and consciousness in them which cannot be reached by the oratory of self-congratulation and self-pity.

LESLIE EPSTEIN

Coming Home

Whuh-en I was a freshman at University High
School in Los Angeles I wrote my first short
story. In it, a crowd gathers at a square in what is
clearly South America. It swells, in both numbers and
excitement. That's pretty much all that happens until the
end, when all faces turn up toward a balcony where, at the
climax, a small figure with a mustache steps out. A great
cheer goes up, the man raises his right arm, and everyone
shouts like crazy, *Viva! Viva Hitler!*

I am almost as surprised now, thinking about that
adolescent effort, as I believe I was then. Where on earth,
or at any rate where in California, with its skies of perpetual blue, did this symbol of evil come from? After all, for
me the Second World War—which had ended a decade
before—had been essentially a matter of Japanese. The
paper drives at Brentwood Elementary, the bacon grease
stored in tin cans, the barrage balloons off Santa Monica
Pier, even the sudden vanishing of the old gentleman who
smoothed our garden with his bamboo rake—all these
were precautions against a threat from the Pacific, where

treachery had already descended upon our nation out of the peaceful heavens.

Not only were Germans absent from my childhood, so were Judaism and Jews. Neither I nor my brother, Ricky, was bar mitzvahed or set foot inside a temple. We celebrated Christmas with a tree whose star of Bethlehem grazed our eleven-foot ceilings, and Easter with chocolate eggs hidden in the sofa cushions, not to mention a dinner with what may well have been a glazed and clove-studded ham. In the public schools of California I played a shepherd during the nativity pageant and piped out the mysterious words—*myrrh, roundyon,* the three kings of *orientare*—of the carols, just as in prep school later I bellowed the more lucid "Onward Christian Soldiers."

Yet all the indoctrination of a Christian culture (how bright that star in the heavens, how moving the wise men and their gifts, how sweet the animals about the little halo-headed fellow before whom all dropped to their knees) could not have had what I believe was a profound effect upon me had I not possessed some hidden psychic affinity for a religion that stressed forgiveness for prodigal sons and had I not been a son, myself, of such resolutely secular parents.

In this my mother and father were typical of an emancipated second generation hell-bent on sparing their own children the kind of Orthodox regime they had had to undergo themselves. What was atypical, and decisive, was the position my father and uncle held in the film industry. Together these identical twins wrote *Arsenic and Old Lace, The Man Who Came to Dinner, Strawberry Blonde, Casablanca,* and dozens more. By the midthirties, when Phil and Julie arrived in Hollywood, the men who ran the studios had decided upon such a stringent policy of ethnic cleansing that throughout the whole of the Second World War the words "Jewish" and "Jew" appeared in not a single film about American life (with the sole exception, it pleases me to say, of the Epstein Boys' *Mr. Skeffington*). It is not surprising that the words were rarely spoken in my family, either. If Julie and Phil were busily creating the American dream in, say, *Yankee Doodle Dandy*, their children had little choice but to join the great national audience of white, blank, indistinguishable faces that made up the home front of American culture.

Which brings me back to the question of how Herr, or Señor, Hitler made his appearance at the end of my first short story. Is it possible that after all I had noticed something hidden in those wartime films? Or heard a few whispered remarks about the dinner table? It's not unlikely that I had glimpsed, either in *Life* or in the newsreels that preceded my usual diet of cartoons and westerns, some blurred image of what would later become familiar photos: a bulldozer at work on a mountain of corpses, the surviving wraiths peering through the wire fences. Were there ovens? Chimneys? Yellow stars?

The truth is, I had always known—in the same way that everyone knows, from childhood on, the laws of gravitation. What goes up must come down. From childhood? I might have been born with an innate grasp of the fate of the Jews. What we learn later, the formulas for the mass of objects and the square of their distance, only confirms what we carry within us like the weight of our bones. Hints, hushings, inflections: these pass by a kind of psychic osmosis from child to child and from Jew to Jew. I have not mentioned one more thing that may account for the gravitas of my first piece of fiction. My laughing father had died less than a year before I wrote a word. Even at that event my brother and I did not enter a synagogue. Instead of attending the funeral, a friend of the family took us to see *The Lavender Hill Mob*. We laughed our fool heads off. How hilarious Alec Guinness was, attempting to flee down the Eiffel Tower with his suitcase full of golden statuettes. At the end of the comedy, however, the hero is led off in handcuffs, a victim of the production code that in those innocent days insisted that crime not be portrayed to pay. I preferred my weekly ration of cartoons, in which the characters, no matter how greatly endangered—blown sky-high one moment, flattened by a fall from a cliff the next—have nine lives. Would that my father, dead at age forty-two, had had eight more to go.

If the film industry did not respond to the plight of the Jews when the enemy was Fascism, what would it do when the country fell into the grip of anti-Communist hysteria? When Yellow Peril was replaced by Red Menace, the panic was greatest in Hollywood, which, as Adolphe Menjou told the House Un-American Activities Committee, was "one of the main centers of Communism in America." I don't suppose it is surprising that most of those who found themselves on the blacklist were Jewish; for practical purposes, both Senator McCarthy and Adolf Hitler, in struggling against Communism, were also waging a war against the Jews.

That war affected my own family in the late forties, when Jack Warner gave the committee a list of subversives largely consisting of those with whom he had contractual disputes. It included Philip G. and Julius J. Epstein, Roosevelt Democrats, on the grounds that they always seemed to be on the side of the underdog. Little wonder, then, that the chairman of HUAC should send the twins a two-part questionnaire. The first question was, *Have you ever been a member of a subversive organization?* The second was, *What was that organization?* To question one the boys dutifully answered, "Yes." To question two they answered, "Warner Brothers."

The twins did not hear from the committee again; their careers flourished. Others in the family, however, did suffer, and greatly. It's clear to me now that the combined effects of my Jewishness (inevitably there were incidents when my friends turned on me with either fists or dirt clods, crying "Kike, Kike!"), my political idealism (I went about the neighborhood knocking on doors for Harry Truman when I was ten years old), the mood of the country, and above all the death of my father—that all these things caused me to withdraw. Certainly my imagination withered. The adolescent who wrote that story set in Buenos Aires, and another story about an old man in the desert who sees a bright flash in the sky that turns out to be a test of the atom bomb (no novel of manners for me!) put down his pen and did not write another word of fiction for many years.

What I did instead was flee—flee California, flee what was left of my family, my religion, and any vestiges of the film industry. I could have gone to the University of Chicago, I could have gone to Columbia, but I battered my way into Yale, where the Jewish quota was a miserly 10 percent. I lay low. My only approach to Judaism in those years was the overcoat I bought at Fenn-Feinstein's and my excursion to Ratner's on Second Avenue in New York. There I sat, a freshman, wearing that coat, which was three sizes too large, reddish brown, with what looked like horsehairs sticking out of the lining. On my head, a snappy hat. Round my neck a Lux et Veritas tie. There might even have been a pipe. After studying the menu, I raised a finger to the waiter. "I'm not electric," he said, hobbling by. A quarter of an hour later a second old man shuffled over.

"What's this *ma-ma-li-ga?*" I inquired.

Said he: "Not for you."

The waiter was right. Not for me. Not yet. Meanwhile I continued what I now see was for me a pattern of expulsion—not just from the Eden of California and my childhood and my religion, but from whatever Citadel of Christendom I found myself in. First was the Webb School, where I'd been sent, with several dozen other products of broken or unhappy homes, two years after my father's death. "What's this?" asked one of my tablemates, perplexed by the platter of mystery meat set before him. "This week's profit," I replied, and was expelled the next morning. Next came Yale, where I insulted the mayor ("What's the mayor doing?" asked a classmate, on seeing his honor go from Fenn-Feinstein's to Phil the Barber's and then J. Press. "Thursday. Three o'clock," I replied, rather loudly. "Time to collect.") and from which I was rusticated until a public uproar got me readmitted. Last was Oxford, or Oggsford, as my coreligionist Meyer Wolfsheim calls it in *The Great Gatsby*. I threw myself out this time, mostly from sheer boredom—though I threw myself in again when I realized that if I came back to the United States I would be drafted.

The best thing about an education at Oxford is the great deal of time you don't have to be there. I went, of all places, to Israel. It was there, in the Jewish State, that I began once again to write. The story, my first as an adult, was called "The Bad Jew," and the title character—a cool Californian, aloof from the faith of his fathers, unmoved by the traces of the Holocaust he sees about him—in no small measure resembled myself. What is most telling, I think, is the way contact with the Holocaust and its survivors transforms this Angelino, if not into an angel, at least into not such a bad Jew after all.

Why did I write this tale? I believe that the return to Israel, the sensation of being immersed in Jews and Judaism, must have represented in some sense a return to my own past and not just to that of my coreligionists. I have long believed that the work of every artist is in no small degree a recapitulation of his earliest experience. E.T.A. Hoffmann claimed that the imagery for all his fiction was nothing more than the residue of the impressions he had formed on a two-week trip in a chaise longue, while at his mother's breast. And there stood I, at the birthplace of my people. No less crucial to my stirring imagination was a heightened awareness of the Holocaust. During that stay in Israel I was surrounded not only by its survivors, but confronted by their persecutors. For this was the precise moment that, in a large stone building in Jerusalem, Adolf Eichmann went on trial. For the first time I had to confront in my conscious mind the nature of the Holocaust and the history of anti-Semitism in general.

The Jews of the world were to be a light unto the nations. That was, and is, their crime. For the nations of the world have behaved toward the Jews with that same animosity that darkness feels toward light or that, in an image I wish were my own, flour must feel toward the yeast that will not allow it to subside.

More to the point, I do not think it an exaggeration to say that the war of the Germans against the Jews was a war against certain qualities of the Jewish mind, and that, to twist the famous aphorism of Heine, before the mobs in Berlin and Munich and Dresden could burn the Jews, they first had to burn their books. What is in these minds and books that bedevils so many who come in contact with them? I think the hated element is the continuous exercise of what Coleridge called the primary imagination: the "repetition in the finite mind of the eternal act of creation in the infinite I Am." It is the Jews who took the imaginative leap of comprehending out of an empty whirlwind, a burning bush, *The I Am That I Am*. It is the Jews who substituted the *story* of Abraham and Isaac for the reality of a father killing a son and a son killing his father. If in some measure Christianity longed for a return to the original form of sacrifice, it was German paganism that made that hidden wish a fact of life. And it is the Jews, too, who have maintained in their finite minds a belief in the infinite; when that belief, that supreme fiction, which is that *we matter*, that *existence has meaning*, became a rebuke to our age's countervailing faith, which is that *everything is possible*, then those finite minds, and all that they held within them, had to be destroyed.

I had not formulated these thoughts on that long-ago trip to Israel. But I do think it possible that it was there that I began to form the association, or the nexus, between Jews and their sufferings, my own childhood, and the wish, no, the necessity, to exercise my imagination. In other words, I knew that, from Haman to Hitler, the nations had been trying to eliminate the Jews and that perhaps the only way I could protest this history was to make sure a No. 2 pencil was in my hand.

This much I know for sure: when I returned to Oxford I spent all my time reading about the Holocaust—and in particular, Gerald Reitlinger's *The Final Solution*, most especially page 64, on which was printed a single paragraph about Chaim Rumkowski, the leader of the

Łódź Ghetto. Eighteen years later, when I published *King of the Jews*, a novel based on what I had read on that dog-eared page, a celebrated Holocaust historian wrote my publisher the following blurb: *Not only did Hitler kill six million Jews, now Leslie Epstein comes to dance on the graves of the dead.*

That response from the world without was the first sign of far greater trouble about to arise from within. I knew that in the year I spent researching *King of the Jews*, I had drawn a psychic shutter between myself and the suffering of my people; or, as Chekhov has advised all writers, I had turned my heart to ice. The punishment for that pact with the devil, or my instinctive life, came well *after* the publication of my novel—and it very much resembled the imaginative paralysis I had experienced as an adolescent. Suddenly I could no longer write—rather, everywhere I looked in my new manuscript I saw pain and death: amputations, autopsies, disinterments, acts of torture; whole armies crossed rivers, like Caesar's men, on the backs of their fallen comrades. I realized that all the horror I had kept from the pages of my Holocaust novel was now returning, as if in a reflex of revenge, in this tale of gold rush California.

Why was it so difficult to put down the words of *Pinto and Sons*? I do not think the heightened self-consciousness that followed the success of *King of the Jews*, nor the emotional censorship I practiced while researching and writing that novel, can account for this return of what I believe is called the repressed. When, at what other time, had I purposefully turned my back on such feelings? Was it not when my brother and I had gone off to see a comedy the day after our father's death? What kind of bargain, I wonder, was I making in my thirteen-year-old mind when I

said I did not wish to attend the funeral? Did I think that if
I ignored the proof of my father's death he might return to
us in the guise of his identical twin? Did I retain in me the
dregs of the surrounding Christian culture that assures us
that no death need be final? What were those gold statuettes that Alec Guinness has in his suitcase? Miniature
Eiffel Towers? Or Oscars? My father's Academy Award?

No Dancing on the Graves of the Dead! That is the slogan of the young resistance fighters in *King of the Jews*.
They're warning the residents of the ghetto not to go to a
play (*Macbeth*, as it happens) while their people suffer. Was
this meant to be a flag waved in my own direction? For
going to the movies on the day my father was buried? For
writing a novel about these millions of victims, in some
sense ancestors too? For my laughter on both occasions?
For the voice of that novel's narrator, so lively, jaunty,
glad-to-be-alive? One would have to be a resistance
fighter in a different, more Freudian, sense to untangle
these knotty questions, though perhaps no less heroic for
that.

It took me eleven years to write that next novel. I
found I could only finish it by transforming Adolph Pinto
from a nondescript Austro-Hungarian into a Jew. That
was part of what I had to accomplish in order to reclaim
my imagination. I also had a journey to make. I had fled
California, the film industry, my own Judaism, and my
own family. I went to the other end of the country. I disguised my identity. I became an academic. I wrote in a
highbrow, literary manner, far removed from the popular
culture that my family had helped form and in which they
had thrived. I may have had a long way to go, but *Pinto and
Sons* took more than just a single step. Not only was the
main character of the novel now a Jew, but he traveled by

accident to my home state, in which he then spent the rest of his life. Not only that, the Modoc Indian War, the dramatic center of the book, was all too clearly a psychic recapitulation of the plight of the Jews, with the lava beds of California replacing the streets of the Łódź Ghetto.

The journey backward, the long, circuitous, and largely hidden return to the past, continued in the books that followed. In *Pandaemonium*, the European émigré also arrives in California, where he creates his own chaotic version of Hollywood. In *Ice Fire Water: A Leib Goldkorn Cocktail*, we are not only in Hollywood but involved in a love affair with three of its goddesses, Sonja Henie, Carmen Miranda, and Esther Williams. *San Remo Drive: A Novel from Memory* takes us full circle: to California, to Hollywood, to Jews and their relation to the film industry, to the McCarthy era, and finally back to my father, my mother, my brother, and the very house we lived in, 1341 San Remo Drive.

What these three books reveal, with enough clarity for even me to discern them, are the entwined themes of my work and life: Jews and Jewishness on the one hand, and family, films, and California on the other (though the use of the word "entwined" suggests yet another theme, twins). What is ironic, and, to me, moving, about these themes is that if I had not turned my back on both of them, neither would have played a role in my fiction; indeed, there is some question as to whether I would have become a writer at all.

What I mean by this is that if I had had a Jewish upbringing, or even consciousness, as a child, I surely would not have attempted to fill what I suppose I must call a spiritual vacuum as an adult. Similarly, if I had never left California and all that it represented—the cork trees on our lawn; the glamour of the movie business; my mother, in a white bathing suit and gleaming cap, swimming endless laps in our pool; the yip-yapping laughter of Phil and Julie in our library; my brother, cross-legged, burning an incense stick; and the flat, unceasing sunlight, the blue of the real and the blue of the fake Hollywood skies—I would not have been longing for it ever since in my work.

I'll leave the last word to Richard, who speaks for me throughout *San Remo Drive*: "So it is, I discovered, that all art is created: not from the actual objects or the life we see around us, but from the images of our childhood, with its early sorrows and many joys, that we carry undamaged within."

ALAN LELCHUK

The End of the Jewish Writer?

Let me start with two anecdotes concerning Saul Bellow and the varieties of ethnic displeasure he has caused. In Jerusalem in the 1970s, I was sitting in the living room of Gershom Scholem, the great scholar of Jewish mysticism and one of the tribal chiefs of secular Judaism, when the discussion turned to American literature. At the mention of the name Bellow, Scholem, normally cool and relaxed, immediately grew livid, stood up and, striding back and forth, began to downgrade Bellow as a writer and to berate him personally. At the bottom of Scholem's ire, it turned out, was Bellow's remark after he had received the Nobel Prize that he was "An American writer first, and a Jew second." How could an intelligent man who was Jewish say such a thing, Scholem charged, instead of acknowledging his Jewish identity first and foremost? To Scholem, the claim was either stupid or cowardly, the product of an assimilationist culture and/or personality, and Scholem would never forgive Bellow for it. For Scholem had not come to primitive Palestine in the early 1930s—abandoning his civilized Germany to be mocked by family and assimilationist friends—only to hear a Jewish Nobel Prize winner de-emphasize his Jewish heritage.

The second incident took place in a somewhat duller setting, at the 1978 commencement ceremonies at Brandeis University, where I was teaching, when Bellow and Lionel Trilling were among the recipients of honorary degrees, and Bellow was the official commencement speaker. His talk, that hot Sunday, was unusual in that it bypassed a public topic in order to track his own life as a young writer. He recounted his early days in Montreal, where he studied in a Hebrew school, and then in Chicago, where he composed on a table in the kitchen while his aunt made Russian borscht and argued in Yiddish with family members. With affection and humor, Bellow recalled his student days at the University of Chicago, too, and his growing mixture of college sophistication and homespun wisdoms. Characteristically, along the way, Bellow offered rich autobiographical glimpses into the making of a novelist.

•••

For me, a young writer about to have yet another commencement address inflicted on him, it was a wonderful surprise—an honest and detailed talk, free of the usual piety and palaver that clutter those speeches. Trilling, however, thought otherwise. Speaking with him later, I asked how he liked Bellow's talk. His face tightening, Trilling retorted, "Not at all." Why not, I wondered? "It was inappropriate. Highly inappropriate."

Inappropriate. Trilling announced it like a judge repeating the jury's verdict, "Guilty." Clearly, for Trilling, Bellow had committed a gross act of violence, a violation of the strict code of academic behavior. Poor Bellow—in his way he was being an errant patient, a wayward Jew, not quite in touch with reality. You just didn't talk about your personal life, especially not a Jewish ghetto life, at a university ceremony.

Now, what was inappropriate for Bellow in life, according to Scholem's terms of identification for a writer and Trilling's standards for a public speaker, was also not appropriate—in terms of ethnicity—for Bellow as a novelist at an earlier point in his career. It was Katherine Anne Porter who, after *The Adventures of Augie March* won the National Book Award in 1953, complained that this reward might start a dangerous trend, since the author in question was "bastardizing" the English language and lowering the standards of the American novel with his use of "foreign"—i.e., Yiddish—inflections, words, syntax. Although strains of anti-Semitism have always existed in the literary community, Porter's genteel attack found few believers, perhaps because it was already clear to most, including Edmund Wilson and Philip Rahv, that not only was Bellow a gifted talent but also an outstanding new stylist. But once again Bellow was paying the price of not behaving appropriately—this time in his fiction, not leaving off his ethnic ways and acting as if he were a well-behaved gentile writer. Naturally, this was a bit difficult, since he wasn't one, and since one of his greatest strengths was precisely in playing out his strong ethnic suit, in language as well as landscape.

The issue here is not Bellow, though the example speaks for itself. And, of course, much has changed in literary and social history in the last few decades. But the example gives us a starting point for discussing the complex issue of a writer's ethnic origins and their (possible)

uses in his work. Now, to put my foot in my mouth immediately, if anything is "appropriate" for a writer to write
about, surely it is to write about what he/she knows. So
that if he grew up Jewish—whether believer, skeptic,
rebel, or secularist—then that upbringing, that sensibility,
will shape and at times constitute his fictional world.

It is surprising to see how often narrow definitions of
the Jewish writer are voiced or projected by critics who
should know better. And yet need it be said at this late
date, that the return to one's origins by itself is not enough
to sustain a book's literary interest, let alone make it a
work of art? I fear it does. It seems unfortunate but true
that the pendulum has swung the other way and the fashion of the times has been to celebrate the "ethnic writer,"
trying in part to catch up with the recent shifts in American social history, in which ethnic groups have fought
hard to assert themselves and gain their share of the
American pie. So the culture of the past decade, both popular and literary culture, has rewarded those returns to the
ethnic past that have brought back a measure of certainty,
of celebration, of lament. And I don't mean the enormous
success in the mass media of full-blown pageants like *Roots*
or *Holocaust*, but the many works that have come along
and been hailed as works of art or literary masterpieces
when really they are no more than sentimental journeys to
the past. This critical pattern is dangerous, for it demeans
works of fiction that are deeply and obviously rooted in
ethnic sources, at the same time that they move beyond
to art.

Consider a work like *Call It Sleep* by Henry Roth, that
small gem published in the 1930s, then buried for several
decades, precisely because it appeared too ethnic. Yet it is
clear to me that to name Henry Roth as an ethnic writer

and leave it at that is a disservice; he is a writer, period. *Call It Sleep* is distinguished by its strong sense of character and rich play with language, as well as its resonant evocation of Brooklyn immigrant experience viewed from the perspective of a young boy. Henry Roth was not merely taking a trip down memory lane; he was creating the complex world of a childhood. Now, without the landscape of the ethnic, *Call It Sleep* would have been impossible to imagine; but in the hands of a lesser writer, it would not have been a novel to remember. It would have been a period piece.

I must cite here another recent development, not altogether pleasant. The danger of pushing primarily ethnic works as serious literature has unfortunately been extended to novels of the Holocaust as well. In recent years we have witnessed a deluge of novels that have been debasing to the actual experience. The Holocaust is In. At first, there was simply the tendency to describe the horrors and document the victims' plight; next, the tendency to universalize the particular, to turn the Jew into mankind and, recently, a new wrinkle—to show the "humanness" of the torturers. Ah, imagination!

For the best of intentions, *maybe*, the cheapest books have been manufactured. And, in the process, the very few pieces of genuine literature about the terrible experience have been passed over, forgotten. *Sophie's Choice* is far better known than *This Way for the Gas, Ladies and Gentlemen* by the tragic Pole Tadeusz Borowski. And *King of the Jews* enjoys greater renown than a much finer novel written in the early 1960s, *An Estate of Memory*, by the Polish Ilona Karmel. This long, flawed, but serious novel traces and contrasts the experience of three very different women in the camps, where the author herself lived for four years, and yet, despite its high merits, it has remained obscure. In both Borowski and Karmel, the emphasis is on character, motive, detail, tone, rather than on the horrors themselves; in short, they focus on the literature to be made from the world they knew.

For Borowski and Karmel, Auschwitz, Maidanek, and Treblinka were their New York playgrounds and hangouts, their Chicago streets or Pennsylvania farms. It was the turf they knew and were, literally, condemned to, and it is a measure of their courage that they stayed with it and honed their talent on that forbidding subject matter. And, for readers, the horrors are more authentic within the context of everyday routine—in a Borowski tale 3,000 Jews disappear to the crematorium between throw-ins at a camp soccer game. These novels, among a few others, not to mention the important nonfiction accounts of Lucy Dawidowicz, are dishonored by the easy and spurious novels exploiting the issue.

Now the aims of literature are, as we know, not so much to comfort or celebrate as they are to confront and disturb. Literature is a force for disturbing the complacencies of our reason, the prejudices of our emotion, the formulas of our language. In other words, it is a force for restabilization—at times revaluation—all in the interest of removing our bondage to the received wisdom of family, country, religion, whatever tyrannizes us in the helpless years of childhood and youth. It is no surprise therefore that the returns home of adults, in literature as in life, are fraught with violent ambivalences and paradoxes. For most of us, the real wars take place in the family trenches, not the battlefields, and those form the stuff for rich imaginings. To miss out on this human dilemma and concentrate on the newly discovered meaning of this or that ethnic ceremony is to sacrifice literary possibility for sentimentality.

Having said that, let me counter by adding that richness of all sorts takes place when the ethnic can be joined with the familial to provide conflict. Let me give a brief personal example of where the two—ethnic and familial—coalesced for me and how I look to make fiction from it. When I was approaching my thirteenth birthday, my father began to give me lessons in preparation for my bar mitzvah ceremony. My father, possessor of a fine self-taught Hebrew and no less fine singing voice, decided he would be my teacher instead of the usual hired teacher, for reasons of economics and pride. So, several times a week, we sat at the wooden table covered with oilcloth and, armed with haftarah and Torah texts, went through my assigned portions. Interestingly, many of my friends envied me, since they were forced to put up with the hired tutor, usually a middle-aged rabbi of unfailing severity.

...

Now it might be "appropriate," and certainly easy for me, in looking back, to write of the warmth and coziness of the scene—father and son learning together, the ancient Jewish ritual rehearsed with meticulous care and warmth, and so on. Unfortunately—or fortunately—reality proved far more complex. In fact, I was the one who secretly envied my friends their stranger-tutor, for my father, a perfect gentleman in public, changed masks when alone with me. He was unforgiving of error, impatient with my weak Hebrew and poor singing voice—an attitude that made both Hebrew and voice worse, of course—and frequently wound up chastising me with choice epithets and sharp slaps. Moreover, those occasions were opportunities for him to get back at me for siding with my mother in their long-standing marital conflict.

The result for me was an ordeal that lasted for three or four steamy months, during which the upcoming ceremony lost whatever joy or wisdom one was supposed to get from it. And when it was over and I passed through it well in the small synagogue on Strauss Street in Brooklyn—a few doors away from the barbershop where Bugsy Siegel used to assist the barber with his shaves—my father took full credit for my "success." At the reception, through my restrained smiles with friends, I swore a cold Sicilian revenge.

What was a long trial and semiweekly torture for the young boy turned into fruitful material for the adult writer; because of the heat between father and son, scenes of greater emotional power were available than any offered by a renewed celebration of the bar mitzvah experience, at the same time that the religious ceremony provided a nice backdrop of irony.

Being an American is no less easy, if taken seriously, than being a Jew, if taken playfully; and the one without the other is a thinner experience, if an easier one to comprehend. Like most native types, whether Midwest Lutherans, Boston Catholics, inner-city blacks or chicanos, Brooklyn Jews know that we are richer *because of the other*; and they in turn are enriched by us. One tries fiction to understand if not actually dramatize this duality, to be genuine about one's origins while reaching out beyond, to other worlds. In my heart, I have always remained as loyal to Jackie Robinson stealing home in Ebbets Field as I have to memories of Hebrew school.

Of course, it should be remembered, there have been Jewish writers who have declared open war on their ethnic experience. In our time, Philip Roth has waged a continuing battle against various aspects of middle-class Jewish life, secular and religious, a battle that has incited the wrath of critics and rabbis. And most recently, Joseph Heller has turned to the Old Testament in an effort to give contemporary voice to ancient stories and religious pieties. But there have been earlier novelists, less known but perhaps even fiercer in their struggle for independence from the clan. A little more than one hundred years ago in Warsaw, Joel Linetski wrote *The Polish Lad*, which was such an outspoken, insider's attack on the Hasidic way of life that the writer was expelled from the community, never to return.

•••

And in the early 1900s a Russian Jew began writing stories and novellas about Jews and Jewish questions that exemplify the toughest love-hate relationship of all. In his novel *Breakdown and Bereavement* and in novellas such as *Nerves*, Josef Hayim Brenner reveals his exquisite torment over Jewish traditions, aspirations, ideals, failures. Steeped in self-conscious Dostoyevskian anguish, Brenner's antiheroes suffer the crippling fates of hearts that desire Jewish salvation and emancipation, but minds that perceive the insufficiency of ideas, land, and people to achieve them.

This cosmopolitan, skeptical spirit, who lived in London before settling in Palestine in 1909, was obsessed with the Jewish experience and its many paradoxes. The "ethnic" issue itself, with debates over assimilation versus tribal attachment, Palestine versus the Diaspora, was the source of his drama, and he attacked all traditions fiercely, forever undercutting his protagonists' positions by his own lacerating ambivalence. For those of you who have never read Brenner, a provocative experience awaits you. Dead at forty-three, in 1921, he made his mark as a kind of Nietzschean tough guy, as passionate a critic of all things Jewish as he was a passionate Jew.

In America today, the predicament of the Jewish writer is no less uneasy because of acceptance than it was in the many years of rejection. No longer does one have to guard the Yiddish phrase, clean up the ghetto grocery, explain the bar mitzvah ritual. These formerly esoteric particulars have become a part of the literary lingo of the times. The Jewish writer, like the Holocaust, has made it. But the paradox is, America has made it too, using success to take its toll on the rebellious spirits—accepting them, celebrating them, co-opting them. When the enemy, imagined and/or real, becomes one's ally, what does one do?

We have come a long way from Abraham Cahan's *The Rise of David Levinsky* (1917), that story of a Russian immigrant's rise on the fabled East Side that embarrassed the decent liberal critics as well as offended genteel professor-reviewers. Poor Levinsky, alone and lonely at the end of that interesting, raw book, dares not cross the ethnic barrier and propose to the gentile woman he loves. And indeed, since Levinsky we have witnessed various steps and stages—the trials of just such a mixed marriage in Ludwig Lewisohn's neglected tale of the Jewish professor and his upper-class wife *The Island Within*, and after that, in Bellow's *Dangling Man*, the declaration by Joseph of his full literary and philosophical independence from the dominating voice and code of the Hemingway man. We are no longer startled by Portnoy's desire to deflower every Mayflower shiksa as a way of getting back at Protestant America.

One response to the easing of the Jew into the majority (literary) society has been a turning backward, a return
to the religious shell, the old neighborhood, or the recent
nightmare of Europe, in an attempt to stem the flow of
assimilation. But what about that "other" Jewish writer,
who recognizes with exacting honesty that the European
grandparents and parents have left or are just leaving us,
for good, and that with them the language and manners of
a whole way of life will depart?

In other words, that world of riches is on the edge of
vanishing, both as fact and as potential fiction. Oh, he or
she might scratch out a Yiddish word here, a ritual there,
but the truth is, a species and a culture are disappearing.
And there is little use in pretending otherwise, in calling
for a "new Yiddish-American" lingo, in euphemizing or
sentimentalizing the truth. Yes, there is American Jewish
life, but that is mostly a religious affair, available to a narrow minority. For the rest of us, the loss is the truth, and
we should face the matter squarely. The felt experience of
the Viennese, Berlin, Warsaw, Budapest, Moscow Jew,
found in the generation of immigrants and passed into the
literature through their sons and grandsons, is becoming,
if it is not already, a thing of the past.

Paradoxically, however, the time of this inward loss
for the Jewish writer coincides with the time of his greatest gain outwardly. Once again, we are speaking of this
"other Jewish writer," this skeptical, exuberant, and more
independent fellow shaped by the odd Enlightenment
called America, not the fragile, harried European gentleman molded by the Dark Ages of Mosaic Laws and tribal
codes and institutionalized anti-Semitism. This more
modern Jewish artist writes under the handicap of recent
American success. He is a freer man in certain respects.

He has more or less rid himself of the scars and wounds of his uniquely disfigured history. Though this may violate the ideas, if not the out-and-out-prescriptions, of critics such as Cynthia Ozick, I myself find it coercive, not to mention subtly exploitative, to carry around the luggage of that disfigured history and count it as some sure sign of artistic superiority, let alone merit. After all, each ethnic group has a disfigured history of its own; to rely on it alone for art is a mistaken strategy.

So if what I am saying is that the time has come for the modern Jewish writer to become just the writer, a writer, I consider this no small victory for this time, this place. He will certainly have given up something of value, but also in the process gained something. He will have given up his special claim to ancestral injury and European wound, and taken up instead his American passport—to confusion, paradox, mystery, pleasure.

I am describing here an emancipation of sorts, but not the kind imagined by the Messianic-projectors or decreed by the prophet-critics. This is a more ambiguous emancipation that leads only to native challenge, the wide-open challenge perhaps best visualized in our great crisscrossing highways, where we are led to disaster as often as to destination, to the despair of nowhere as much as to a locale of purpose. No longer bound by insulating landscape, language, or experience, we mustn't pretend that we are, for that is a disingenuous paranoia in place of historical reality. The writer who grows in childhood here, endures adolescence here, matures and breaks down here, marries or divorces here, ages here, is celebrated or defeated here, well, he *is here*, whether he wills it or not; his imagination, the rich computer of his work, must start at the starting point to open his true file. If he chooses not to let it, he will be escaping his turf, his audience will remain partisan, his work marginal.

•••

If I seem to be speaking about the end of the Jewish writer as an ethnic entity, I am not speaking of the end of things Jewish in his work. The sensibility that is skeptical and ironic, especially about its own failure and misfortune, like a Kafka; the temperament that is emotionally high-pitched and accepts itself as such without seeking refuge in cooler realms, like a Bellow; the imagination that is humorous and serious simultaneously and that perceives in one quality the beginning of its opposite, like an Italo Svevo; these I associate—as much as, or really more than, particular objects and rituals—with Jewishness. When Elizabeth Hardwick, a Southerner, explains that she came to New York to make herself over into a Jewish intellectual or John Berryman avers that he considers himself an honorary Jew, they describe the sort of ethnicity most appealing to me. The opposite of pious, chauvinist, sentimental, this version of Jewishness is defined by emotional breadth, critical inquiry, tactile curiosity. It prefers the historical to the absolute, the concrete to the abstract, the American to the European.

Let's say this, the Jewish writer should resemble others of his international troupe, writers performing in the peculiar circus of literature. At times they play the clown; at times they play the impresario; sometimes they fly high on the trapeze; sometimes they attempt to walk the tightrope. In all this, independence is the Jewish writer's play, and beauty and excellence his purpose, imperfection his only premise. In other words, accomplishment is all, at last.

MAX APPLE

Max and Mottele

Lives are distorted, or occasionally salvaged, by questions of identity, and people are sometimes consumed by who they are or, even worse, who someone else is. Yet this is a struggle I've never felt in my own bones. Identity is someone else's problem; I've always known who we are. In this compact body that barely seems to fulfill the requirements of one, there are in fact two: Max and Mottele.

You could think of us as the American and the Jew, or the modernist and the traditionalist, or the nonbeliever and the believer, but none of these categories wholly fits either of us. Mottele, who knows almost nothing about the real America of politics and economics, is uncritically in love with Yankee ways, while Max, who does understand America, is a European socialist.

Of course, Mottele isn't really a citizen. He's the son of immigrants. He grew up among Yiddish-speaking parents and grandparents in a place called Michigan, which he thinks is a province of Lithuania. With his mother's milk and his grandmother's Sanka coffee he took in the shtetl. The things he knows about happened before 1920—many of them closer to 1920 B.C.E. Thanks to his grandmother's favorite book, *Tsena Urena*, the women's Bible commentary, he's as comfortable with Abraham and Moses as Max is with Bill Clinton and Shimon Peres. Mottele believes that his ancestors keep tabs on him, even after their death. And, as if that's not enough, God checks the record every year between Rosh Hashanah and Yom Kippur and has been known to make unannounced appearances. This constant checking keeps Mottele close to the fold, but within his limits he likes to have a good time. America is made for him: it's a gigantic amusement park filled with good-natured clowns in every shop and office.

Max, however, knows better. Max discarded the shtetl. He realized at an early age that by speaking English and reading books he could please his Gentile teachers. He knew these pleasant women were Gentiles by their failure to talk about cholera or pogroms or Hitler. They passed out gold stars and, later, scholarships. Max understood a good deal when he saw one. To impress his teachers he memorized the Gettysburg Address. He practiced every night at bedtime as his grandmother marveled at how well he said the *Shema Yisroel* in English. He read so many books that his grandmother was afraid he would ruin his eyes and never get a good job, and she was right. After more than twenty years in school he became merely a teacher.

While Max immersed himself in Shakespeare, Milton, and Christian humanism, Mottele stayed away— more than that, he disappeared. In the seminars and classrooms Mottele was a forgotten remnant, a Yiddish Puff the Magic Dragon. Then, with formal education behind him and his head filled with the glories of English literature, Max began to write stories. He wanted them to sound like the stories he read in the anthologies. He hoped for British characters who would experience epiphanies, those obscure but luminous moments that reveal the human condition. But all of his people turned out to be Americans, and none of them even knew what an epiphany was. They were good-natured folks, clowns in every shop and office.

Mottele had not disappeared. He had been there all along, busy taking notes on the raw material, mostly Max. When Max started up with women and memorized "To His Coy Mistress" to impress them, Mottele almost died laughing. When Max lectured on Christian humanism, Mottele took quiet revenge for the Crusades. And when Max started writing stories, Mottele squeezed in his characters, the kinds of Americans he loved to laugh at: ballplayers, truth seekers, entrepreneurs, and vegetarians. Max, of course, did the serious work of being an American. Mottele stayed in the background unless Max carried seriousness too far.

"You live in the Garden of Eden," Mottele said. "Everything around you is funny, and you don't know it because you spend all your time in the library."

"The life of the mind exists in the library," Max said. "My Garden of Eden is the card catalogue."

"Then why are you always looking around at the girls?" Mottele said. "Be honest about it. Let's go to a mall—there you can read a book *and* look at girls . . . as well as at shoes and dry goods."

"I can't write in a mall," Max said. "I need a quiet place to work."

"That's why there's a Christian Science Reading

Room," Mottele said. "Meet me there in two months and I'll give you a book of stories."

After Mottele delivered the stories as promised, Max gave him a freer hand, and over the years they've collaborated so well that no outsiders recognize the differences between them. Yet the differences are all over their stories. They squabble like the president and Congress, and, like them, they pretend to do so for the common good. For example, Mottele noticed that Max was getting a little too full of himself. His picture was in the paper, people paid him to read aloud to them, and he got free tickets to ball games. So Mottele wrote a story about a fellow just like Max, a sports-loving lightweight who thought he was a big shot ready to enter the arena of letters. Mottele set the story in a boxing ring, where Max had to prove himself against a real heavyweight, Norman Mailer. Max danced around in the story, threw a few jabs and metaphors, but when he landed his best shot, Mailer took it in the midsection without even noticing the punch or Max. The lightweight disappeared, engulfed by Mailer.

"I did you a favor," Mottele said. "Now you can see where ambition will lead you."

To return the favor, Max wrote a story about Mottele's favorite couple: a boy and his mother. He made the boy resemble Mottele. "You like boxing so much," Max said, "try this." The boy, almost middle-aged, had had enough of Mom. One day he punched her and went off to Saudi Arabia to find a good job.

It took Mottele a long time to recover from that fictional blow. "Nobody hits a mother," he said. "You're worse than a lightweight, you're avant-garde." After that punch the mother said she wanted no part of any of their stories, so Mottele wrote a whole book about his grandmother.

Still, none of their internal bickering caused any problems, because the commotion took place in literature, one of the quietest neighborhoods in America. And even within that neighborhood Max and Mottele spent most of their time in the real boondocks, the short story.

Then they moved briefly to a much more expensive neighborhood, the movies, and there they encountered for the first time questions about Who They Were. Max will explain:

> I wrote a book called *Roommates*. The main characters were a grandfather, Yerachmiel, and his grandson, Max. They spoke Yiddish. Yerachmiel prayed three times a day. He wore a yarmulke on his head, a *tsitsis* under his shirt. It was not hard to guess his tribal identity—or mine. About a year later a movie came out, also called *Roommates*. The film, like my book, featured a grandfather and a grandson, and their religion and ethnicity are also easy to identify. They're Polish Catholics.

Max and Mottele, that solid couple, seemed to have split down the middle: one wrote the book, the other the movie. Many people noticed this split and didn't like it. Max received angry mail from Jews. One letter he can quote in its entirety. "So," wrote a Brooklyn rabbi who'd read an excerpt in *Reader's Digest,* "if you weren't ashamed for the magazine, why were you ashamed for the movies?"

Max tried to explain. "There is no shame," he wrote, "in imagining what it's like to be someone else. That's what I do for a living. The world is full of writers writing about characters like themselves—lawyers writing about lawyers, alcoholics about alcoholics, Jews about Jews. There is no danger that this will come to an end. Our like-nesses will always be among us. The writer's job is to make you believe a character is real, not Jewish. This is called 'verisimilitude,' and it evokes empathy, the attempt to put yourself into someone else's skin. Hath not a Gentile skin, Rabbi?

"This is what writing is all about, and in order to do it the writer must be free to imagine anything, even a non-Jewish version of himself and his grandfather. If you need examples of great freedom of imagination, may I suggest that you check the Midrash.

"As far as causing you confusion, for that I do apologize. I assume that you went to the movie expecting it to be the same as the book since the title was the same. I can tell you that you're not the first to be fooled by a movie title. About twenty years ago a Hadassah chapter in New Jersey bought out an entire showing of a movie called *Tora! Tora! Tora!*, a World War II epic. They didn't pay attention to spelling, so instead of Rashi and Rambam they got Guadalcanal and Iwo Jima. The lesson, Rabbi: Buyer beware."

Mottele read Max's reply to the rabbi and tore it up. He wrote his own reply:

Dear Rabbi,
    Business is business. The movie people wanted goyim. They thought that would sell more tickets. The movies are about millions, not about who counts for a *minyan*. If they had left us alone we could have made a nice Jewish picture.

Max tore up that reply and was about to do the same to the rabbi's letter when Mottele stayed his hand and held the sheet of paper up to the writer's face.

"Look who you're writing to about freedom and imagination. Instead of preaching to him about empathy, use a little yourself. Does this look like congregational stationery? Are there names of rich people down the left-hand side of the page? Don't mistake this rabbi for the kind you know, men who play golf and give speeches and have closets full of suits. This man probably lives in a few miserable rooms on Avenue J and supports his five or six children by working nights for a caterer. While people stuff themselves at weddings and bat mitzvahs, he's in the kitchen making sure there are no bugs in the broccoli or the cauliflower. And don't flatter yourself. He didn't read *Roommates*—he said *Reader's Digest*, didn't he?

"His boss, the caterer, a rich nonbeliever, probably tossed him a smeared magazine and said, 'Rabbi, here's something you'll like.' He did like it, and a few weeks later when he saw the movie poster with the picture of Peter Falk, he took a chance.

"This is a man who had never gone to a movie before. The closest he'd come to excess was a video of street dancing on Simchat Torah. Because he liked your characters so much, he went to a movie house and risked sitting next to a woman. Don't lecture to him about empathy and freedom. In Crown Heights those words don't mean anything. Send him a refund for the movie ticket and throw in an autographed book. And be sure to sign your name in Yiddish."

Max refused. They fought to a standstill, and the rabbi, still awaiting an answer, has probably been taken in by *Tora! Tora! Tora!* on video.

In their second movie adventure, Max and Mottele stayed away from Jews. They wrote a film called *The Air Up There*, which featured a college coach and his would-be recruit, a six-foot-nine African youth. No rabbis complained, but a New York sportswriter skewered Max. The sportswriter said that a white man shouldn't have written the film. And he took literally a line from the press kit that quoted Max, a five-foot-four, white writer, as saying he liked to imagine himself as a six-foot-nine, black power forward. "If you want to imagine black heroes," the sportswriter said, "forget basketball, write about real heroes."

"Mazel tov," Mottele said. "You got what you always wanted. You made it to the sports page."

Max threw the paper down with disgust. "Who does he think he is giving me directions about what I'm allowed to write? Didn't Shakespeare imagine Othello, and Mark Twain, Jim? Didn't George Eliot, a Gentile and a woman, create a male Jew? The sportswriter has a lot more chutzpah than the rabbi."

"Relax," Mottele said, "the man had a column to write, it's just business. Anyway, your ballplayer is not exactly the Moor of Venice."

"The principle is the same," Max said.

"Every time someone in a newspaper criticizes you, you're ready to call in Shakespeare as a character witness. He's a journalist. Don't forget we tried that too."

To calm him down, Mottele helped Max recall their first journalism assignment—an investigation of beef barbecue. When Max accepted that job Mottele turned up his nose and kept it in the air. Throughout East Texas, where they inspected pits, Max interviewed, Mottele sniffed. Max quoted happy eaters, adults in paper bibs tearing into their dripping meat with two hands and a clean shirt. Mottele took in the beef and mesquite aromas.

In a switch from their usual roles, Max leaned toward the meat and potatoes while Mottele hankered for the spiritual. He even quoted one of Max's favorites, John Keats: "Heard melodies are sweet / Unheard sweeter still."

"He was talking about poetry," Max said, "not bar-becue."

"So what," Mottele said. "It's also true of beef. You can have the food, I'll take the hunger. Do you think Kafka was the only Jew who understood hunger?"

While Max talked to cooks and managers who thought he was from the health department, Mottele analyzed smoke and emptiness. Max concocted a tomato, Worcestershire sauce, and onion recipe. *Esquire* decorated their reportage with drawings of Texas longhorns and sizzling fat. Together they received this response from their sister: "So for a thousand dollars you ate *treyfe*."

"If our own sister didn't understand that our work is about aroma and hunger," Mottele said, "what can you expect from outsiders? The people who try to tell us what we should be doing are always 'ones.' They can be pious ones like the rabbi or politically correct ones like the sportswriter, but they're all singles, not a twosome like we are. They see one thing; they know one thing. How hard is it for one to be right? A one is always right. Anyway, they just have opinions; they don't do research like we do."

In their research they're sometimes subtle, like private detectives on the trail of a suspect emotion, but most of the time they're daydreaming, or at the ballpark studying statistics, or in the midst of nature staring at ants to sharpen their sense of destiny. But whatever else they do, they're always conducting their ongoing primary research. They eavesdrop so lasciviously that they are now required in certain public places to wear T-shirts emblazoned with the warning "I'm Listening."

Age has not altered them, nor has a half-century of squabbles caused them to consider breaking up. They understand how much they need each other. Without

Mottele, Max knows that he would be a pale imitator, a John Updike without Protestants. And Mottele alone would be exactly that—Mottele alone. Born into Yiddish at the exact moment that murderers were extinguishing it, he would have the language without the people. He needs Americans to populate his shtetl.

Of course, these two are just a couple. The great ones like Shakespeare and Tolstoy aren't mere couples—they're more like corporate Japan: they take in a whole society and guarantee full employment. Max and Mottele resemble their recent ancestors, the peddlers, more than they resemble the great writers. With their wares they roam the neighborhoods: an essay, a story, a novel, a screenplay—they're just glad to have customers. Since they're a twosome they can't enjoy solitary pleasures, they can never be single-minded or even focused. Like all couples, they hold harmony as their highest goal, and they find it above all in the lively carnival of America, in the English language, in words like these, which are to their ears music.

ERICA JONG

How I Got to Be Jewish

*News of America travelled quickly around the European shtetls.
Word was that even if the streets of the "Golden Land" weren't
paved with gold, at least a Jew had a chance.*

Jeff Kisseloff, *You Must Remember This* (1989)

D id you ever wonder why Jews are such relentless
scribes? You may have thought it was because
we are people of the book. You may have
thought it was because we come from homes where reading is stressed. You may have thought it repressed sexuality. Yes, yes—all that is true. But I submit the *real* reason is
our need to constantly define our class. By writing, we
reinvent ourselves. By writing we create pedigrees. Some
of my heroines are West Side, New York Jewish girls like
me. But the heroines I love the best—Fanny in *Fanny
Hackabout-Jones* and Jessica in *Serenissima* and Sappho in
Sappho's Leap—are to the manor born, good little equestri-
ennes, and you can bet they have high cheekbones. Fanny

grew up at Lymeworth, Lord Bellars's country seat. Jessica grew up on the Upper East Side of Manhattan, in the Golden Rectangle. Her pedigree was very gin and country club. Sappho was a noble girl of Lesbos, born to reading, writing, and the lyre. She thought herself the equal of the gods.

Why does a West Side kid like me invent such heroines? Am I trying to escape from my *schmearer-klezmer* class? Interestingly enough, my heroines always escape too. Fanny runs away from her aristocratic upbringing, becomes a highway woman, a whore in a brothel, and a pirate-queen. Jessica leaves the Upper East Side for Hollywood. Sappho becomes a rebel and political exile. And all three of them come to regret it, and find their final happiness back in their own backyards. The heroines who are *apparently* more like me—Isadora Wing and Leila Sand—change their status, or else establish it, through creative work. I guess my writing tells me something that I didn't even consciously know about myself: I write to give myself a class, to invent my name, and then to leave myself a country seat!

I suspect the process is not so different with other writers—however uninvolved with class their books may seem. Saul Bellow's heroes start out as drifters and end up professors. But his very best picaresque hero, Henderson the Rain King, is a WASP to the manor born who goes to Africa and embraces his multiculturalism, thereby finding his true identity. Philip Roth's heroes are equally concerned both with questions of class and with questions of Jewishness. Though they themselves are almost always Jewish, they aspire to fuck their way into WASPdom—a familiar gambit for American Jewish (male) creators. We could call it the Annie Hall syndrome. Surely Woody Allen defined it forever when his autobiographical hero, sitting at Annie Hall's Midwestern dinner table, amid the WASPs, suddenly sprouts *payess* and a big black hat.

The archetypical Jewish American fear! If we eat *treyfe*, we may suddenly grow *payess!* Perhaps the reason Jews in America have adopted Thanksgiving as their own special holiday is that we hope by claiming the Pilgrims as our fathers, we will fool the rest of America too!

Howard Fast is a perfect example here. His best books, the fictional *April Morning* and nonfictional *The Jews*, are oddly connected. They both chronicle rootless people. They testify to the fact that Americans, like Jews, must constantly define themselves.

A Jew may wander from Egypt to Germany to America to Israel, picking up different languages and hair and eye color, but he remains a Jew. And what is a Jew? A Jew is a person who is safe *nowhere* (i.e., always in danger of growing *payess* at inopportune times). A Jew is a person who can convert to Christianity from now to Doomsday, and still be killed by Hitler if his mother was Jewish. A Jew is a person who will be given away by his penis. This explains why Jews are likely to be obsessed with matters of identity. Our survival depends upon it.

Americans, too, are obsessed with defining identity. In a melting pot culture, where aristocratic titles are considered laughable (witness Count Dracula or Count Chocula, as kids are introduced to him—a breakfast cereal), we must constantly test the limits of identity. Andy Warhol's remark that in the future everyone will be famous for fifteen minutes delineates the quintessential American dilemma. We can become famous, but perhaps not *stay* famous. And once having known that fame, how will we live out the rest of our lives? More to the point, how will we ever get into the Hebrew Home for the Aged?

Many American lives seem doomed by Warhol's definition. Remember the first George Bush struggling to stay president against the historical tide? Or Stephen King aspiring to top all three best-seller lists at once? Or Bill Clinton wiring the White House to become its own media network? Americans can never rest. They can never join the Corviglia Club in St. Moritz and amuse themselves skiing down into the picturebook village. The grace of their skiing is *never* in itself enough. They must always climb back on the chairlift and do it again, do it again, do it again.

I see that the Corviglia Club (which I visited once as a guest of an aristocratic friend) has become my symbol of *sprezzatura*—a lovely Italian word which means the art of making the difficult look easy. Perhaps I select that image because it evokes a world of blessed people who do not have to *do* anything, they only have to *be*. I long for such status as only an American Jew can. How nice to have an entree into the world that cannot ever be revoked. How nice to be *born* into an identity. I say that even though I know many such people who envy my status as a writer and think they would happily change places with me. They find their lives wanting. They want to write novels. Yet they seldom do—for lack of the fierce drive I and my Jewish compeers have. They cannot give up their other status as languid aristocrats. Meanwhile I, who grew up wanting languid aristocracy, find myself now glad to have been born a fevered Jew.

The older we get, the more Jewish we become in my family. My mother's father declared himself an atheist in his communist youth, so we never belonged to a synagogue or had bat mitzvahs. But we wind up in Hebrew homes for the aged and in cemeteries with Hebrew letters over the gates. Thus does our heritage claim us—even in

America, our promised land. In my family, if you're still protesting you're Unitarian, you're just not *old* enough. (I refer, of course, to one of my ex-husbands, who having married a shiksa, worships at the local Unitarian Church. That will change, I predict.)

My father, on the other hand, sends money to Israel and carries around a card that supposedly will expedite his admission to Mt. Sinai Hospital, and after that heaven, identifying him as a Big Donor. This is the sort of thing he would have done riffs on in his vaudeville days. Now my daughter Molly does those riffs. The young are cruel. They *have* to be to supplant the old. The old are such a burden, so territorial, so inclined to hold on to their money. The young have to be tough to make it at all.

After all, what does the ritual of circumcision say to a Jewish son? *Watch out. Next time I'll cut off the whole thing.* So Jewish boys are horny, but also full of fear about whether their cocks will survive their horniness. Alexander Portnoy is the archetypal good Jewish boy. The good Jewish boy and the bad Jewish boy inhabit the same skin—if not the same foreskin. Jewish girls are luckier. Their sexuality is less damaged—whatever those jokes about dropping emery boards may imply. Girls are allowed to be sexual as long as they keep it in inside the family. Marriage is sacred as long as you marry an oedipal stand-in. Jewish adultery is an oxymoron. We read Updike for that. Jewish men who cheat end up like Woody Allen. In big trouble. Even Jewish lesbians are required to have silverware and bone china from Tiffany's. Jewish lesbians are required to fall in love with women who remind them of their mothers—and, in today's feminist times, are doctors or lawyers.

How did I get to be Jewish?—I with no religious training? Jews are made by the existence of anti-

Semitism—or so says Jean-Paul Sartre, who knew. And despite myths to the contrary, there is plenty of anti-Semitism in America (otherwise we'd be saying "Next year in Oyster Bay or Grosse Pointe" instead of "Next year in Jerusalem"). But American anti-Semitism takes the clever form of class snobbery. Let me show you what I mean.

We say that America is a classless society, but really it is not. It's just that our class distinctions are so much subtler than those of other countries that sometimes we don't even see them as class distinctions. They are uniquely American class distinctions and they follow us all our lives. We go happily into the Hebrew Home for the Aged, having learned that where aging and death are concerned, only our own kind *want* us. When we're young and cute, we can hang out with *goyim*—but as the sun goes down, we revert to knishes and *knaydlach*. We do mitzvahs—of the sort that I have done by getting my wandering, memory-impaired aunt into the Hebrew Home.

When I was growing up in a New York that seemed dominated by Jews whose parents or grandparents had fled from Europe, I never consciously thought about Jewishness. Or about class. And yet invisible barriers ruled my life—barriers which still stand.

Even in childhood I knew that my best friend, Glenda Glascock, who was Episcopalian and went to private school, was considered classier than me. We lived in the same gloomy Gothic apartment house near Central Park West. We both had parents who were artists. But Glenda's name ended with *cock* and mine did not. I knew that names ending in *cock* were intrinsically classier.

What was my name anyway?

My father was born Weisman and became Mann. My

mother was called Yehuda by her Russian Jewish parents when she was born in England, but the intransigent Englishman in the registry office had changed it first to Judith and then to Edith ("good English names")—leaving the resultant impression that Jews were not even allowed to keep their own names. The dominant culture around our (mental) ghetto required names that did not *sound* Jewish or foreign. That left a strong impression too.

There were categories of Americans in our supposedly egalitarian country and I did not belong to the better (as in "better dresses") category. Glenda did. Her last name bespoke this. Even her nickname—Jewish girls did not have nicknames like Glennie then—bespoke this. And yet we were close as twins, best buddies, in and out of each other's apartments—until we took a bath together one day and she accused me of making peepee in the bathwater because that was "what Jews did." I was outraged, having done no such thing. (Unless my memory censors.)

"Who says they do that?"

"My mother," said Glennie confidently.

So I reported this conversation to my parents and grandparents and mysteriously my friendship with Glennie cooled.

She went off to private school. I did not. I was in some "Intelligently Gifted Program" at PS 87 on Seventy-seventh Street and Amsterdam Avenue—a great Victorian pile in those days, with girls' and boys' entrances. There I discovered other class stratifications. The closer you lived to Central Park West and the "better" your building, the more classy you were. Now I had status. Below me were poorer Jewish kids whose parents had fled the Holocaust and lived in lesser buildings farther west, Irish kids who lived in tenements on side streets, and the first sprinkling of Puerto Rican kids to arrive in New York. They lived in other tenements on *West Side Story*–ish side streets. In the forties, New York was far from being racially integrated. I did not meet black kids from Harlem until I went to the High School of Music and Art, where talent, not neighborhood, was the qualification. The only African Americans we met—called Negroes then—were servants. In childhood, my world was Jewish, Irish, Hispanic—with Jews lording it over everyone else.

The WASP kids were, by this time, off in private school meeting their own kind so they could go to Yale, make their fortunes through cronyism, run the CIA, and rule the world like the Bushes. Jewish kids did not go to private school in *that* New York—unless they were superrich, had disciplinary problems, or were Orthodox.

I figured out pretty soon that in my school I was high class, but that in the world I was not. The kids on television shows and in reading primers did not have names like Weisman, Rabinowitz, Plotkin, Ratner, or Kisseloff. Certainly not Gonzales or O'Shea. There was another America out there in televisionland and we were not part of it. In that other America, girls had names like Gidget and boys like Beaver Cleaver. Our world was not represented—except when the credits rolled by.

Kept out of this *proper* America, we learned to control it by reinventing it (or representing it—as in agent). Some of our parents already did this as actors, producers, or writers, so we knew this was a possible path for us. Others were businessmen, or artists-turned-businessmen—like my father. The point was: We were outsiders longing to be insiders. In those days, we knew that Princeton and Yale might not want us unless we were rich enough. We knew our initials were ICM, not CIA. We knew we were

not born into the ruling class, so we invented our own ruling class. Mike Ovitz, not George Bush. Swifty Lazar, not
Bill Clinton.

How much the world has changed since the forties!
And how *little*! Except for Henry Kissinger, who has
changed these laws of class and caste? Not even Mike
Ovitz. What you see your parents do is what you think *you*
can do. So are we defined, designed. Since my father was a
songwriter-musician turned importer, my grandfather a
portrait painter, my mother a housewife and portrait
painter, I just assumed that I would do something creative.
I also just assumed that I would graduate from college, and
live in a "good building" forever. I also assumed that I
would never turn out to be anything like those American
families I saw on TV.

My family was fiercely proud to be Jewish, but not
religious—unless our religion was buying new English MaryJanes at Saks and English leather leggings
and velvet-collared Chesterfield coats at de Pinna. We
were dressed like little English princesses; I understood
that this was the class to which we aspired.

Dress tells you everything about aspiration. I hated
the damned leather leggings but had to wear them because
Princesses Elizabeth and Margaret had. How did *they* get
to be Princesses of the Jews? Better not ask. It was tacitly
understood just as it was understood that Glascock was a
better name than Weisman (or even Mann).

I smile writing all this. I am trying (clumsily, I fear) to
reenter that world of 1940s New York with its "air-
cooled" movie palaces (complete with towering matrons
and wrapper-strewn children's sections), its striped awn-
ings on apartment buildings in summer, its bus transfers,
its candy stores, its big marble lunch counters that sold the

most delicious bacon, lettuce, and tomato sandwiches and fresh-dipped ice cream cones.

Gone, gone forever. But just as sunlight on a series of paving stones or the taste of tea-soaked cake returned Proust to his halcyon childhood, I sometimes stop on a street corner in New York and am taken back to the forties. The smells do it. The mouths of the subway stations still, on occasion, blow a blast of cotton candy/bubble gum breath, mixed with sweat and popcorn, with piss and (its precursor) beer—and inhaling deeply I am taken back to my sixth year, standing in a subway train, staring at a forest of knees. In childhood you feel you'll never grow up. And the world will always be incomprehensible. First you are all mouth, then you have a name, then you are a member of a family, then you begin to ask the hard questions about better/worse which are the beginnings of class consciousness. Human beings are naturally hierarchical beasts. Democracy is not their native religion.

It was in junior high that my world opened up beyond Seventy-seventh Street and the West Side. Because my parents and I were terrified of the violence of the local junior high, I went to private school—a deliciously comic place where the paying students were mostly Park Avenue Jews and the scholarship students mostly WASPs from Washington Heights whose parents were professors, clergy, missionaries.

The teachers were genteel and WASPy like the scholarship students, and they had proper American-sounding names like the TV people. The school had been started by two redoubtable New England ladies named Miss Birch and Miss Wathen who were probably lovers—but in those days we called them spinsters. One of them looked like Gertrude Stein, the other like Alice B. Toklas. They pronounced "shirt" as if it had three *i*'s in the middle, and they pronounced poetry as if it were poy-et-try. I knew this was classy. I knew this was WASP.

At Birch-Wathen, most of the Jewish kids were wealthier than me. They lived on the East Side in apartments hung with expensive art, and some of them had German names. They went to Temple Emmanuel—my nephews now call it Temple Episcopal—and took dancing and deportment—what an old-fashioned word!—at Viola Wolf's. Again my sense of class was up for grabs. With my Russian grandparents and my West Side bohemian home, I didn't fit in with these kids either. And the scholarship kids all stuck together. I thought them snotty—though now I realize they must have been scared to death. The paying students got bigger allowances—and some of them came to school in chauffeured Cadillacs, Lincolns, or Rollses. That must have seemed daunting to kids who rode the subway. It seemed daunting to me. Cliques splintered us. The Park Avenue kids stuck with their own kind. The scholarship kids did the same.

I floated between the two groups, now shoplifting at Saks with the rich kids (the richer the kids, I learned, the more they shoplifted), now wandering up to Columbia with one of the scholarship kids (whose parents were professors). I felt I belonged nowhere. Ashamed that my father was a businessman, I used to wish he were a professor. If you couldn't have a name that ended with *cock*, you ought to have a Ph.D. at least.

When high school began, I joined still another new world—a world that was racially mixed and full of kids from the ghetto. Chosen for their talent to draw or sing or play an instrument, these kids were the most diverse I'd ever met. Their class was talent. And like all insecure people, they shoved it in your face.

It was in high school that I began to find my true

class. Here the competition was not about money or color or neighborhood but about how well you drew or played. At Music and Art, new hierarchies were created, hierarchies of virtuosity. Was your painting in the semiannual exhibition? Were you tapped to perform in the orchestra, or on WQXR? By now we all knew we did not belong in televisionland America—and we were proud of it. Being outsiders was a badge of merit. We had no teams, no cheerleaders, and the cool class uniform was early beatnik: black stockings, handmade sandals, and black lipstick for the girls; black turtlenecks, black jeans, black leather jackets for the boys. Stringy hair was requisite for both sexes. We experimented with dope. We cruised the Village hoping to be mistaken for hipsters. We had found our class at last.

Many of us rose to the top of it. I count among my high school classmates pop singers, television producers, actors, painters, novelists. Many are household names. A few earn tens of millions of dollars a year. Most went to college—but it was not finally a B.A. or a Ph.D. that defined our status. It was whether or not we stayed hot, were racing up the charts with a bullet, were going into syndication, had made the best-seller list, were translated into twenty-five languages. Even the professors envied *this* status: money and name recognition override all classes in America. Hence the obsession with celebrity. Even in Europe you can pass into the "best" circles, though the rules of class are quite different there.

Americans are intrinsically unclassy—so the Jews almost fit in. All we talk about is our work. All we want to do is make our first names so recognized we don't even *need* a last (Ms. Ciccone is the ultimate American here). We believe in change as fervently as Europeans believe in the status quo. We believe that money will buy us into heaven (with heaven defined as toned muscles, no flab at the chin, interest on interest, and a name that cows maître d's). Once that's accomplished, we can start to save the world: plow some money into AIDS research, the rain forest, political candidates. Maybe we can even run for office ourselves! (Witness Mr. Perot.) In a society where pop name recognition means everything, celebrities are more equal than everyone else. But celebrity status, like an aging body, is hell to keep in shape. It needs a host of trainers, PR experts, publishers, media consultants. Plus you have to keep turning out new product—and new scandal. (Witness Woody Allen.) Maybe the reason celebrities marry so often is simply to keep their name in the news. And maybe—whether they know it or not—they create scandal to hype their movies. (Again, witness Woody Allen, né Allen Konigsberg.)

Ah—we are back to the question of Jews and names. Can we keep our names? As long as we keep them *hot.* Otherwise, we also have to change them. We may have, as political theorist Benjamin Barber says, "an aristocracy of everyone," but not everyone can be hot at once. Thus, the drive for class becomes as relentless and chronic in America as the diet. No matter how hot you are, you're always in danger of growing cold. It's a lot like mortality, isn't it? No wonder *carpe diem* is our motto. This is what makes America such a restless country and her top-class celebrities so insecure.

Ah, friends, I long to be born into a membership in the Corviglia Club. But I suspect I would never then have written any books.

My yearning is real even though I know dozens of people born into such identities who use them as excuses to become drug addicts and drifters. I know it is not easy to be noble and rich. Yet, like F. Scott Fitzgerald, something in me insists: "The very rich are different from you and me." Fitzgerald tested that hypothesis in *Gatsby*, showing the carelessness of the very rich to life, limb, and love. And yet the longing *remains* in American writers. Perhaps that's why this rather slight, beautifully written American novel has become a bona fide classic. It embodies the American dream of identity and class.

The jumped-up bootlegger, Jay Gatz, dreams of a world where he wouldn't have to *work* to be Gatsby. And that is still the primal American dream. Even lotteries play to it, promising houses and yachts. Rootless by definition, we dream of roots.

American novelists are usually good examples of this. The first thing they do after a best seller is to buy a house and land. Alex Haley bought a farm in the South. He didn't become a slave owner, of course, but he became a landowner. Gore Vidal settled in a villa in Ravello fit for an Italian aristocrat. Arthur Miller bought a Connecticut farm for a Connecticut Yankee. So did Philip Roth.

I'm no different. After *Fear of Flying*, I bought a house in New England. Believing that when writers died and went to heaven, heaven was Connecticut, I bought a piece of that literary state. To a writer, used to making up the world with ink and a blank piece of paper, roots and gentrification are the same thing. And you get them both with *words*.

Rootless people always gravitate to those fields of endeavor where class has to be repeatedly self-created. Perhaps that's also why creativity flowers during periods of great social turmoil and often among former underclasses. Perhaps that's what draws Jews to the word and the image. If you think of the vitality of Jewish American writing in the fifties and sixties, the vitality of women's writing in the seventies and eighties, the vitality of African-American writing in the eighties and nineties, you see that there is a clear connection between change of status and productivity. As a group becomes restless and angry, it produces writers.

I may dream of what I would have done with my life if I had been born on a plantation with plenty of coupons to clip, but probably my literary ambitions would have never blossomed. Perhaps I would have written inscrutable poetry, readable only by advanced graduate students. But most likely the anxiety and aggression needed to finish a whole book would have been denied me. For writing is not just a question of talent with words, but of drive and ambition, of restlessness and rage. Writing is hard. The applause never comes at the end of the paragraph. The rotten tomatoes often come at publication time. And given the hours put in, the money isn't that good. Counting taxation and time spent, most writers make less than dental hygienists.

But we don't do it for the money. We do it to elevate our class.

JOHANNA KAPLAN

Tales of My Great-Grandfathers

One morning in the clamorous early 1970s—that hectic, electric time of flower power, angry demonstrations, saffron-clad gurus, and their chanting, shaven-headed acolytes—one morning, waiting for a New York City bus in that gaudy, psychedelic time, I ran into a woman with whom I had gone to high school and college. The daughter of artists, she had grown up in sophisticated Greenwich Village, while I, a teacher's daughter, had emerged from the subway provinces.

We had never really been friends, Mara and I; still, we knew each other and had many acquaintances in common. So, standing there together, waiting for the bus, we fell into an uneasy early morning exchange. All too quickly, though, we exhausted the juiciest gossipy good stuff and an edgy silence overtook us, until suddenly my old schoolmate—who was at that juncture, she had just informed me, a member of a women's guerrilla street-theater troupe—said: "You know, I was just thinking about you recently. In my consciousness-raising group . . ." And then, very guardedly, "You were like really always into being Jewish, weren't you?"

"I guess so." I said this with reluctance, immediately feeling defensive.

Because in a time of so much ferment and ecstatic disruption, who could believe it? Hear about Johanna? Pathetic, really—still into her same old boring *Jewish* trip. But this, it turned out, was not at all what she had in mind. What I did not know, and would never have guessed, was that Mara herself was even then inching her way toward reclaiming a Jewish inheritance she had been raised to disdain. On that long-ago morning, as she stood peering down the yet-to-be gentrified Upper West Side street for a glimpse of the bus, she carefully avoided my eyes as she finally blurted out, "What did you—I mean, how did you get *into* it?"

But the bus was at long last arriving, and I took incoherent refuge in rummaging for my fare. "Oh well, you know . . . my parents," was all I managed to summon up before we climbed on and became separated by the determined stream of onrushing passengers.

As it happens, Mara would eventually find her way to an unfamiliar and decidedly not home-inspired sense of Jewish belonging by way of klezmer music. You just never know: Jewish destiny is a great mystery, said the illustrious Rav Kook, Israel's first chief rabbi. So for Mara, the world at large, or the zeitgeist, filled in the blanks, and she did not need what should have been my answer.

Which might have been what, exactly? Surely, even in that perfervid time, I could have offered her at least a few surface details—for instance that my grandfather had been a cantor, that I was raised in a moderately observant but specifically Zionist family, and that my intense adolescent years of membership in the Zionist youth movement Habonim were in my own mind still, precious and formative. But suppose I hadn't left it there? What if I'd done better?

Suppose, for a moment, that I'd let whistle through the stale air of that crosstown bus a shiver of my earliest memories: a child's tentative, barefoot decipherings of only the close-by world. That child (we lived then with my mother's parents in Massachusetts while my father was far from home in the Army)—that unkempt, backyard little girl who squints out at me from a scatter of snapshots—was first of all, absolute primary identity, an *eynikel:* a grandchild. So, as my cantor grandfather's *eynikel,* I sat, on Sabbath mornings, within the grandeur of a deep, high-backed, wine-red chair on the *bimah,* entranced and even dizzied by the lofting space and swaying worshipers to sing, as my first songs, what were in fact prayers. The cadence of my diminutive, combative grandfather's voice—its clean, climbing intensity—can sometimes come back to me still when I hear the yearning penitential High Holiday prayer *Avinu Malkeynu.*

And I was just as much *eynikel* to my grandmother— my murmuring, *tichl*-clad grandmother—whose pantry wall, on late summer afternoons, would become so gorgeously ablaze with row upon row of many-colored sun-dazzled *pushkehs* that often she would find me staring up in baffled delight at this shifting, rush-of-color display. But these radiant rows were no mere design of pretty boxes meant to excite my infant eyes—this my grandmother made sure I learned as she put coins into my hands so I could drop them in with my own fingers. They were charity boxes, money to help poor Jews in faraway places, places where terrible things happened, things so terrible they could make her cry.

What were her tears about? In my parents' new, postwar apartment in the Bronx, I would find out. There, from a leafy, unremarkable New York City neighborhood, I came to rudimentary consciousness at a time of Jewish enormity: a rift moment when awesome events masqueraded as ordinary days. The stunned remnant Jews of Europe were trickling into grief-pierced American freedom; at the same time, in a sun-toughened, orange-fragrant sliver of Palestine (then still usually a long ship's travel away), an independent Jewish nation was flailing to be born. Exactly how distant were those abstract events? In my mother's kitchen, over cups of tea that got cold, newcomer survivor-neighbors—two blondish, small-boned sisters with ugly blue markings on their arms—whispered their horrific accounts. In Polish, so I wouldn't understand.

But as soon as they left, my mother always translated; more than that, she always explained. (After all, it would forever be my born-in-America responsibility to help Jews from foreign countries.) A few steps away, in the living room, my father, still buttoned into his shirt and tie, hunched over a shortwave radio: any minute now, he might—just might—be able to pick up a broadcast straight from the *yishuv*'s own airwaves. (You could never know beforehand if their signal would get through.) Despite the radio's awful crackling, I sat beside him, and I listened, too: Lake Success, Czech arms, British troops, Jews, for weeks and weeks on boats, now forced back to Cyprus. I was in kindergarten. What did I understand? Like nothing else was this drama of Zion, this all-senses-raw throb of tightrope elation—could it really happen—that after so many long, terrible centuries of danger and suffering our own old-new flag might unfurl to start flying among flags of the nations. How could I understand? How could I miss it?

Still, no matter how much I might have confided to my old schoolmate on that crosstown encounter decades ago, I know I would have been incapable in those years of formulating the deeper, more elusive answer that her poignant, baffled plea, "How did you get *into* it?," deserved.

···

I think now that every family has its significant myths, its agglomerations of told and retold stories, memories, and experiences, and that these myths, even as they may diverge from literal truth or documentable historical facts, lay out a felt but invisible path, a subterranean template that defines and sometimes even determines, if you will, a kind of barely traceable spiritual DNA. Because these myths are the very air we breathe in childhood, we tend to take them for granted, to be a little bored with them—they can seem foolish, even embarrassing—so that it becomes impossible for us to recognize what makes them, after all, our *own*, unique or remarkable. Perhaps it is only later, with life's perplexing turns and middle age's apprehension of the shocking flight of time, that they come back to us in new and sharpened focus.

In my own family, I might have told Mara, the formative myths arose from the very different life stories of two of my great-grandfathers. I call them the Tale of the Great Rabbi and the Tale of the Simple Jew.

The Tale of the Great Rabbi

Usually stories about great rabbis—and nearly every Jewish family has one, somewhere—center on their singular wisdom and prodigious learning. Not so for my mother's grandfather, Rabbi Jacob Meir of Minsk: in his case, the family stories were about his austere, remote, otherworldly aspect and character, and his countless (if sometimes highly peculiar) good deeds. This improbable combination—*Twilight Zone* manner and one-man social-service-agency activity—is said to have inspired awe in the surrounding *gubernya*, or district, and to have led some, Jews and Gentiles alike, to attribute to him nearly magical powers, though he was most definitely *not* a "wonder" rabbi, *not* a Hasid. "Reb Jacob Meir of Minsk, a saintly *Mitnaged*" (or anti-Hasid), is how he is characterized by Zalman Shazar, Israel's third president, in his autobiography, *Morning Stars*. How Shazar in particular came to regard him as saintly is something I'll return to, but first let me provide a taste of the stories I grew up on.

Before the Sabbath—every Sabbath—Rabbi Jacob Meir would not only empty out the pockets of his coat in order to give whatever money he had to the needy, he would actually give away his coat. When the members of his congregation remonstrated with him about this highly idiosyncratic practice, he would say only, "God will provide." But clearly it was those same congregants who would each time be obliged to provide, and though this exemplary story would always, in childhood, fill me with a terrible frisson—how reckless and unnatural to give away your brand-new coat!—it is apparent to me now that my great-grandfather's famously remote gaze harbored a surprising shrewdness. However his congregation might guiltily begrudge its numerous coatless poor, it could hardly deny its own rabbi.

But here is a more substantial story. Scattered throughout the *gubernya* of Minsk were children known as Rabbi Jacob Meir's *mamzerim*, bastards. Who were they? When a woman had a baby she knew she could not keep—in telling this story, my mother, mindful of my sheltered, childish ears, would always suggest extreme poverty as the reason for the woman's dilemma (though she sometimes darkly murmured, "or who knows?")—the anguished new mother would bring the baby to my great-grandfather's house. He became godfather to these infants, each of whom he would place with a family in one or another of the surrounding shtetls. The given-away children would bear the last names of the families who raised them, but to each distraught birth mother my great-grandfather pledged that he would personally watch over the education and development of her child, that he would always consider himself to be bonded with that child—to remain forever as a special presence. And these were not mere empty consolatory words: my grandmother grew up knowing some of these children and regarded them as semi-cousins.

In one instance, the dynamic of this special relationship was to take a dramatic twist. In the turbulent early days of the new Bolshevik government, a nephew of my great-grandfather's, a pharmacist, was arrested and thrown in jail for "economic crimes"—I suppose he had his own little store, and as such was regarded as a bourgeois parasite. His prospects looked exceedingly grim until my great-grandfather thought to seek the help of one of his *mamzerim*, who had grown up to become first a fervent revolutionary and then, rising very quickly, a local commissar. The newly minted commissar sprung the hapless pharmacist and hurriedly arranged for him and his young family to get to Warsaw, where they could take up a new life. (But in the twentieth century, too many Jewish stories did not have happy endings. So, lucky once, but only once: the Warsaw pharmacist and his family were to perish during World War II in the Warsaw Ghetto.)

Perhaps the strangest, most legendlike story I heard in childhood about this great-grandfather refers back to Czarist times, when an extremely onerous tax on kosher meat was levied against the Jewish community. So burdensome was its effect that my great-grandfather went to the local official to plead that it be rescinded. Denying him even the most minimal courtesy, the official peremptorily refused. The next day, that man's young son fell ill—so ill that it appeared the boy would die. At this, the father became convinced that his harsh dealings with the Jews and specifically with Jacob Meir were the cause of his misfortune. The official rescinded the tax; his child recovered; and from then on, rumors began to spread among the local peasantry about Rabbi Jacob Meir's powers.

But what did my great-grandfather himself regard as the most important undertaking of his life? The curious answer to this question I learned only from reading Shazar's memoir. It was Jacob Meir's firm belief that the *geulah*, the long-awaited redemption of the Jews, could never come about as long as there was a chance that the holy name of God might be "trodden underfoot . . . whenever a page of an ordinary *siddur* [prayer book] or *chumash* [Pentateuch] fell on the floor." What did he do? Writes Shazar: "Very carefully . . . he had [typeset] pages of a siddur where the letters of the Name were scattered and printed on a slant, so that even if the page became loose and dropped out there would be no desecration."

To raise money for the printing of these special volumes, Rabbi Jacob Meir went from shtetl to shtetl, escorted to the homes of the wealthy by local *heder* (religious primary school) boys who were judged capable of appreciating the significance of his mission. And that is how a very young Zalman Shazar came to encounter my great-grandfather, and ultimately, to offer the only physical description of him that I know: "a tall, thin old man wearing a black velvet hat and a long robe that reached to the top of his shoes; he walked along with me, splashing in the mud, while his lean, yellowish hand shielded his eyes to keep him from looking at that forbidden sight—a woman."

Now, there is no way, today, that you can look over a photocopied page from that bizarrely set siddur, as I did only recently—a giddy, nearly expressionistic swirl of Hebrew letters swooning before your eyes like the guilty, fevered visions of a dying, errant Jew—without immediately acceding to the darkest suspicions about at least one thread in the psychic component of your own genetic makeup. How, then, can a rational contemporary mind make sense of so deeply premodern a preoccupation? For myself, I have reached the conclusion that to my great-grandfather, the world-to-come was at least as real as the muddy roads he splashed through daily. He believed absolutely what he read every Sabbath in the rabbinic treatise *Ethics of the Fathers:* "This world is a vestibule before the world-to-come; prepare yourself in the vestibule so that you may enter the banquet hall."

So totally did he believe this that when his daughter, my great-aunt, decided she wanted to go to medical school in Moscow, it never dawned on him to forbid or discourage her, even though the only way a Jewish girl could get the requisite identity permit to live in Moscow was by allowing herself to be declared a prostitute. What difference could it make to Rabbi Jacob Meir: what was all this anyway but the vestibule? When his outraged *balabatim*, his money men, stormed to his door to protest such a shocking prospect—*their* rabbi's daughter, bearing the papers of a prostitute?—and even threatened to fire him if he did not change his mind, he gave them this reply: "She will go to Moscow; she will become a doctor; she will serve her people." And she did just that, my stern-faced great-aunt. She left Russia for Palestine to become the doctor for a company of pioneers who were draining the swamps of the Huleh valley.

At his death, the family story had it, Jacob Meir was given a state funeral by the local Soviet government, and was hailed as "the rabbi of the people," ostensibly because of his lifelong devotion to the welfare of the poor. And although this was true—and although it was also true that, contrary to the usual rabbinic practice, he had never accepted money for resolving ritual disputes—the family myth held that the real reason for his state funeral lay in the profound superstition of the local peasant populace and their age-old fear of offending the spirit of the powerful dead.

The Tale of the Simple Jew

There are no literary accounts of my *father's* grandfather. In fact I do not even know his first name, though my guess is that it would have been Joseph—Yosef, Yussl— since that was the name of my own father's eldest brother, my grandfather's firstborn son. What I do know was that his last name, my original family name, was not

Kaplan. Was this change in our family name the peremptory doing of some ignorant Ellis Island immigration clerk? Far from it: my great-grandfather never came close to leaving Russia. His story is much darker. His entire life's trajectory was defined by a particularly horrific episode of child persecution in Russian Jewish history that is not particularly well known. My great-grandfather was a cantonist.

This strange-sounding designation—it names a devil's detour from childhood, not a religious or political splinter group—was the brainstorm of Czar Nicholas I, who, like a latter-day Haman, had conceived a specific plan to rid his realm of Jews. This was the so-called Plan of the Thirds, according to which one-third of Russian Jewry would be compelled to emigrate, one-third would die of starvation, and one-third would be forcibly converted to Christianity. It was in brutal pursuit of that last third that my great-grandfather's fate was sealed.

At the age of seven, he was ripped from his family in a Lithuanian shtetl, swooped away from his birthright life among Jews, kidnapped by the dreaded *khapers*—snatchers—and transported, along with other seized, impoverished little heder boys like himself, to a remote, frigid outpost of the Russian empire. Officially, all these captured, terrorized, often ailing small boys, abruptly torn from their mothers' arms and thrust into stiff soldiers' overcoats, were made lifetime conscripts in the czar's army, and in that guise were housed in army barracks called cantonments (hence "cantonists"). In those dismal precincts, they were subjected to the harshest military discipline and relentlessly tortured to give up every vestige of their Jewish lives—robbed of their ritual fringed garments, forbidden to pray, prohibited from speaking Yiddish, and, finally, the true goal, forced to perform the rituals of the Russian Orthodox Church. These were small children, after all. How hard could it have been? Any who resisted were starved till they acquiesced or died.

So, though this was never part of the family myth, to me it is clear, from my reading, that my great-grandfather must at some point have submitted to baptism. What *was* told to me was that from the age of seven, he had spent his entire childhood on a frozen, isolated waste of a farm in Siberia, in servitude to a peasant family that required him to do their foulest, filthiest, most backbreaking work. And here the *Enyclopedia Judaica* confirms the family account: "The cantonists were sometimes sent to Russian farmsteads in remote villages where they performed exhausting labor and were forced to change their faith." In other words, he was a slave—an isolated, forcibly baptized, brutalized child slave.

But maybe, just maybe, that harrowing reality was something he could in some inchoate sense recognize— even hang on to—as a measure of spiritual resistance. After all, it had happened before: *avadim hayinu,* "We were slaves unto Pharaoh in Egypt." Through all those lonely years, did he retain—could he have retained—from some dim corner of another life, the memory of a seder table? Or was it perhaps the hazy echo of a buzzing heder bench where he'd studied the Book of Exodus? "We were slaves unto Pharaoh in Egypt. And the Lord delivered us from there with a mighty hand and an outstretched arm." Because something, surely, did sustain him. Through years of howling Arctic blasts and blinding blizzards, he remained a stubborn, solitary child Marrano—and one who was denied even the Marrano's small solace of occasionally glimpsed secret brothers somewhere in his environs.

At the age of eighteen, eleven years after his first kidnapping, he began his mandatory twenty-five years of duty in the czar's regular army. He was forty-three, then, when he was finally released, his sole, unlikely possession in the world a plot of land in Siberia, given him in return for his service to the czar. After thirty-six years, at last delivered into freedom, what could he have been by that time but an odd, remote, rough, uncommunicative man? Decades of military rigors, numberless privations, involuntary servitude, and confused, hidden identity had ensured that he had missed just about every ratified stage of normal human development. Yet out of that prolonged nightmare half-life at the ends of the empire, he made his way back to the shtetl of his birth in Kovno Gubernya, there to request a bride.

And who could she have been, my great-grandmother, but a penniless orphan girl, utterly without prospects, to have accepted a match with a strange, hardened old soldier who barely spoke Yiddish, who had had no bar mitzvah, known no calendar of Sabbaths, fast days, and festivals, let alone any ordinary family tenderness or communal nurture? Who else could she have been to find herself under the *huppah*, tearily bedecked, circling seven times around a groom who would promptly take her off to, of all places, Siberia?

But in Kayinsk, Siberia, there was, as it turned out, a small community of other released cantonists who had retained their Jewishness—enough for a prayer quorum, enough to form a tiny congregation, the Soldatski Synagog. There, in remote Kayinsk—a place so cold that a party of determined visiting cousins were discovered frozen to death in nearby woods en route—my own grandfather was born and did become bar mitzvah. And when, as a young man, this grandfather of mine set off on his own long-planned journey from Kayinsk, Siberia, to New York harbor, ship's passage clasped hard in hand, he, too, traveled first to his father's birthplace in Kovno Gubernya, there, hurriedly, to gain a bride: my grandmother, the undowered orphan daughter of an itinerant coopersmith.

And the name? Well, in fact, Kaplan was the name of a rich boy—a boy whose father's resources had ransomed him out of the dreaded schoolboy conscription. Was he perhaps the pink-cheeked pampered son of a grain merchant, the honey-licking firstborn of a timber dealer? I'll never know. I only know that shoved in under the name Kaplan in his stead was my luckless, destitute great-grandfather.

Still, I had always assumed—it was the family myth—that Kaplan's bribe had been paid to the czarist officials. Not so: on this point, the *Enyclopedia Judaica* provides a highly disturbing correction. It was the Jewish communal authority, the *kehilla*, that was compelled to furnish the quota of conscript heder boys; it was the kehilla that made up the list, and a member of the kehilla, a Jew, who would have accepted the bribe, and consigned a helpless, expendable child into the pit of oblivion. A little uncanny, then, that my great-grandfather should have been named Joseph. Like that Joseph in the Book of Genesis—the Joseph whose story is the prelude to the Passover saga of redemption—he, too, had been bundled into slavery by his own brothers, his own people.

But they *were* his people still. That he never forgot this, but clung to it with all his might to survive and prevail as a Jew against the grimmest of odds—in itself an amazement—is surely the luminous lesson of his haunting, impenetrable life.

...

These days when I think about the two disparate family myths that made up the household hum of my childhood, I am struck by their odd, asymmetric link. I am the great-granddaughter at once of an eccentric, lofty-minded rabbi who rescued abandoned children and of a desolate, kidnapped child conscript whom no one in his community ever made the smallest attempt to save. How could I not, then, as a writer, be drawn to the paradoxes and disruptions that stumble through generations of Jewish families' lives? How could I not be preoccupied, in my fiction, with the terrible deforming power of history's privations when I know that its remnant anachronistic tendrils are still so alive within me?

As a child, I read Jewish history with the rapt reader's out-of-body removal that only in adolescence would I begin wholly to derive from fiction. And this is not surprising. I knew early on (but at best in an inchoate way) from my own family's life and all those curiously instructing undulations of my upbringing that the past, and with it, the force of external events not only shapes the arc of lives, it infiltrates even the most private spaces of the imagination. Yet I knew and I didn't know at the same time. Both a chapter in a children's Jewish history book about the Mortara case (the nineteenth-century Italian-Jewish boy baptized by his Catholic governess and taken away from his family) and equally then, a library-discovered children's story about a girl on the American frontier kidnapped and raised by Indians—each of these drew me in with a sickened lingering fascination. So I was captivated by stories of captives, though I did not even remotely intuit the lurking family source.

A storytelling family, a story-*laden* family, the whole

strange whirl of lives I could observe around me—relatives, neighbors, strangers, even, and beneath that surface, the enigmatic trudge of all those oddly clothed antecedents who leaned in so vividly from the past—all that overheard bustle gave me a sense of the phantom quickenings of stories, of characters always already *present*, always already streaming, waiting maybe, somewhere above the TV aerials, in the ether. I wanted to catch hold of these phantom stories, these phantom characters—to write them down. And now when I write fiction, I think of history as an implicit presence—in a way akin to the world of dreams: perhaps not always clearly recognized, yet undeniable, a ground bass in people's ordinary, surprising day-to-day lives.

Still, linked forever to that unquiet sense of history is the hovering imperative I gleaned as a child: the primacy of peoplehood. If, as the Talmud tells us, all Jews are responsible for one another, then isn't this my larger, latent, hidden family—my *nistar* family, call it? And that vast *nistar* family—though at times flying under the radar, and always so far-flung—is at least as generous with its anguish, arguments, exasperations, but also nourishments as the small one I grew up in. So even though I cannot, with my rabbi great-grandfather, negotiate the day-to-day world as if it were a mere waiting room for the Redemption, I am sufficiently inhabited by both family tales to cling, with bemused intensity, and under conditions of American ease my cantonist great-grandfather could never have begun to apprehend, to a complicated, vexing people. Somewhere, among their ancient, unlikely dreams and far-fetched adventures toward fulfillment, lies my own ineluctable walk-on in a drama of catastrophe and renewal any imaginative writer would be hard put to equal.

STEVE STERN

After the Law

Two decades ago, the late Irving Howe uttered a pronouncement that made an impression in the circles where such things matter. He predicted that, with greater distance from the immigrant experience and without some authentic connection to community, so-called Jewish American fiction would become attenuated; "it must suffer a depletion of resources, a thinning out of materials and memories." It would, in short, dry up. Now Mr. Howe was an honorable man, and twenty years since his assertion, no serious challengers have yet emerged to threaten the sovereignty of the generation of Roth, Bellow, and Malamud. After them, implied Mr. Howe, what can we look forward to but ever-diminishing returns, a gradual shading into the American mainstream? After them, the desert: works too leached of Jewish identity to bear comparison to their predecessors; and who could argue with that? It's certainly not my intention to question the authority of Irving Howe (who was an honorable man), for the evidence still remains more in favor of burying Jewish American fiction than praising it.

Mr. Howe's dark forecast brings to mind the Hasidic parable concerning the forest, the fire, and the prayer. This is the one where the Baal Shem Tov, when he has a problem, goes to the forest, lights a fire, says a prayer, and finds wisdom. The next generation has forgotten the prayer, but they can still go to the forest and light the fire; the generation after that has forgotten the prayer and can't make a fire, but they can still go to the forest. But the following generation is unable to find the forest, light the fire, or remember the prayer, though at least they know the story about forest, fire, and prayer—and that must suffice. Then along come the children of the children of the immigrants, so divorced from tradition and community that they can't even recall the story.

I offer myself as a case in point. Born at a considerable cultural and temporal remove from the Jewish East Side, in farthest Memphis, Tennessee, I grew up in a Reform congregation that—but for some residual Hebrew in the liturgy—may as well have been Methodist. When I felt the first pangs of a desire to write fiction back in the bracing climate of the sixties, disaffection and alienation were the themes; antic nihilism was the method, its propagators a host of brainy *shaigetzes*. There were Thomas Pynchon, John Barth, illusionists such as Nabokov and Borges who played their intrepid games above the abyss, Samuel Beckett who managed eerie echo effects from his voices in a vacuum. In light of their artful inventions Jewish American fiction (wasn't Jewish American an oxymoron?) already seemed to me out of date.

Of course, one might contend that the pet themes of those authors had their source in the work of a Jew. For it was Kafka, the undisputed master of disaffection, who early in the century struck chords that still resonate like a tuning fork in the bones of his successors. Take his parable "Before the Law," which might serve as a signature piece for the literature of marginality. In it, you'll recall, a man spends his life waiting for admission to the Palace of the Law, too timid to challenge the doorkeeper who forbids his entry; then just before the man's death, the doorkeeper reveals that this particular door had all along been reserved exclusively for him. In the tradition from which Franz Kafka was disaffiliated, Law and Torah are one and the same, an identification that would not have been lost on the parable's author. He would have known from infancy that Torah is the Book that the Jews are the people of. "The text is our homeland," remarked George Steiner, paraphrasing generations of rabbis before him; and by that logic, insofar as we are denied access to the Law, we are also homeless.

We're all Kafka's timid petitioner, anticipating neither Messiah nor Godot; we're a people for whom waiting has become a vocation. Problem is, for a writer of fiction, you're liable to get bored and impatient with a career predicated on the act of waiting. You want to break ranks, stretch your legs, take a walk—and again I offer the example of myself; for sometime during the mid-1980s I took a walk, turned a corner at Poplar Avenue and North Main Street in my hometown of Memphis, and stumbled quite unintentionally out of history proper. I fell through the fabric of time—which is especially thin around these blighted old ghetto neighborhoods—into a street populated by ghosts. There, in a city remarkable for erasing its own past, was an immigrant community of East European phantoms; in broad daylight they performed the timeless rites of poverty and superstition they'd imported wholesale from the Old Country. Naturally, being an orthodox spiritual bankrupt of a distinctly postmodern turn of mind, I didn't *believe* in ghosts, but seeing them was nonetheless eye-opening, and their antics made for diverting stories.

So I wrote a story about a North Main Street neighborhood that existed in symbiotic relation to, while at the same time remaining independent from, history. In other words, a place where anything could happen.

"The air is full of souls," wrote the Hebrew poet Judah Halevi, and Martin Buber: "All men are the abode of wandering souls." They were speaking figuratively, of course, but I'm here to tell you the atmosphere around North Main Street was thick with figurative souls, and each one had a story. I chose the tale of an old man who refuses to die and is dragged off to Paradise alive by the Angel of Death. "Original, no?" I thought, believing it safe to take credit for a tale whose source did not technically exist. Then, as if to disparage my vanity, the story aged before my eyes and sloughed its own skin; and beneath it, palimpsest-wise, was another story. This one was the Hasidic tale about Rabbi Ben Levi, another obstinate, deathless old man, who deceives Malach Hamovess, the Angel of Death, into admitting him into Paradise alive. But Rabbi Ben Levi's story turned out to conceal yet another about Elijah the Prophet, also deathless; and Enoch, transformed while alive into the archangel Metatron. Thus did I sink into ever deeper strata of narrative, not touching bottom until I arrived at Genesis 5:24, a single line that spawned a whole literature: "And Enoch walked with God, and he was not; for God took him." And those were the generations of my piddling story.

I felt like Jonah, having discovered that the fish who swallowed him had been swallowed by a larger, and that one swallowed by an even larger, world without end.

The old wisdom, now defunct, has it that Torah prefigured the world. God used Torah as a blueprint for creation, then handed it to Moses on Sinai, and Moses read in it the tale of himself. He was a person of the Book, Moses, his story already told, while it was also in the process of unfolding; he was a character out of a fiction, who was nevertheless given an opportunity to determine his own (and his people's) historical destiny. It's said that on Sinai the oral Torah (the interpretation of the Law) was revealed along with the written, and for centuries thereafter the Jewish scribe viewed his work as the unfolding of revelation. His work was *received* even as it was *created*, which is a paradox, and in paradox you can confound the rational categories; you can conceive a vantage from which it's not unlikely to see ghosts.

Paradox can dissolve the distance from authenticity that Irving Howe cited as fatal to the Jewish branch of regional American fiction. History flows from Eden into exile, past landscapes strewn with carnage, washing us up high and dry on the brink of another millennium; but myth contains both Eden and exile and consecrates their respective truths. "Eternity," says William Blake, "is in love with the productions of time," and vice versa. Time embraces timelessness the way the evil husks in Kabbalah surround the scattered sparks of the divine; the way secular stories contain the sacred. Crack the husk, strip the story from the tale, the folk narrative from the midrash, peel away apocrypha, pseudepigrapha, and Talmud—a very sexy operation—and you arrive at the glimmering source, the once and future Book itself. Or at least it's pretty to think so.

But let's face it, paradox is a trick of the intellect, and I'm inclined to agree with Mr. Howe that what's lost is lost; you can't get there from here. At this late date, what can harkening back to the archetypes result in but pale imitation, distant echoes of a once joyful noise? Once ritual was the means of bridging the gap between the sacred and the profane, but with the collapse of community, the rituals that myth requires are largely forgotten. All the traditional means of transcendence have had their day. Jacob's Ladder, doubtless gathering dust backstage in some abandoned Yiddish theater, is missing too many rungs; the Tree of Life is in need of a surgeon. And even should you stumble accidentally into the Garden through some neglected back door (at the corner, say, of Poplar Avenue and North Main), chances are you could never negotiate a safe return.

The ancients had a system of interpreting Scripture to which they ascribed the acronym *PaRDeS* (literally Hebrew for *garden*, or *Garden*). They moved in their exegesis through four stages: *peshat*, *reshev*, *drash*, and *sod*, which corresponded to literal, metaphorical, allegorical, and mystical readings of the Text. In this way their program involved a virtual ascent from the mundane to the sublime. There's a fable called "The Four Who Entered Paradise" that cautions against the perils of that ascent. In it four rabbis make a pilgrimage to the celestial Garden. Upon entering, one dies, another goes mad, another loses his faith, and only Akiva gets back to the world in one piece. Which is to say that the return to the sources is a journey beyond mere nostalgia; it is fraught with hazard, and finding your way there is no guarantee you will find your way back. Enter the dreamtime, wherein you're a contemporary of the patriarchs, the martyrs, the exiles, the immigrants, and you stand to lose your own moment in history.

Follow the example of Akiva and his cronies and,

lacking their credentials, you're likely to die an obscure death, lose the little credibility you have (your faith is already forfeit), and catch hell from critics anxious to remind you that "You're no Roth, no Bellow—*tahkeh*, you're no Akiva."

Best to play it safe. Irving Howe left no prescription for the restoration of the Jewish wasteland—the literary landscape would merely become increasingly parched, the distance between fiction and truth as regards the Jewish American endeavor becoming an ever wider divide. Certainly my generation, already (at least in my own case) rapidly aging, lacks the authority and experience to attempt any such *tikkun*, an exercise that from this vantage appears frankly imprudent. Besides, haven't we got heartache enough, what with a chronic spiritual homelessness that not even the emergence of the State of Israel could mitigate?

Of course, there's always a lunatic fringe, hotheads who assert that, homeless before the Palace of the Law, we are also lawless, which is a condition less compatible with pathos and passivity; a stance that paradoxically inspires a certain chutzpah in the face of paralysis. We're outlaws, they bluster, renegades who, with no license to enter the Palace, might just storm it . . . But who are they kidding? Better they should bow to the wisdom of their elders, acknowledge the rectitude of the honorable Mr. Howe, and learn to grow old with dignity outside the Palace walls.

Still, I have this recurring dream. In it I'm the old man in Kafka's parable, sick of waiting but too broken in spirit to do anything else. I'm nodding off as usual, when up walks this scrawny kid, bold as you please, sporting an outlandish getup—long caftan, skullcap, earlocks, impish grin. Without ceremony, with maybe a whooping taunt, he scrambles between the legs of the giant doorkeeper, who chases him into the Palace. The next thing I know, from a narrow casement above me the scrolls of the Law drop into my lap; then the kid himself leaps out and hits the ground running. That's when I recognize him from a story I didn't know I knew. It's Hershel Ostropolier, the Jewish Eulenspiegl, hero of a whole cycle of trickster tales, and having escaped some story for the sake of performing this theft, he's no doubt on his way back to another. Above me the doorkeeper is stuck half-in and half-out of the window, shouting bloody murder, while Hershel calls over his shoulder as he runs away: "Life is like a glass of tea!" "Nu?" say I, noticing that my old bones have begun to stir; I'm in motion for the first time in memory, following Hershel. "Why is life like a glass of tea?" I holler, and he answers without breaking stride, "Shmendrik, what am I, a philosopher?" Wondering if that's my name, Shmendrik, I hug the scrolls to my chest and continue to give chase. When last seen we're still running.

REBECCA GOLDSTEIN

Against Logic

O nce upon a time, I resolved to live a rational life. This was a long time ago and I was very young, having just emerged from the allegedly enchanted age of early childhood. I exited a skeptic.

My plan for rationality called for hypervigilance in the matter of my beliefs. Beliefs, not deeds, were my focus. My circumstances were such that I had restricted determination over my actions, far more restricted than most American girls of my generation and class. I was born into an Orthodox Jewish family, and the rules for my conduct were largely entailed by that fact.

But beliefs were private, especially if severed from their natural behavioral concomitants. Nobody could enforce my beliefs; nobody even need know them. They were mine to determine for myself, and one of my self-determined beliefs was that this sort of freedom was all the freedom that I required. The only force that I'd allow to compel me in the matter of beliefs would be logic itself.

Accordingly, I resolved to examine each of my beliefs for blemishes, much as my mother examined her chickens, which in those days she used to have to *kasher* herself—gutting, then soaking and salting, to remove all traces of the taint of blood. We had chicken almost every night, so the image of my mother at her gruesome task of evisceration is still vivid after all these years. I would watch her as a child, fascinated and repulsed, resolving that I would never serve my family chicken when I was a mother if this is what I'd have to go through. My father, a cantor, supplemented his meager income by various jobs, including *shokhet*—or ritual slaughterer—at the local chicken market (though I recoil at appending the brutal term "slaughterer" to the memory of that most gentle of all men). The chicken market paid my father in poultry, which is how my parents managed to keep their large family fed.

Whenever my mother opened a chicken and found something questionable—a perforated lung, a spotted liver—she would proceed with caution, seeking rabbinical guidance as to whether the chicken was acceptable. As it was with my mother and her chickens, so it would be with me and my beliefs. I would examine each one for the taints of wishful thinking, submission to authority, faulty logic. Never would I allow the accidental features of my particular situation, the group of people into whom I happened to have been born, influence me in the matter of my beliefs, which were mine alone, and for which I took full and solemn responsibility.

Epistemology is the branch of philosophy that examines the grounds for beliefs, asking such questions as what constitutes good grounds for various sorts of belief and whether there are limits to attaining these grounds. In epistemology the difference between grounded and ungrounded beliefs makes all the difference. I certainly didn't know the fancy word "epistemology," but I had an idea of the concept. Epistemology for me meant *kashering* my beliefs.

Given my preoccupations, it isn't so surprising that I was drawn toward the study of philosophy. I started studying it before I got to college, though certainly not in the high school that I attended, an all-girls ultra-Orthodox school in which we were discouraged from going to college at all. If we were determined to go to college, we were told, then we ought to study practical subjects that could help out our future husbands were they to have difficulties earning a *parnosa*. The humanities in general were *assur*, forbidden, infected as they were with alien values. But the worst thing that one could possibly study was philosophy, a field that promiscuously questioned everything, even the existence of *Hashem*, the Name.

The pernicious nature of philosophy came up in our class in *historia*, or Jewish history. We were learning about that *apikorus*, or heretic, Benedictus Spinoza. Benedictus wasn't born Benedictus, but rather Baruch, which means "blessed" in Hebrew. He changed his first name to the Latinized version of "blessed" after his excommunication from the Portuguese-Jewish community of Amsterdam, in 1656. See what happens, little girls, when you think you're so smart and start questioning everything? From Baruch to Benedictus!

The very word *apikorus* testifies to the deep suspicion with which the Jewish tradition regards philosophy. The word derives from the name of that famous Greek philosopher, Epicurus, who taught of the fundamental importance of pleasure in justifying our actions and also had such a horror of beans. The far more approving adjective and noun "epicurean" is also derived from his name. But for the Jews, the Greek philosopher yielded the word for heretic—more on account of his pleasure principle than his phobia for legumes.

Philosophy was *assur*, but its pull proved too strong for me. Even before I had graduated from high school I used a summer vacation to audit a philosophy course at Columbia, and when I got to college I majored in it. I had already married, having gotten engaged my senior year in high school, not so uncommon in the circle into which I was born. Marriage considerably widened my prospects, for, as my disapproving mother put it, "You're your husband's problem now." But my husband, although Orthodox, didn't in the least disapprove of my interests. He, a physicist, is devoted to philosophy as well.

Studying philosophy, going on for a doctorate and a career in it, was, for many years, the only indication I ever gave (though, of course, it's a mighty big one) that my private beliefs weren't totally in accordance with my outward conduct as an Orthodox Jewish wife and mother. My two daughters were sent to an Orthodox day school, though one that was (a bit) more enlightened than the Bais Yaakov school that I had attended. One of my daughters even seemed to flourish in the school, her ready imagination stirred even by its anachronisms and contradictions. Her reaction to her upbringing can be read in her own contribution to this volume.

And I, with my childhood plan of hypervigilance in regard to beliefs still firmly in place, in spite of the Orthodox life that I had passively adopted, became an analytic philosopher. I had received my doctorate from Princeton, and then returned to Barnard, where I had studied as an undergraduate, and became a professor. If my story ended there, it would make some sense. But against logic, I also became a writer of fiction. My hopeless passion for fiction had seemed to me, back in the days when I thought of myself as a real philosopher (which I no longer do), a rather shameful little aberration. If the brand of Judaism from which I derive has little use for philosophy, the brand of philosophy that I adopted has little use for fiction (though this has changed somewhat in recent years, especially through the work of such philosophers as Martha Nussbaum).

I remember once being interviewed by a reporter as we sat in the beloved Hungarian pastry shop at Amsterdam and 111th Street near Columbia University. It was soon after my first novel, *The Mind-Body Problem*, had been published, and the reporter had a copy of the book on the little rickety table. (My colleagues in the philosophy department weren't thrilled about my having published that novel, and I preferred to meet reporters outside my office.) Someone I had known as a fellow philosophy student came up to say hello, and the reporter told him that I was now an author, and she held up the book as proof. "You wrote a book on the mind-body problem?" he asked, with real respect breaking out in his face and voice. The mind-body problem is, of course, a standard problem in philosophy, the question, basically, of whether the mind's properties are, ultimately, physical properties. (My Ph.D. dissertation had, in fact, been on a technical aspect of that very problem.) "It's a novel," I felt compelled to tell him, in the interest of truth. "Oh," he said, the respect visibly and audibly melting away, as I knew it would. My precipitous fall in his estimation was so obvious even to the reporter that she ended up making the little scene the focus of her article about me.

Philosophy's suspicion of fiction has, like Judaism's suspicion of philosophy, a long history, also going all the way back to the ancient Greeks. Plato, as we can read in his monumental *Republic*, had planned to rid his utopia of the epic poets, who were the novelists of his day. Fiction writers are enchanters, those who spread their dreams abroad; and Plato—whom I still revere—thoroughly disapproved of enchantment. From the point of view of straight-thinking philosophy, intent on the hard work of grasping the objective nature of reality, enchantment is at best a diversion, at worst a saboteur, infusing its pleasures into the formation of beliefs, so that they deform with the bloat of seductive untruth. Ironically, Plato was himself an artist of the highest order. His dialogues are not only philosophical but literary masterpieces. Knowing the full power of enchantment as only a true creative artist can made the philosopher all the more leery.

Plato's banishment of the artists from his utopian plans, his denunciation of them as inimical to rational aims, still pains me, and when I write fiction I am always hearing Plato's voice in my head. (Strangely, Plato chastises me in Hebrew, calling fiction a *"bitul z'man,"* a waste of time. I suppose the phrase comes to me because it carries the apposite suggestion of moral condemnation, as in anything that isn't the study of Torah is a bitul z'man.) Hearing the philosopher as I do, I try to write the sort of fiction that might possibly appease him, that might have some sort of philosophical justification to offer for itself. But I know that my plan for rationality began to unravel when I allowed my love for fiction's enchantments to swell into the desire to become an enchanter myself.

Even more implausibly, my fiction is often tied up with Jewish themes. This, to me, is truly weird. For though I have reconciled myself, even philosophically, to my love for fiction, I still chafe at allowing "the accidents of precedents" (as one of my own characters, in *Mazel*, once put it) to determine the borders of my points of view. I've always cherished my inner freedom, cherished it all the more for the many years when my outward conduct had little connection with the ideas I held. It's important to me that the stamp of my origins be absent not only from my epistemology, but from my imagination as well. Write only Jewish stories, peopled by Jewish characters? Why? Doesn't such a choice indicate a limit of the imagination, an inability to grasp the stories of people not of one's own kind? For the writer, the entire category of "one's own kind" ought to have no relevance whatsoever.

And so, unlike others with whom I sometimes find myself grouped as representatives of the reawakening in Jewish American letters, I don't write exclusively on Jewish themes or about Jewish characters. My collection of short stories, *Strange Attractors*, contained nine pieces, five of which were, to some degree, Jewish, and this ratio has provided me with a precise mathematical answer (for me, still the best kind of answer) to the question of whether I am a Jewish writer. I am five-ninths a Jewish writer.

But even this fraction of Jewish is far more than I would ever have anticipated being back in the days when I was determined to let my mind roam free from origins. Cynthia Ozick once said that her goal is to dream Jewish dreams. My own early goal could not have been more different. I wanted (like Descartes) to know and not to dream, to know that I did not dream. And I wanted, too (like Spinoza), to leave my Jewishness firmly behind, at least in the privacy of my own self-determining mind.

In Spinoza's magnum opus, *The Ethics*, he tries to demonstrate where we would all end up were we each, despite the accidents of our precedents, to commit ourselves to the process of transforming our *passive* ideas, which bear the marks of contingency, including the accidents of our birth, into *active* ideas, derived through seeking explanations. According to Spinoza, the only freedom that we have is the freedom to change our minds; but it is the only freedom that we really need. The passage, by degrees, from passivity into activity changes one's personal identity in the most fundamental way possible.

I once loved above almost all else the sense that I was reconstituting my mind, transforming the passive ideas that had been handed to me by the conditions of my birth into the active ideas I had derived through arduously seeking rational explanations. I loved that all of us who so dedicate ourselves to this rational pursuit could, at least in principle, end up with the same ideas; that, in a sense, we could end up with the same mind, the mind of objectivity itself—one approximating *Deus sive Natura*, as my beloved *apikorus* Spinoza put it.

Grasping Plato's Forms, or Spinoza's *Deus sive Natura*, or Gödel's incompleteness theorems, it didn't matter a hoot who I was, whether girl or boy, rich or poor, Jewish or not. I called the object of my desire "objective knowledge" and the taste of it in my mind was of pure sweet water.

Yet here I am, five-ninths a Jewish writer, and that is five-ninths more than I can rationally explain. I am dreaming, and at least five-ninths of the time, I am dreaming Jewish dreams. Deep down in the regions of psyche where fiction is born, regions supremely indifferent to criteria of rationality, being Jewish seems to matter to me more than I can explain or justify; and in this way my own small and personal story might be offered up as a metaphor for the very reawakening in Jewish American letters. For here some of us are, after several generations that have tried their damnedest to shrug off the accidents of our shared precedents; here we are, having sufficiently assimilated the culture at large to be able to inhabit, should we so choose, the inner worlds of characters to whom Jewishness is nothingness; here a significant number of us are, against logic, dreaming Jewish dreams.

A few years ago, the literary critic Sanford Pinsker found cause, like me, to comment on the goal of Jewish dreaming that Cynthia Ozick once appropriated to herself. He called it "an honorable effort," but asserted that it was one that "a writer like I. B. Singer never had to undertake. Every dream he had was, by definition, a Jewish dream. . . ."

I would respond to Pinsker that none of us writing today can be a Jewish writer in the same sense that I. B. Singer was. For we are all of us perfectly capable of dreaming non-Jewish dreams, so perfectly capable that what calls out for explanation is that we choose, at least sometimes, to dream Jewishly. At this particular, perhaps transient, stage in Jewish history, it takes a distinctly anomalous desire to become a Jewish dreamer, as it takes, as well, a sustained effort.

For it is a very real problem to be able to discover how to do it, this Jewish-dreaming thing, in terms that make contemporary sense. We obviously can't express the Jewish difference by testifying, as other generations of Jewish writers have so eloquently testified, to the yearning to be let into the Other's dream: to go to the good schools, live in the fine neighborhoods, mix with and marry the goldenly Christian girls and boys. Yearning flows in some other direction.

I've found, like several others linked in this suggested

revival of Jewish American letters, that my Jewish dreams, at least sometimes, take me backward in time, into a past in which the texture of Jewishness was more richly felt. Perhaps it can be argued that some gathered strands from that textured past must always find their way into the Jewish dreams we weave, that to experience the world Jewishly is to experience it historically.

To experience the world Jewishly also is, at least for me, to experience it through the scrim of a certain tradition of storytelling. Deep in my soul where philosophy and fiction are always slugging it out, the Jewish stories I loved as a child give me the means to try to argue with Plato. Storytelling has a high moral role to play in Judaism. I experienced this firsthand, not only through my traditional Orthodox education, which placed so much emphasis on the Bible stories, but even more intimately. Friday nights my father would sometimes put me to bed and he would tell me beautiful tales about downtrodden beggars for whom the gates of heaven opened wide and the angels on high called out their awe and love. He would tell me about simple acts of charity that reconfigured reality. My father's stories were good stories, filled with vivid details and unpredictable reversals. The gentle singer of Israel knew how to tell a good *mysah*. But I think I knew even as the littlest child that my father's storytelling had ulterior motives. He was more concerned with making me a good Jew, the possessor of a good Jewish heart, than a contented little girl who would fall asleep easily. (In fact, his stories often got me so stirred up that I wouldn't be able to fall asleep for what seemed like hours.) He was trying through his storytelling to make of his child one of the compassionate people in the world, one who would look beyond the tempting vanities and who would never forget the unknowable mystery that another human being always is, no matter the lack of outward glamour. Like Plato, my father was trying to instruct me in the higher beauty, though, unlike the philosopher, he chose storytelling, Jewish storytelling, to inculcate his lessons.

He would invariably make me cry with his stories, my father; it was the only time he would look on my tears with satisfaction, smiling as he dried my wet cheeks. And in fact I've never finished writing one of my own stories or novels without my face drenched in tears, even if it's primarily a funny work. If I'm not crying, the work isn't finished. Someone once asked me what the major difference was between my work on philosophy and on fiction, and I answered, "My cheeks are dry when I work on philosophy." And this, too, this particular sort of wetness, I associate with the nature of Jewish stories, with Jewish dreaming.

But whichever way we choose to dream Jewishly these days, it is a choice among many. And knowing, as we do, so many ways of being, other than being Jewish, it is only by desire, by mysterious, irrational desire, that we delimit our imaginations so that they occupy this particular region in the spread of possibilities that are open to them.

And what explains this desire? I can only say that for me this pull away from dry and impersonal objectivity and back into a particularity wet with Jewish history and sensibility has the unmistakable feel of love. It's a love far too complicated to yield me joy (only pages), but it is, nevertheless, love.

And love, luckily or not, makes a habit of silencing logic.

JONATHAN WILSON

How I Became a
Jewish Writer in America

At the age of twenty-six I came to America to be a
Jewish writer because I did not think that I could
become one in England, certainly not in any
meaningful way. This isn't altogether true, but I wish that
it was. When I arrived in New York on July 3, 1976, on the
night before the Bicentennial (Firecrackers! Tall ships! A
perfect immigrant's welcome), my ambitions were not
particularly directed toward the creating of fictions,
except for those that might impress girls I hoped to meet
in either of the two bars that had been recommended to
me: the Gold Rail and the West End. I was a graduate student from Oxford over to spend a semester at Columbia.
My thesis, seriously unfocused at this time (and for all
time), purported to be something about radical Jewish
American writing in the 1930s. There were books in Butler Library that I needed to read.

My first forays into Jewish American fiction, and
therefore into imagining a Jewish life in America, had
begun, it now occurs to me, with J. D. Salinger. At age

fourteen, in the summer of 1964, a friend, Robert Lipman, had passed on his copy of *Franny and Zooey* to me while we were spending a fortnight at my Uncle Simey's strictly kosher "Happy Holiday School" (the word "camp," because of its awful associations, was not used to describe the summer vacations of Jewish children in England). I had previously read *Catcher in the Rye* and been both delighted and baffled by it. The bafflement came because I couldn't imagine what Holden's little brother Allie's baseball mitt looked like. I had never seen one and Salinger didn't bother with a lengthy description. However, neither the Glass family in *Franny and Zooey* nor the Jewish characters surrounding and including Moses Herzog, whom I came across a year later in Bellow's great novel *Herzog*, prepared me for the Portnoys of Philip Roth's *Portnoy's Complaint*. By 1969 I was in the middle of what felt like a yearlong shouting match with my mother about *that* book. The arguments were fueled, it must be admitted, both by my newly developed intimate friendships with gentile girls and my world-historical-event behind-her-back ordering of a nonkosher seafood pizza in a local restaurant (she picked up the plate and threw it in my face).

Imagine, if you can, dinner in a small northwest London home, in a sky blue kitchen newly refurbished by two brothers, one competent, one incompetent, whom my mother refers to as "Mr. Hayden and *Schmerel* Hayden." A high-voltage literary debate is in progress with all the cuts and thrusts that our tart tongues can muster. I am wild with anger because *Portnoy's Complaint* has become the sacred text of my life. It matters more to me than any of the "banned books" by D. H. Lawrence, Henry Miller, and the Marquis de Sade that for reasons determined by the vast prairies of open time that I spend alone in my room with my older brother's "library," I have gulped down by the age of fourteen and returned to with frequency in the last five years. *Portnoy's Complaint* is also, if only she could see it, the book of my mother's life. Sophie Portnoy IS Doris Wilson: the only difference as far as I can tell is that Doris Wilson has an English accent. Like Sophie Portnoy, Doris Wilson will stop at nothing to protect her youngest and most vulnerable child from the temptations and dangers presented by the gentile world. If private letters need to be opened and read, so be it; if phone calls must be listened in on, then what is wrong with that? If unsuitable girls *and their parents* need to be phoned and told "leave my son alone," what mother in her right mind would criticize the action? That inspired jailer, my mother, turns out coat pockets, searches under mattresses, and, if she finds them, rips up photographs of my (gentile) girlfriends and leaves the pieces in a snowy heap on my pillow. "I *hate* that book," my mother screams, and she actually has tears in her eyes. "I *hate* that Philip Roth. Horrible horrible horrible book." To which I can only muster the lame and hopeless reply, "BUT YOU HAVEN'T READ IT."

The tension and discomfort persisted so long as I remained in England. Fast-forward to 1974 on a bruised February afternoon in Oxford. I have recently returned from Kibbutz Kfar Azza, where, serving as a volunteer throughout the Yom Kippur War and three months beyond, I fed, reared, and inoculated chickens, immolating the dead among them and sending the rest off for slaughter. I am still flush with the memory of riding high on "my own" tractor: the Jewish farm boy, tanned and muscled, a young man who has heard *real* sirens calling each to each, and spent a night in an underground air-raid shelter with the sad and beautiful wives of men at war. Now, home in England with studies resumed, I am offering my fellow graduate students a paper on Bernard Malamud's novel *A New Life*. We sit around a long table in Merton College's gorgeously authentic fourteenth-century library. A new life for Malamud's Sy Levin turns out not to be the spacious freedom promised by the American Pacific Northwest, but responsible, resigned acceptance of limitation and restraint. Malamud's hero only achieves a breakthrough in the spirit when he accepts the yoke, not of the Torah, but of some unhappily modern equivalent to Mosaic law: thou shalt stick by thy troubled wife (in this case somebody else's), thy sick kids, thy miserable job. Why? Because thou canst etc., etc. I embellish a version of this reading and the room is very quiet; dusky clouds gather in the all-consuming Larkinesque high windows; and then, in response to a polite, murmured question, I characterize Sy Levin as a "schlemiel," and while it may not at all be so, I sense that this is a first for the oak-paneled room. *Schlemiel* circles the rafters, glances off the stained glass, makes its clumsy way around the long table. Sy Levin in America is trapped (but ultimately free), whereas I, for one delicious moment in the pervasive Christian atmospherics of England, and of Oxford in particular, am free (but ultimately trapped).

I came to America not only in search of the freedom to write in an unrestricted manner about Jewish American authors (or to have the feeling that I was doing so), but also to become one. I also thought I was a poet. One day, crossing the Columbia campus in the pouring rain, I met a fellow student, Allison Funk, who really was a poet. She introduced me to the delights of the Ninety-second Street

YMHA. We went almost every Monday night to see and hear the great poets read: Elizabeth Bishop and Robert Lowell among them. Allison had recently converted to Judaism. I can't remember her reasons for doing so, but a Jewish boyfriend was in the picture somewhere. Jews and New York: the terms were more or less synonymous in my mind (as in everyone else's), and what a wonderful feeling it was after a lifetime of Anglo-Jewish minority self-effacement to be a part of the loud majority.

One wintry December Saturday, close to midnight, I helped my friend Barak Berkowitz move a large double bed from 110th Street to his new apartment on 106th. We rolled the bed on its clattery casters down Broadway. I had taken a shower only a few minutes before going out, and the freezing night air turned my hair to ice. Nobody, cops included, seemed to care that we were blocking the road. There were self-dramatizing groups and individuals up and down the sidewalk: idlers and chatterers of all ages, students, boozers, panhandlers, partygoers, all of them mixed, merged, colorful, juicy, and bathed in light like the starstruck fruit and flowers in the bodegas. I felt the way that Scott Fitzgerald describes in *The Crack Up* when he recalls the heady Manhattan days of his first great literary success. "I remember riding in a taxi one afternoon between very tall buildings under a mauve and rosy sky; I began to bawl because I had everything I wanted and knew I would never be so happy again." Only instead of thinking that I would never be so happy again it occurred to me that, whether as principals or bit players in the city's general theater, I had never in my life seen Jewish people have so much fun.

In America, every ethnic group has its celebrated day in the arts, and on that day it is regarded as fully American in its credentials. The hyphenated guidelines—African-American, Dominican-American, Chinese-American—don't get in the way of invitations to the bigger party. Saul Bellow's wonderful sprawling novel *The Adventures of Augie March* begins with a presentation of credentials from its eponymous narrator: "I am an American, Chicago born. . . ." It is a solid and powerful statement. There's no "Jewish" qualifier in there, and no need for one. Augie's creator, as it happens, hailed from Lachine, Quebec, and moved to the United States as a nine-year-old child. Nothing wrong, of course, with an author inventing any kind of background for a character. But I have always been taken with this particular feint. Saul Bellow had no problem negotiating the early switch that brought his own citizenship into line with Augie's. Nor does anyone, apart perhaps from some territorial Canadians, imagine that he is *not* an American author. But what compels me is this: the kind of confidence that rallies behind the first line of *Augie March* was and is entirely absent, I believe, not only for Jewish writers who move to England and take British citizenship but also for those, like myself, who were born there. It may even be the case that because nostalgia (along with hostility) adheres to old colonial attachments, it is easier for Indian- and Caribbean-born writers living in England, like Rushdie and Naipaul, to be seen (and to see themselves) as English than it is for a Jewish writer. The great wave of Jewish fiction that swept over America from the 1950s into the 1970s—novels and stories by Bellow, Malamud, Roth, Heller, Paley, Ozick (we should not really include Mailer)—did not come from the edge of American life but rather arose from its heart. Such acceptance is unthinkable for Jewish writers in England. Does this have to do with either the quality of their work or the small number of Jewish readers in the general population? Both perhaps. More powerfully, however, I believe that it stems from a deep and frequently unspoken anti-Semitism. A Jew can never *really* be English: it's as simple as that.

A Jew can never be English, but is it also possible, despite my insistence on the democratic openness of the world of American letters, that an English Jew can never quite be an American? That has been my experience even though I have lived in the United States for half my life and been a voting citizen for almost as long. When my most recent novel appeared I was variously described by reviewers as "a British Jew who spent many years in Israel," a "British-born Professor," and "the Anglo-Jewish writer, who has lived chiefly in the United States." Only Gershom Gorenberg in *The Washington Post*, an Israeli-American writer who has his own blurred identity, offered the accurate characterization "a British-born American." None of this, of course, matters very much to anyone except me. But I wonder if the "British-born" can ever fall away completely in the manner of Bellow's "Canadian born." But then of course there is the issue of subject matter: and perhaps that is the only issue. To be seen as an American writer, or a Jewish American writer, one must write about America and Jewish Americans. I haven't always done so. I've written two historical novels and two books of stories: one of the novels has American characters, one doesn't; one of the books of stories is set in America, one isn't. What is all this about except a desire on my part to be seen, like my heroes Saul Bellow, Philip Roth, and Grace Paley, as a Jewish American, American writer? And yet, and yet . . . all dreams, Uncle Sigmund tells us, are either wishes or anxieties, so perhaps there is a part of me that doesn't want to let go of the "British-born." A couple of years ago I went back to London to play in a reunion soccer game of a Jewish boys club team that I had played on from the ages of eleven to seventeen. I was crossing the field when I saw a small group of men standing under a grove of plane trees, all smoking cigarettes as preparation for their exertions. A couple of them, Laurence Milton and Brian Solomons, looked up and spotted me. We hadn't seen each other for more than thirty years. "Wilson!" one of them said. "You *fat* fuck." I felt completely at home.

MELVIN JULES BUKIET

Nothing Makes You Free

A rock drops into the center of a pond. Ripples spread. Make that a flaming comet crashing into a boiling tar pit. A tidal wave ensues. Consider the Holocaust as that first event. Call the ripples literature. Name the pit "Europe."

The Jews, poor schnooks, believed that Europe was a temporary residence they occupied while awaiting return to the true Holy Land. Until that day of redemption arrived, however, they lived quietly: working, studying, making sure their chickens were kosher. Most rural Jews engaged in daily worship of the God who drove them from Zion into Babylonia, Rome, Spain, medieval Mitteleuropa, and, finally, the fertile Polish countryside. Even the city sophisticates who read and wrote for newspapers breathed exile. So occasionally a drunken peasant cudgeled a Jewish tot to death. So there were blood libels, pogroms. What did you expect? This was Eastern Europe, where—despite Marx, Rothschild, and Freud; Kakfa, Chagall, and Schoenberg—not much had changed since the Middle Ages. Life was precarious, yet it went on as it had in ages past. How could these people dream that here, in their own time, centuries of fruitfulness and multiplication would come to nothing?

A friend of my family grew up in Oświęcim, a village thirty miles west of Cracow which, due to the German tongue's inability to pronounce the Slavic syllables, came to be known as Auschwitz. He played there with the other children amidst the birch groves where a world of Jews would utter their last prayers before a bullet . . . before a knife . . . before a brick . . . before a doctor, a butcher, a baker . . . before the gas.

Then came D-Day, the Red Army, German surrender. Concentration camps were "liberated," and approximately one hundred thousand Jews were released from hell. Many more emerged from years of hiding in terror.

What a strange world they inhabited. Their homes were burnt, their culture destroyed, their God silent. It was a world without very young or very old people, because most of those who survived were between twenty and thirty and had been deemed fit for work, temporarily. Perhaps most bizarrely, the survivors' was a world without parents, a world of orphans.

Like their literal mothers, their *mameloshen*, Yiddish, was now as dead as Sanskrit. That was appropriate, because the survivors were ghosts floating across the devastated landscape. Much congratulatory celebration is made these days of their vigor, their character, and their mere existence, but let's keep one terrible truth on the table. In fact, Hitler won.

"Oh, no!" people say. "He's dead and we're here." But *we* are not here. An infinitesimal portion of *us* are here. Most of *us* are ash floating over Eastern Europe. The Jews lost, badly. The continent is morally, culturally, essentially *Judenrein*.

Thus, the survivors were expected to remain unobtrusive supernatural phenomena, not disturbing the living with the clanking of their chains and their alarming stories. In return, a guilty world tried to salve its conscience with passports to the United States and other nations that had barred entry to Jews a decade earlier.

For the most part, the survivors obliged. They pretended to live normal lives, to find work, pay rent, eat dinner. A few like Elie Wiesel and Primo Levi chronicled their individual and communal catastrophe in print, but most lived as privately abroad as they had in their destroyed homes. This was the 1950s and the Holocaust had not entered the public consciousness as it would thirty years later. But the survivors could not wait to be discovered, so the tailor in Borough Park, the builder in New Jersey, the housewife in Miami, and their coequals in Tel Aviv and London and Melbourne told their stories to each other over games of gin. They also told them to the only others who had no choice but to listen, their children.

Despite every possible attempt to obliterate them from the face of the earth, these phantoms had returned to the land of the living, and that meant meeting and mating and bearing squawling infants who wouldn't have stood a chance a single decade earlier. Whether they remained in Europe as eighteenth-generation Germans or were born in the United States as first-generation Americans, within Holocaust circles the children are known as the Second Generation.

In a way, life has been even stranger—though infinitely less perilous—for the children than for the parents. If a chasm opened in the lives of the First Generation, they could nonetheless sigh on the far side and recall the life Before, but for the Second Generation there is no Before. In the beginning was Auschwitz. On the most literal level, their fathers would not have met their mothers if not for the huge dislocations that thrust the few remnants of European Jewry into contact with spouses they would never have otherwise encountered except for DP camps or in the twentieth-century Diaspora. The Second Generation's very existence is dependent on the whirlwind their parents barely escaped.

No one who hasn't grown up in such a household can conceive it, while every 2G has something in common. Every one of these happy or unhappy families knows a variation of the same unhappy story. Of course, some survivors spoke incessantly of the Holocaust while others never mentioned it. Of those who didn't speak, some were traumatized while others hoped to protect their offspring from knowledge of the tree of evil.

The Second Generation will never know what the First Generation does in its bones, but what the Second Generation knows better than anyone else is the First Generation. Other kids' parents didn't have numbers on their arms. Other kids' parents didn't talk about massacres as easily as baseball. Other kids' parents had parents.

Other kids' parents loved them, but never gazed at their offspring as miracles in the flesh. Most of us weren't born in mangers, but we might as well have been. Other kids weren't considered a retroactive victory over tyranny and genocide.

So what do you do with this cosmic responsibility? You were born in the 1950s so you smoked dope and screwed around like everyone else. But your rebellion was pretty halfhearted, because how could you rebel against these people who endured such loss? Compared to them, what did you have to complain about?

How do you deal with it? As adults, many 2Gs took

up the "helping" occupations and became shrinks or social workers while others became involved with Jewish charities. And if you were a writer, you wrote.

Lord knows, you weren't alone, because along with your personal maturity the Holocaust has ripened, and the floodgates to exploration of this awful era opened. Why it didn't happen immediately after the war I don't know. Understandably, people didn't want to think about it, but a delayed-action fuse eventually ignites and we are witnessing the explosion right now.

The comet hits at six million miles per hour and the waves spread. From the primary sources of the First Generation to the Second Generation it has swelled to include other Jews (Saul Bellow's *Mr. Sammler's Planet*, Cynthia Ozick's *The Shawl*) and then non-Jews (John Hersey's *The Wall* and William Styron's putative Holocaust book, *Sophie's Choice*, followed by Pat Conroy's *Beach Music* and Caribbean writer Caryl Phillips's *The Nature of Blood*). Over the last few years, I've noticed that virtually every book I've read—an Australian novel about a millennial cult in the outback, a Brazilian novel about gangsters and gem dealers, a gay cross-dressing fantasia, a noirish portrayal of the movie business, a semi-memoir of a young black poet in an L.A. slum—to a greater or lesser extent involve the Holocaust. Some are good books, some are bad, but that's not the point. What's important is that the Holocaust has become a talismanic touchstone before which every writer must genuflect. Try an experiment. Take every tenth book of fiction off the shelves of your local bookstore. A few will actually be about the Holocaust, but count how many others mention, just mention, in passing, as a metaphor, the *H*-word as a kind of seal of literary seriousness. My guess is seven out of ten.

The weird thing is that, contravening all physical laws, the waves do not diminish. They build upon each other, getting larger rather than smaller as history itself recedes. No other event of our time has attained this emblematic significance. The only thing one can compare it to in terms of its lasting effects may be the French Revolution and subsequent ascendance of Napoleon. Fifty years after Waterloo, Raskolnikov tacks a lithograph of the emperor onto his garret wall in St. Petersburg and the world understands why; that image represents the heights and the depths of human experience far beyond its native grounds.

To the extent that the two greatest and most basic subjects for writing have always been life and death—what it feels like to be alive and what it feels like to fear death—the Holocaust offers the greatest opportunity of our era. Indeed, hardly a week goes by without some aspect of the Holocaust in the news. It's transcended the domain of history and become mythic. And no particular myth either. It's a historic Rorschach blot; people see in it what they wish. If you're depressive, you can justify despair. If you're hopeful, you can find redemption. If you're stupid, you can discern the triumph of the spirit.

For a writer, it's irresistible. So irresistible that several years ago it led to the grotesque fraud of "Binjamin Wilkomirski," whose book *Fragments* purported to be a memoir of his childhood in a concentration camp, but turned out to be a fiction by a man who appeared to genuinely believe in his self-adopted identity. This is victim envy, survivor-wannabe-ness at its grossest. Yet the Wilkomirski case reflects something larger than one disturbed consciousness. People can't keep their fingers off the Holocaust.

In the midst of this festive free-for-all, the 2Gs occupy a special place. Whatever wisdom others bring to the matter comes from the heart and head, but for us it's genetic. To be shabbily proprietary, we own it. Our parents owned it, and they gave it to us. Just as John Quincy Adams and Barry Bonds followed in their parents' footsteps, we go into Shoah business. I'd like to tell everyone from the Bellows and the Ozicks to the Styrons and the Wilkomirskis, "Bug off. Find your own bad news," but no one can legislate artistic imperative, and perhaps no one should. Yet if the history really is ours, then the mythos is public domain. Still, even here, we retain primacy. We have been given an obscene gift, a subject of predetermined value that no one can deny. It's our job to tell the story, to cry "Never Forget!" despite the fact that we can't remember a thing.

"Memory" is the mantra of all the institutions that reckon with the Holocaust, but memory is an inaccurate term. For anyone who wasn't *there*, on either side of the barbed wire, Jew or German, thinking about the Holocaust is really an act of the imagination. All we know is how little we know.

Nonetheless you've got this . . . event, the Holocaust, always capitalized. Actually, I don't like the word. "Holocaust" was an uncommon common noun that meant a burnt offering until the 1940s; it then became unique and was almost immediately thereafter debased by overuse. For most of those fifty-plus years it referred to events in Europe, and yet, because of its potency, it's been wrongly extended to other localities—Rwanda, Cambodia, the Balkans, the slums. Because of this, I prefer a more specific term. "Shoah" means essentially the same thing as "Holocaust" in Hebrew, but that seems wrong, too, because it comes from a different culture. So from here on I'll say "Khurbn," the Yiddish for disaster, which, branded with "The," can refer to no other *khurbn.*

The first thing you learn is not to try to explain it. Asking "why" makes you crazy. Of course, there was a sequence of historical causes and effects: World War I, the Depression, the rise of and reaction to Communism, Church antisemitism. But those are insufficient. The only reason the Germans killed the Jews was because they wanted to. Why? Because. Because they were poor or because they were rich. Because they were clannish and isolated or because they wore top hats and attended the opera. Because their tailors and seamstresses were spiritual, unworldly wraiths or because their bankers and journalists insidiously plotted to dominate the world from within the corridors of power. Because they did not believe in the common deity or because they did believe in their own tribal God. Because they drank the blood of Christian children. Because, like Everest, they were there. Because.

The Khurbn is a black hole that devours light. The more illumination cast upon it, the less you see.

Thus, the second thing you learn is that you can't realistically render it. The one picture I have of my grandparents is a formal family portrait taken in the mid-1920s and sent to relatives in America. In it a stiff man in a wide-brimmed black hat stares uncomfortably at the camera while an attractive young woman sits with a baby on her lap. The baby, my father, is blurry. Other children and other relatives fill out the frame. I've heard stories about these people's lives; I will not turn their deaths into fiction.

Still, one yearns to attribute meaning to the blurry baby, as if his motion at the moment of the shutter's opening will keep him moving twenty years later and keep him alive to bear me to describe his motion. In this direction, however, lies vile theodicy.

But if you can't place yourself in the mass grave, you can't quite drag yourself out of it, either. You're left with the existential dilemma described by French thinker Alain Finkielkraut in *The Imaginary Jew*. He says, "I inherited a suffering to which I had not been subjected, for without having to endure oppression, the identity of the victim was mine. . . . The allotment was inescapable: for them, utter abandonment and anonymous death, and for their spokesperson, sympathy and honor. . . . I owed to the bond of blood this intoxicating power to confuse myself with the martyrs. . . . no trace of them remains, except perhaps my taste for poppy seed bread, scorching hot tea, and the way I hold sugar in my teeth rather than let it dissolve."

In other words, how do you cope when the most important events of your life occurred before you were born? What does this do to your sense of time? Of authenticity? As they were ghosts in history, you're a ghost in your own safe little suburban bedroom with cowboy lamp shades. All you know is that you've received a tainted inheritance, secondhand knowledge of the worst event in history. In fact, you see only the most benign effects of The Khurbn, because, by definition, this is as good as it gets. The manifold imaginary offspring of the six million actual dead do not have the Second Generation's opportunities. Perhaps their books are buried on the shelves in some library of the deceased, but we don't have a card to that library.

The library we know by heart is our parents. Maybe some don't fit this image, but I think of all the men as short, round, bald, and tough as spikes, and the women as plump with dyed hair, tough as spikes. I remember one "gathering" many years ago where then vice president George H. W. Bush was addressing about five thousand survivors and their offspring in front of the Washington Monument. I left, because of my politics, and sat in the first of several dozen waiting buses. One elderly woman had preceded me, and a few others followed us. For them, leaving the Mall was a matter of practicality; the first bus filled would be the first to depart.

Unfortunately, there was a problem. The first bus had been reserved for VIPs. As soon as the speech ended and a multitude of survivors swarmed toward the buses, an officious young woman told us we had to vacate the vehicle. We who had been so clever would be consigned to the back of the line. The elderly woman in front of me started bitching. She was saying things like "Hitler didn't beat us, and you won't," and I egged her on. We were ready to link arms and go limp. I could see the bad press take shape in twenty-point type in my mind: "Survivors Arrested in Protest at Washington Monument."

Eventually, authority caved in and told us we could have our damn bus, but the elderly woman was still muttering and cursing. "How dare they?" As the bus looped around the Mall, I leaned forward and said, "But we had fun, didn't we?" and she gave me a smile as bright as sunshine. We had never met before, but we knew each other.

Later that night, I spoke to my girlfriend in New York, whom I'd eventually marry. Not a child of survivors, she assumed we'd be wearing sackcloth and ashes and delicately asked how things were going. I think I shocked her when I crowed, "We're having a great time." Knowledge of death imparts appreciation for life.

Knowledge of death also imparts an unusual kind of

resignation. In the recent *Encyclopedia of Holocaust Literature* there are 129 biographical entries. Of these, more than a quarter are still alive, but of the dead, at least half a dozen were suicides. Larry Amsel, a psychiatrist who studies suicide, says that the probability of this percentage of suicides occurring out of a random sampling may exceed a million to one. The natural supposition is that Jean Amery, Tadeusz Borowski, Adam Czerniakov, Paul Celan, Jerzy Kosinski, Piotr Rawicz, and, perhaps, Primo Levi killed themselves because of severe depression traceable to the war, but I prefer to think otherwise. It's simply that when life becomes unbearable because of debilitating disease or scandal or whatever, then death is not fearsome. These people are so intimate with mortality that at a certain point they can shrug and say, "It's time."

When friends he loves die, my father calls me and says, "Let's go to the funeral," and we do. That's it. No fuss, no bother. His tear ducts have been cauterized. When three presidents of the Cracow Society died in the space of a year and my uncle was asked to assume the post, he said, "It's a dangerous job." Life is a dangerous job.

That same uncle tells about a moment during the liquidation of the Cracow ghetto. Two groups of about fifty men each stood side by side, the first deemed *Arbeiter* or workers, the second, including my uncle, *Menschen*. He didn't know why, but my uncle just felt that it would be better to be a worker, so he moved from one group to the other, a matter of a few feet.

Just then Kommandant Amon Goeth arrived. He asked the German in charge what the two groups were, listened, pointed to the *Menschen* and said, "*Weg mit dieser Scheisse.*" This means "Get rid of this shit." The men were marched into an alley and shot.

But Goeth must have noticed a Bukiet family blur. He

turned to my uncle and said, "Weren't you with the other group?"

"No," my uncle replied.

"What sort of worker are you?"

"Um—a mechanic."

"Where do you work?"

My uncle remembered a mechanic's shop nearby and named it. Still suspicious, Goeth looked at my uncle and said, "If you're lying to me, I'll hang you tomorrow."

So my uncle thought—and here's the punch line—"I'd rather be hanged tomorrow than shot today."

Were the novelists and poets and dramatists and cartoonists of the Second Generation born writers or were we compelled to write by our proximity to extremity? I don't know. I only know that these are the stories I heard at the dinner table. Thus rendering life with people who are capable of saying, "I'd rather be hanged tomorrow than shot today. Pass the salt," becomes one's most enduring subject.

Throughout history, there have been two parallel, millennia-long strands of Jewish responses to catastrophe. First, there is a tone of mournful lamentation that echoes from the psalms of the Bible through medieval poetry through the somber reflections of Elie Wiesel and his kin. Yet off on the side, there was always an unpleasant, hectoring voice of shrieking hysteria that came from the prophets, God-haunted maniacs on hilltops, and segued into the Hasidic messianists who tossed away their worldly possessions every time another fraud promised redemption. Opposed to wishful-thinking realpolitik Zionists who aspired to salvation on earth, they were so doubtful of their era's ability to bring forth deliverance that they could only believe in redemption in connection with the End of Days.

Fifty-some years ago, the End of Days arrived for one-third of the Jews on earth. Nonetheless, the literature of The Khurbn, with few exceptions until now—notably Jerzy Kosinski's *The Painted Bird* and the ferocious *This Way for the Gas, Ladies and Gentlemen,* by Tadeusz Borowski, a gentile—has not been written in the voice of lunacy and apocalyptic frenzy. That voice explodes with renewed vigor in the Second Generation, whose fury at what they have been denied—history, deity, grandparents—comes out on the page.

Two traits distinguish the Second Generation from the canonical Elie Wiesels and Primo Levis of The Khurbn syllabus. The first difference is stylistic. Wiesel and the (mostly) men who have written about the war emerged from a tradition of rabbinical tale telling; their works, driven by the enormity of their experience, reflect that older, more traditional mode, whereas the Second Generation for the most part came of cultural age by reading Joyce, Proust, and the great shapers of modern literature. Their work thereby has a manifestly contemporary texture that could not exist in any other era.

Also, a matter of genre, even when the First Generation claims it's writing fiction, it comes out as memoir. They have no need to imagine; we have no option but to imagine.

A case might even be made that if writing—at least fiction—is more essentially imaginative than representational, then the Second Generation may be more appropriately suited for the task than the First, but I'm hesitant to make this claim. Of course, our perceptions and the manner in which they unfold are also culturally determined in many ways. For example, American children of survivors tend toward a straightforward, in-your-face prose that emphasizes their own struggles, whereas Israeli children of survivors often pathologize their parents—most likely because the nature of Israeli nationhood requires constant strength. For them, vulnerability is suicidal. Also, the farther east one moves in Europe, the more elusive and allusive the prose. Maybe this is because it is still dangerous to be an avowed Jew in Slavic nations, or maybe there's something in those writers' literary heritage that encourages that style.

In imagining, a particular tone bleeds through in all but the mildest of Second Generation writers. Though often literarily exuberant and sometimes "experimental," they are viciously unredemptive, scoured of weakness as they look atrocity straight in the face with barely contained rage. Despite today's insipid fetish for "healing," frequently engaged in by the social workers of the Second Generation, the writers heal nothing and comfort no one with their work. Healing is another word for forgetting. Healing is what movies like *Life Is Beautiful* and *Schindler's List* seek—the former with gratuitous vulgarity, the latter with insidious skill—as they concoct a spurious ray of light to falsely illuminate the night. Instead of closure, the writers prefer the open wound. And should that wound threaten to close, they rip out the stitches. As a young German Jewish writer provocatively titled an essay about tourism and voyeurism, "See Auschwitz and Die."

Sorrow comes from recollection, outrage from reflection. Then, recollecting fury, it grows. The Second Generation's work is angrier than the First's. Not for them the celebration of European *Yiddishkeit*. Not for them the God of their fathers. God? Who's that? Never met Him. Or worse, if God reveals Himself at moments of vastness—what Arthur A. Cohen called "Tremendum"—what more aptly qualifies than Auschwitz, 1944? If God appeared, He was wearing a brown shirt.

"If." There are a lot of ifs in this essay. That's because the only thing the Second Generation knows is the imponderable, which means that we don't know anything and distrust anyone with an answer. The wonderfully equalizing thing about The Khurbn is that it denies all wisdom, throws everyone it touches into the abyss of ignorance.

On the other hand, the only tenderness in the writing of the Second Generation is reserved for those we do know, our parents. Yet even they are portrayed without sentimentality, but that's a testament to their humanity. Some may be noble; most aren't. It doesn't make a difference. If you are a minor person, shabby, greedy, or vulgar, it still doesn't mean that the Germans should slaughter your mother.

No one—not a German and not a Jew—who isn't a child of survivors can begin to understand the bottomless depths of rage inside those born into The Khurbn. No one can understand how we can hold collectively guilty not only the octogenarian perpetrators but the rest of the nation that saw nothing for the twelve-year reign of the Thousand-Year Reich, and their children and their children's children and the yet unborn tainted by their German blood. This is, I know, by any moral standards and by any sane logic, wrong. But because the pure flame of undying hatred is wrong doesn't mean that it isn't true, and if this reflects a deep flaw in my soul, so be it. They put it there. Remember, no particular moral stature adheres to suffering and less so to being born of those who suffered. Jews are different since 1945. Not that the Chosen People were especially saintly Before, but they exhibited a sense of passive acquiescence to circumstance that is no longer. Now, we are strident. Now, we rub the world's nose in our misery. Go to our museums. Go see our movies. Go read our books. Look at what you did. Behold.

...

P.S. 108016 is the secret personal identification number for my bank account. 108016 is also the password for my computer and answering machine at work. Whenever I need a number in this age that compels them, I use 108016. Several years ago, I presented a novel I wrote to German Chancellor Kohl, and signed it "108016." Herr Kohl looked baffled; he probably thought it was my phone number. Indeed, it would be if I could make the arrangement. After a journalist chronicled the encounter, Herr Kohl might have called me, but the only number he had was the only number I had: 108016.

It would be disingenuous for me to claim that those six digits were the first I knew. Presumably I could count, but the artless aniline blue of 108016 tattooed on my father's forearm was an abiding sign of the past in our present. It was his alone and then, as much as such a thing can ever be, it became mine, and now it's yours; we can *share*.

NESSA RAPOPORT

Body of Love

Her Mouth Full of Song Like the Sea

The acclaimed American Jewish writers I read when I was young had the immigrant experience to draw on and quarrel with. They had the music of Yiddish in their ears. They had a tangible neighborhood anti-Semitism to sharpen their mordant wit. Their novels taught a generation of Jews to understand itself—torn between the world of European parents and the wild, seductive promise of America, with its non-Jewish women and its nonneurotic men. It was not possible for those parents to transmit an intimacy with Jewish texts in the *heder* their children endured, longing for baseball.

With some exceptions, this was not the narrative of my generation, and yet the stories we read in Jewish communal magazines were often written in a Yiddish intonation derived from imitating the tone of earlier fiction rather than from authentic experience. They were frequently about the same extremes, the encounter between the circumscribed, nostalgic world of the ultra-Orthodox community and the post-sixties anarchy of secular America. Or they contrasted suburban Jewish life of the synagogue and the country club with an idealized portrait of Israel in which everyone lived on kibbutz.

Like any reader, we looked for books that spoke to us, that offered a vision of Jews or Jewish life corresponding in knowledge and intensity to the wealth our parents had given us: the strong Jewish education at day schools they established when we were children; the music of Hebrew rather than Yiddish, *modah ani lifanekha* or *avadim hayinu* or *bi-shofar gadol yitaka*—those phrases inscribed on the unconscious by life in the community, echoes of prayer repeated each day or year since childhood; and the passion for Israel not as icon but in the bone, after years of travel and weeks of talk inflected with street-slang Hebrew.

In vain we looked for ourselves, the invisible Jews who did not leave Judaism for a universal truth or retreat to a fundamentalist security. What about the rest of us, we wondered, young Jewish women who could read each month in *Ms.* magazine, many of whose editors were Jewish, stories about the tribal rituals of African-American or Chicana women but nothing about the mystery of Jewish ceremonial life. Why weren't our texts, our experiences valuable, we asked, to the overwhelmingly Jewish editorial boards, anthologists, and teachers directing the next generation of American writers?

I dreamed of telling a different story, suffused with the festive joy inherited from my mother's family, girded by a legacy of lost magnificence, the illustrious rabbinic family from which I descend on my father's side. Above all, I wanted to reveal a Judaism capacious and passionate enough to be sufficient.

Here I sit, writing my first novel. I am trying to

describe the moment when my young heroine surprises her great first love by flying to Jerusalem to find him. Already, the chapter in which their encounter takes place is drenched in the language and cadence of the Song of Songs, although I know that a reader unfamiliar with Solomon's song will not hear the allusions, to cypress and cedar, hills of spice, perfume, and Jerusalem as earthly paradise.

But now I have stopped working for three weeks. I cannot find language to express what happens inside this seventeen-year-old girl when her love opens the door on that night.

And then I hear, within, the chant of Hebrew. It is the Hebrew I say each week on Shabbat morning: *ilu finu malei shirah ka-yam*—"if our mouth were as full of song as the sea," a phrase from the beautiful prayer that begins "Let the breath of all that lives praise Your name."

I change the pronoun in the phrase, for I am not speaking as the people of Israel, blessing the One in whose image we are made, but as a lovesick girl, who sees the boy as if he were divine:

> If her mouth were full of song like the sea and her tongue rejoicing like the rushing waves and on her lips praise like the breath of heaven, her eyes the sun, the moon, her arms outstretched like the sea eagles, her feet delicate as gazelles, still it would not be enough to hold what happened then.

The moment I noticed our sacred texts flowing through me without cease was the moment I became a Jewish writer. Standing in the aura of Shai Agnon and A. M. Klein, I beheld a radiant vista that seemed almost uninhabited—the prospect of writing in English that could reflect not only Jewish lives but Jewish letters.

The Jewish novel has been a book for Jews, about Jews, or even against Jews. But the Jewish novel could also resonate with Jewish language and draw its structure, its mode of thought, its allusions from the Jewish books that came before it. These books are not fiction as we make it today. But they are imaginative readings of sacred texts; I see the Jewish novel as a descendant of that tradition.

I do not mean that a Jewish writer of fiction should replicate the forms of those materials by composing midrash or commentary, but that the text of the novel be informed by those earlier texts, respond to them in syntax and diction, immerse itself not only in the great works of Western culture but in the mostly unknown body of Jewish writing—the exuberant conversation that took place among centuries of sacred books and their creators, the talking on the page that resulted in law, myth, parable, argument, and praise.

Unshackled, if I ever had been, by the constraint of mimesis, I was impelled by a vision that until today entices me, a steadfast, unquenched love.

What did I understand? That as a daughter of the tradition, I could play with the sources that run in my blood *yomam va-lailah*, by day and by night, faithful to the rabbis who preceded me, honoring my maternal grandparents' unique mixture of Canadian noblesse oblige and patrician pity for any Jew who did not understand that one can be observant and do anything. Most thrilling, I could escape the predicament represented by Northrop Frye in his teaching at the University of Toronto. For him, English literature aligned tidily, perfectly, with his theology as a Christian. For me, an ancient and obscure literary tradition, the words shaped by the mouths of my people, could be art.

The Jewish Writer Unmasked

My great-aunt Bella, asked how she sustained her spirits in the face of loneliness and old age, answered simply: Poetry. In the middle of the night, when Jerusalem slept, she walked back and forth in her room reciting the Yiddish poems that were her beloved companions since her youth. At such times, she told me, her brothers and sisters—all dead, one murdered by the Nazis—were summoned: the songs of childhood were in her ears.

My great-aunt was brought up in a house in which her parents, hearing a crash in the next room, would call out, "It's only a thing, only a thing," before they knew what had been broken. When Bella, the youngest, left her beautifully furnished apartment in Warsaw to follow her new husband to impoverished Palestine, her in-laws importuned her father in Canada to intervene. My paternal great-grandfather wrote back: "Better that a daughter of mine should starve in the streets of Eretz Yisrael than live in plenty in the streets of Poland."

On January 15, 1991, I am drinking coffee in Jerusalem with Meir Shalev. We speak of our writing and our children. And we speak of the war, which may break out tonight. Meir has the familiar Israeli panache; it is business as usual for him. He is writing in his office today and would not even prepare a sealed room against a possible chemical attack if not for a conservative feeling of parental responsibility.

When I behold Jerusalem on this day, I hear old words: "Ten measures of beauty descended upon the world," the Talmud says. "Jerusalem was adorned with nine." In the prelude to war, these words are juxtaposed with those of Chaim Nachman Bialik in his poem of pogrom, "In the City of Slaughter." When I look out the window at the unblemished sky, I hear the poet's Hebrew: *ha-shemesh zarhah, ha-shitah parhah, ve-ha-shohet shahat,* "The sun rose, the acacia bloomed—and the slayer slaughtered."

Bialik was crying out against a universe and God that allowed one cruel constancy: Jews can be murdered, and yet the created world proceeds to manifest its beauty, untouched.

On the radio, Galei Tzahal, the army station, is instructing people all day about how to adjust their masks and how to seal their rooms. "*Gemar atimah tovah,*" the announcer ends his hour cheerfully.

It is for my laughter at this pun that my father's father studied Hebrew in Poland, and my mother's mother founded the first progressive Jewish day school in Toronto, and my mother keeps a Hebrew novel and dictionary at her bedside, and my father spends his sabbaticals in Israel, where my sister will move within the year.

Gemar atimah tovah, or "a good sealing [of your room against chemical warfare]," is a phrase parodying the words with which Jews take leave of each other between Rosh Hashanah and Yom Kippur: *Gemar hatimah tovah*— "a good sealing [in the Book of Life]."

For a Jewish writer, this witticism on Israeli radio heralds what we call in our prayers "the beginning of the flowering of our redemption." So does the Hebrew word for tie as the outcome of a soccer game: *teiku*, the Talmudic term that means an unresolved debate whose outcome must await the Messiah.

"We have been through many things before this and will see this through as well," my Israeli friends tell me in

Hebrew. I have not been through anything like this, except in my Jewish dreams, for just as every Jew is obliged to see herself as if she, too, stood at Sinai, so every conscious Jew of my generation has imagined herself in such a possible catastrophe.

When my soul cries out in terror, what language does it speak? What if my parents had not bequeathed me this gift, access to the Jewish tongue? Nessa, my son says, confused by my former name, Mommy, his cousins' mother's name, *Ima*, and the urgent "Nessa" that precedes the words of someone who knocks on the hotel door in the middle of the night to be sure we've heard the siren telling us to run upstairs to the sealed room.

When I come back to New York, how will I tell this? I who have lived for words and by them do not have any language to convey what happens in my body when the insistent siren blares in the Jerusalem night and I wake my sleeping child to race up the stairs.

Two stories are colliding in my head: the North American one that, Cold War and Cuban missile crisis notwithstanding, was a tale of increasing security, prosperity, and acceptance of me as a Jew; and the older tale, the blood tale, the one I learned first about how in every generation a tyrant arose and who knew from whence our salvation.

Now, in the war, which Jewish body am I, the cosseted Jewish body of my childhood or the vulnerable Jewish body of our historic nightmare?

We Diaspora Jews who made our first trips to Israel in the early seventies certainly know how Israel changed our bodies. To descend from a plane into the redolent air, shocking in its potency, was to identify the land forever with youth and sensuality and a tactile freedom undreamed of by our sincere Zionist parents. Has anyone fully described the eros of Israel to the *galut* Jew, the beautiful dark men, the profusion of flowers, the tropical landscape so alien, so ours? Shivering Canadians who lived for a brief fling with mutable summer tasted paradise in a country with certain, unwavering light and heat for nearly half a year.

Following a sleepless night of three alarms, my family in Rehovot calls.

"How are you doing?" my father's cousin says.

"Fine," I tell him. "You?"

After the first alarm, he says dryly, *"Tafasti et ha-princip"*—I got the idea.

This is the third tale, the sober and confident tale of the people who speak Hebrew, who created this country. Of the God who declared this language holy. And of the mothers who ingeniously covered the floor of their children's plastic tents with candy, so that they would hurry in without complaint.

Meanwhile, I am holding my son in my arms, staring at the plastic tent on that first night. "Get in, Popsky," I say to him. He is crying. His cousins are helping each other put on their masks, but I have disobeyed the instructions of the hotel security staff to don mine before helping my child; I cannot bring myself to frighten him.

"Get in, sweetie," I say, paralyzed.

"I don't want to," my son cries out, and for a minute literature is mute.

"Tasimi et ha-ben shelakh bifnim"—Put your son inside, someone directs me.

And so he must crawl in, and I must invent stories for him, projected through my mask and his tent in a calm, controlled voice for the hour it takes until the TV announcer says: "*Efshar le-hasir et ha-maseikhot*"—you can take off your masks.

My great-grandfather said: Yiddish is my mistress, but Hebrew is my wife.

I say: English is my mate, but Hebrew is my lover.

As for my nights in Jerusalem, I cannot translate this experience for anyone.

Summoned to the Feast

Most days, I inhabit an Anglo-Saxon sovereignty, composed of the English language, founded on the British literature I devoured in my Commonwealth youth, and imagined through the Canadian Jewishness devised by my maternal clan. Then there are the other days, when I write according to the injunctions left by the greatest catastrophe to befall us.

In the twentieth century, a cultural fuss was made of the growing divide between art and science. My mother's mother, Mattie, coming of age in the Edwardian era of colonial Canada, had a mind that could shuttle effortlessly between Thomas Hardy and the theory of relativity.

The eldest of ten children, she was a "flash," the slang applied to her at the turn of the twentieth century. From her earliest years she excelled in school. Her grandchildren knew she had read all of Shakespeare by the time she was twelve.

Bub, as we called her, had a mind that seemed to retain everything she read or heard. She might quote a lively conversation conducted with a stranger while she was on her European honeymoon in 1924, recite a cherished poem by Tennyson, or use a witticism contrived inadvertently by the woman who helped her in the house when her children were young.

For nearly thirty years, she wrote and broadcast her commentary on the CBC, Canada's national radio, on a program devoted to women's issues called *Trans-Canada Matinee*. When I was growing up, we had in our house a recording Bub made in April 1943. In a country where, it emerged long after the war, the policy toward Jewish refugees was, literally, "None is too many," my grandmother gave a detailed report of the Final Solution, condemning Western nations for their indifference: "Asking themselves the question, 'Am I my brother's keeper?' the democratic nations of the world, our country among them, answered: 'No.' "

She ended her talk with these words: "Some action must be taken at once. If it is not, within a few months six million people will have been murdered, and the nations of the world will not be able to escape the charge of being accomplices to the bleakest crime in history."

Bub spoke English beautifully, of course. She pronounced the *h* in "white," her diction so precise that my friend Rose's mother, a survivor of Auschwitz, improved her newly acquired English by listening to my grandmother's broadcasts.

Writing and broadcasting were not, however, the sole domain of my grandmother's accomplishments. Bub was one of twelve women to take "M & P"—Math and Physics—at the University of Toronto, graduating with a B.A. in 1921. In 1926, pregnant with the second of her five children, she completed the formal requirements for a Ph.D., the first woman and first Jew to receive a doctorate in physics from the university.

In our family, the desirability of a book was measured

by the degree of sleep deprivation one was willing to suffer in order to reach the last page. There was no higher accolade than "I stayed up all night to finish it."

Whatever our duties, my grandmother, mother, three sisters, and I were always pining to return to our books, although it cannot be said that we read the same material. On a summer afternoon at the cottage, I can be found on the porch, suspended in Nancy Drew's peril. My mother is imbibing a Hebrew novel, dictionary at hand, while my grandmother sits in the rocking chair, rereading for pleasure *Black Lamb and Grey Falcon*, Rebecca West's two-volume history of the Balkans.

I am also the descendant of a rabbinic and priestly family, the Rapoports, that can trace its ancestry to the sixteenth century, among the only Jewish families with a coat of arms. My sisters and I are the direct heirs of one scholar, Shabbetai ha-Kohen, known as the ShaKh, whose acronymic name, inscribed on my grandfather's tombstone, elicits a reverence close to awe when it is uttered among learned Jews.

My father's father, Yisrael, cherished eldest son, an *iluy*—child genius in Talmud—fled Russian conscription for a struggling life in Canada as a grocer and a milkman. In Poland, his sister Tzippele and her children have no tombstone. I picture my grandmother Nezia, for whom I am named, weeping in her Toronto kitchen in the mid-1940s when she understood with finality that her mother, my great-grandmother Sheindl, had been murdered.

Without mythologizing the past, I feel tenderly protective of all that was desecrated and then annihilated by the Shoah. My father was born into the first generation of his family since the 1500s without a rabbi. He could not inherit from his father the intimacy with sacred texts bestowed by an intact world. That patrimony was abrogated by the shattering of the Jewish people in the twentieth century. But he did impart to me the memory of splendor that his father had conveyed to him.

In redress, my father studied Jewish history. He was a pioneer, the first Jewish clinician in a hospital that had refused to hire even the most talented Jewish doctors before him. To his lasting regret, he did not have the ease with his people's letters and observance that my mother was given by her parents, who defied the cultural attrition surrounding them.

And so my life is fashioned by the round of celebration that is my mother's legacy, yet in the clasp of my father's birthright.

Daf Yomi with Mom

When I was twenty, I believed that by the time I turned forty I would play tennis, know Italian, and be able to read a Hebrew novel for pleasure. Twenty years later, I had given up on tennis and Italian. I also despaired of reading contemporary Hebrew, having opened several Israeli novels only to abandon them after a few pages, frustrated by my sluggish, dutiful pace.

Last summer I turned fifty. In the fall, I read an article in a women's magazine contending that although many people seem to transform themselves overnight—"One morning I gave up smoking after thirty years"—in fact, they try and fail, contemplate and do not follow through, again and again until at last they are able to change.

And so, fortified by a weekly conversation in Hebrew with an Israeli friend, I began once more.

My mother is never without a Hebrew novel. She is a long-standing member of an Agnon reading group and an Israeli literature reading group. Apparently, she spoke only Hebrew to me in my first weeks of life.

Perhaps that accounts for my love of this language. Or perhaps it is the inimitable power of the Hebrew Bible. Or dozens of trips to Israel, the music of the *alef bet* electrifying my body from the moment I enter the El Al lounge. Or the knowledge that spoken Hebrew is a miracle, the only successfully revived language in the history of nations.

Whatever I might call it, the infantalizing act in which I am at last engaged is not yet reading. It bears no resemblance to the addiction that has soothed my desolation and augmented my ecstasy since I was five. It is certainly not effortless. Still, I am reading Hebrew every day, consoling myself by the inspiration of my mother and by the courage of all our ancestors who fled their countries, forsaking their birth tongues to learn a new song.

Emulating the Jews around the world who begin each day at dawn by studying one page of Talmud, an activity known as *daf yomi*, and influenced by my sister-in-law, who learns Maimonides each week with her father over the phone from Jerusalem to New York, I am now reading Amos Oz's *Sippur al Ahavah ve-Hoshekh* with my mother, by phone, New York to Toronto, reversing the journey I took when I chose Manhattan over the city of my birth, intoxicated by the uniquely nonmarginal status that only New York City could grant an observant Jewish feminist writer, working woman, and mother.

Of course, my mother finished this book long ago, but she is patient with me, as she always has been, reflecting her past as a teacher. I read the sentences aloud, she compliments me on my pronunciation, gently correcting me when I make the inevitable mistake. Then we divide up the task of finding words in the dictionary, although often she already knows the word or can glean it by its three-letter root. Unlike the children of immigrants, I am far behind her.

My mother gave me and my sisters the gift of Hebrew literacy, and now she gives me a more direct gift—her presence and perseverance. I hope that my children see me inscribing in pencil, in the margins of Oz's novel, the words I painstakingly look up, often more than once. And I hope they absorb the idea that for Jews study is lifelong and Hebrew is their inheritance.

The Song of Songs

My husband is a painter and sculptor. His vocabulary is entirely visual. New York born, he likes to say that English is his second language. I live for English, to read it, write it, and savor it on my tongue.

Several years ago he invited me to write the meditations that would accompany the museum show of his ceremonial art. I said no, and then yes.

The voice that emerged in the prayers I created honors my rabbinic ancestry, my devotion to English literature, and my passion for Hebrew sacred texts, especially the Song of Songs, whose ravishing words anticipated my first love and accompany my love for my husband, until—and perhaps after, who can say?—I meet the One in whom my soul delights.

Meditation for a Simhat Bat

On the naming of a newborn daughter

Leap into our lives, from the hidden places to the hills of spice, garden of pomegranate, apple of paradise, awakened by the perfume of your name, we sing you into our mothers' house and listen for your voice.

LEV RAPHAEL

Writing Something Real

All through college, my creative writing teacher kept predicting that I would be published someday, even win prizes, but not until I wrote something "real." I didn't know what she meant at the time, although I can see it now. I was dashing off comic sketches about working-class couples, and what I thought of as high English farce. I even attempted a gothic romance about a girl locked in a tower by her father who played Beethoven in the gloomy parlor below, while she lamented her fate and wrote tearful sonnets. I'd read one too many Victoria Holt novels, I guess.

My writing was as far away from myself as possible, and by that I mean, as far away from my world, my own observations, my own truest knowledge. It was second-hand, drawn from other people's books.

Yet it was two classic novels I read in my senior year that first opened me up to my own depths, connected me to myself in such a way that I could never quite return to falseness and hiding—at least in my writing. Edith Wharton's *The House of Mirth* and Henry James's *The Portrait of a Lady* had a lasting impact on me by forcing me to begin confronting my own demons: the fear of being gay and my unwillingness to claim a positive Jewish identity.

What was in these two books that kept me reading into the middle of the night, breathless, transfixed, aware of myself as utterly changed? Wharton's masterpiece is the story of a woman destroyed by a society that offers her one choice alone: marriage. There is no other way for Lily Bart to live the life she has been trained to expect as rightfully hers because she is beautiful, graceful, and gifted with impeccable taste. Perhaps the most crushing moment in the book takes place on the Riviera, when Lily is publicly and unmistakably branded as an adulteress. Soon after, she discovers that she is virtually disinherited by the aunt who has not too generously taken care of her since her parents' death, in part because of that scene. Twin humiliations: two moments in which Lily Bart is alone, stared at, the object of scorn and pity, and irrevocably cast out. Life's hopes and possibilities continually elude and defeat Lily.

James's heroine, Isabel Archer, a free-spirited, optimistic, and challenging woman, finds that a huge inheritance leads her into a blind alley. In the novel's most poignant chapter, Isabel understands that the man she married, hoping to give herself a wider view of life, is really the exact opposite of what she expected. He is petty, mean, and shallow. She feels hopeless and trapped; her imagined home of free expression and love openly given and received is really "the house of dumbness, the house of deafness, the house of suffocation."

That was the emotional house that I lived in. Although I had known I was attracted to men from first grade on, I had never allowed myself to carry this attraction forward into anything more than furtive hugs and soppy poetry. Instead, I dated women, compelled by the dictates of a society that even in liberated 1970s New York hated homosexuals. I could not face the possibility of being scorned and cast out as Lily Bart had been.

But it went further back. Exile and isolation were in the air for me, growing up as the child of Holocaust survivors who had been shipwrecked by history. Their homes were stolen, their families were murdered, the Nazis stripped them of everything they owned and even tried to take their humanity and pride. They ended the war tossed ashore with nothing but memories, each one of which was surrounded by barbed wire. I knew almost nothing of this past, but breathed in its miasma anyway.

Like many children of survivors, I grew up with few family photos and little sense of connection to the past—even through objects. My parents had nothing from their former lives. Unlike my friends, I had no grandparents, and barely any family at all. My parents got upset and tearful if I asked too many questions about those who were not there. So I didn't ask. But I wondered, and I felt their absence all around me, all the time.

At first, I didn't comprehend why they were gone. The explanations that came to me in pieces were hard to assimilate. My parents, my missing relatives, had been locked up in camps. Why? What had they done? Nothing except being Jewish, and being alive. A few had survived the camps, in the war. The others had not, dozens of them, whom I know only by their names, and sometimes just their last names.

The camps were in the same strange category as "the war," that mysterious thing that was a combination of thief and mystery. I didn't really know what it meant, but my parents had survived it—barely.

I, too, was Jewish. But what did that mean? I certainly wasn't like the German Jewish kids in my grade school classes with their to me oh-so-American first names of Ronnie and Michael and Eric. They had large allowances and summer vacations and expensive toys and multitudinous after-school activities—a life that seemed glamorous and always out of reach.

They looked down on me. Their parents did, anyway, and so did some of my teachers. We lived in a bad neighborhood, didn't have much money, and we were from Eastern Europe. Never mind that my mother had started university before the war arrived in her city, never mind that between them, my parents spoke Russian, French, Flemish, German, Czech, Polish, Ukrainian, Slovak, Hungarian, Romanian. And English, of course.

They also spoke Yiddish, that inferior, debased form of German—as the *yekkes* saw it. These snobs and their kids belonged to a Reform temple, and I had no idea what was being reformed or what this temple looked like inside, what people did there. There was another such temple near my father's place of business, and I always felt ashamed walking past its high steps and Moorish arches. It was beautiful and forbidding. I felt I didn't belong there, that the very stones themselves judged me.

So what did we observe in my family? We lit Hanukkah candles (except on the days we forgot) and if my father was at the menorah, he mumbled quietly over them. I had no idea what he said or why. My parents lit *yorzeit* candles for their parents and on Yom Kippur. My brother and I always got a bag of Hanukkah coins made out of chocolate, though I could never figure out what to do with a dreidel and it bored me. Both of us were kept from school on Jewish holidays, on which my mother cooked something special. And we listened to Kol Nidre on the radio from Temple Emanuel in New York. I found the sobbing, melodramatic voice embarrassing. I had no idea what the cantor was saying. That was the extent of our observance, and I hated if anyone inquired about our Passover because we never had a seder.

Ah, but my parents were Jewishly observant in a very different way. Oy-yoy-yoy, were they observant! They combed the newspapers for any article that reflected badly on Jews, looking for Jewish wrongdoing in its criminal form. Jewish triumph of any kind was also noted, but an article about a Jewish crook always seemed more important and noteworthy.

As did Jewish origins. An actress would appear on TV, Judy Holiday, for instance. My mother would tell me she was born Jewish and changed her name. The radio would announce a symphony conducted by Michael Tilson Thomas and I'd learn his real name was Tomashevsky, and his father (or was it grandfather?) had been a famous Yiddish actor.

What was I supposed to draw from these revelations? That once a Jew, always a Jew? That Jews were always being watched, always in hiding? That if my parents knew who they were, so did everyone else?

My parents read a Yiddish newspaper, spoke to each other in Yiddish (except when they cursed in Polish or Russian and I knew it was smart to stay out of the way), but being Jewish did not seem something they were consistently proud of. So it's no wonder that when friends or acquaintances in junior high or high school made anti-Semitic jokes or remarks, I never challenged them. Being Jewish was somehow shameful to me, and being the child of Holocaust survivors was beyond shame—it was not even a topic to think about, let alone discuss.

A fierce admirer of Martin Luther King from fourth grade on, I didn't have the courage to speak up for my own people in my own voice. I rarely identified with Jewish causes, except for a visceral support of Israel, though I wouldn't march in any Independence Day parades. How could I? My parents had urged me to never, ever sign a petition, because it could be used against me somehow, it would be *recorded*. And they criticized how I loosely sealed my envelopes, because they could be easily opened by the wrong people.

When I asked my parents why they hadn't gone to Israel after the war, my mother said she didn't want to live among all those Jews after the war, after the Vilna ghetto and the camps. But didn't my parents play cards with Jews? And go for weekend drives with Jews, and shop with Jews, and have coffee with Jews? How did this make sense?

When I started writing fiction in earnest in high school and college, it expressed my desire to erase my difference, to flee into another reality, any reality. My writing was profoundly un-Jewish, it said nothing about the Holocaust, and ignored sexual conflict. I was afraid of outrage and retribution both from non-Jews for being Jewish and from Jews for being gay. I had seen and studied the incredible uproar in the Jewish community generated by Philip Roth's *Portnoy's Complaint*, which was published as I entered adolescence. This book terrified me for its blatant sexuality and blatant Jewishness. Roth wrote that what made the book so infamous is that no one expects a Jew to go crazy in public. Not Jews, and especially not non-Jews, who, as Portnoy says, "own the world and know absolutely nothing about human boundaries."

This was not mere rhetoric to me, this was real. My

parents had seen their neighbors in Poland and Czecho-slovakia eliminate human boundaries. And so I was afraid not only of betraying them if I were to acknowledge my sexuality, but also of exposing myself to potentially hostile non-Jewish eyes. No wonder my fiction was full of disguises. It read like a series of desperate flares sent up for help.

My creative writing teacher in college understood those flares, and she was the first person I came out to. I did it on the phone one evening, because I figured if it went badly I could always hang up.

"Kris," I said. "I have something to tell you."

"Do I need a drink to hear this?" I didn't catch the irony in her reply, just the warmth.

"Yes—a big one."

"Wait a minute—hold on—don't hang up!" I heard a cabinet door open, the clink of bottles, glassware, ice. "I'm back."

Whispering now, unable to hang up, driven by the urge to tell someone and captured by the momentum of release, I said, "I have these feelings—" I couldn't go further, but she did, nonchalantly.

"Feelings about men?"

Her insight and lack of surprise made me laugh. And later I found out that two other students in the same class had come out to her, not long before. Also on the phone. But her ease wasn't mere practice or pedagogy, it was the natural expression of a nurturing, wise woman whose gift was seeing in her students potential of many kinds. I registered for every class she taught.

It was in her novel classes that I read authors who took me deeper into myself: Samuel Butler, Dreiser, James, Fitzgerald, George Eliot, Edith Wharton. In her writing workshops, she kept up the pressure on me to write something, anything, that was real. Yes, my medieval fantasies were amusing, but I was floating on the surface of the story. Every story. My own stories.

My senior-year conflicts about whether I should marry a non-Jewish girl I was in love with, in combination with reading Wharton and James, finally propelled me into writing that was unmistakably more real. Writing that dealt with characters' feelings as facts and not fantasies, writing that traveled into uncertainties of the heart and not mere plot complications, writing that didn't constantly pat itself on the back for being so clever. This new depth was unexpectedly aided by the theater courses I was taking. Not because—as one might expect—I learned about myself in rehearsal and onstage, but because I had never before felt so tantalized and so completely an outsider. Never truly their equal or even their colleague, I was moved to observe and write about the other students in this self-dramatizing, cliquish, mean-spirited, viciously witty department. I was suddenly a budding anthropologist, recording details of an alien world. I slowly realized that I could turn that observation on myself, my family, my missing past.

In my graduate writing program at Amherst a year later, I was drawn on to new discoveries, not all of them pleasant. I learned that the need for a man had been so stifled in me by internalized homophobia, by my own shame, that I could not only accept an unsatisfactory and even demeaning relationship, but glory in it as if living an opera. Surely I deserved to feel tormented? But I also learned the joy of being with other writers and of taking myself seriously as a writer.

There in Amherst, for the first time in my life I gave

way completely to the admission that I wanted another man. This wasn't a fantasy, this was the provocative presence of someone in my dorm. I said the words—I wrote it down in my journal. He had dropped by my room one night to chat—a large broad Viking of a man, easygoing, sensuous, relaxed. That week, I had been reading two novels of obsession: Susan Hill's eerie *The Bird of Night* and *Wuthering Heights;* I was primed for an explosion of some kind. While Fred and I talked, suddenly I saw him with complete clarity at the same time that I knew I wanted him, desperately, with such force that the frenzy of my pulse made me wonder why every item in the room didn't burst apart.

The revelation devastated me afterward. I could feel a tremendous shift inside, and knew I was in the middle of a crisis in which the decision seemed to be: Stop writing and hide, or keep writing and open up. To write at all, to write honestly, was to stir up everything inside of me that was painful and unresolved.

I had written a paragraph describing a character's father and knew it was the entrance into a story I had to tell—and was afraid to tell. When I called Kris and read it to her on the phone, she urged me to keep writing, in fact, made me agree to write a section, call her and read it to her, write another, call her, and so on, until it was done a day and a half later. I was terrified—I was alive.

It was a story about the son of Holocaust survivors who felt alienated by his parents' past, and crushed by it—as I was. Writing that story, staying open, was a choice, and a liberation from silence about at least one aspect of my life.

My writing workshop hated the story, and so did the professor. It's thus very satisfying to report that two weeks later, Martha Foley, editor of *The Best American Short Stories*, awarded it the Harvey Swados Prize. A year later, when I was twenty-four, it was published in *Redbook*, which then had 4.5 million readers. I was being taken seriously as a writer, I was making money on my work. But publishing in *Redbook* led me into typical New York blindness. Starting there, winning a prize—weren't those natural first steps of an easy ascent to cash and fame?

For five or six years after that, every story I sent to national magazines and even the major literary quarterlies was rejected. Opening the mailbox I felt assaulted by the manila envelopes, sometimes five in a day, defeated, crushed. It was my own misjudgment; I thought that everything I wrote was as good as my first publication. I thought the only place worth publishing was in a magazine like *Redbook*, or better. In Michigan, which I'd moved to in 1981 to pursue a Ph.D. in American studies, I could slowly cut loose of those expectations and ask simple questions: What did I have to say in my writing? Who was my audience?

A story I wrote in one evening was the first to break the drought. It was accepted immediately by a Jewish magazine, and my stories began to appear in a widening range of Jewish publications. I became something of a Jewish celebrity in East Lansing, but was afraid that coming out would make me lose respect. I had started attending Orthodox services locally and though I learned a great deal there, and felt welcomed, I suspected the welcome would be withdrawn if the congregation knew I was gay. Finding another congregation was not difficult, and it was there that I studied for my bar mitzvah, and officially entered the Jewish community at the age of thirty.

Feeling deeply connected at last as a Jew, and restored

as a writer, hopeful again, I was still only halfway there. It wasn't until I fell in love with my partner, Gersh—who is Jewish—that I was able to begin bridging the two worlds. It was loving him and being loved (feeling safe) that gave me the courage to write my first gay and Jewish short story—an early version of the title piece of my collection *Dancing on Tisha B'Av*. And when it was included in a national anthology of gay fiction a few years after being published in an obscure Jewish magazine, I suddenly had a new audience developing. Ultimately what brought me the most attention as a writer was adding another circle of readers by stepping out into a gay audience, but unmistakably as a Jew. Together Gersh and I have been part of a gay Jewish group in Michigan and moved on from that to join an accepting Reform synagogue as an out gay couple. Our level of observance has ebbed and flowed over the years; at our most intense, for three years we studied Torah on Shabbat, entering the text that belongs to each and every Jew.

My writing is deeply Jewish not just in subject matter, but in its sense of the urgency to break every constricting silence. The refusal to accept silence and marginalization, the importance of speaking for ourselves, of telling stories, have been recurring themes of my fiction and essays. Indeed, Jews have always been enjoined to tell their stories: the Book of Amos says, "Tell your children of it." But telling our stories does more than keep memory alive, it creates something new. It builds bridges between communities, helps people find pride in their identity, and breaks—or at least weakens—the hold of silence.

Through the stories I tell in my fiction, I hope to create a greater understanding among non-Jews of the continuing impact of the Holocaust. I hope that Jews and non-Jews will appreciate the parallels between society's oppression of gays and anti-Semitism. I hope straight Jews will come to see the place of gay and lesbian Jews in the American Jewish community. And for lesbian and gay Jews in particular, I want my fiction to say what Jews say after someone has had an honor during a Torah service, *yasher koach*, may your strength be multiplied.

There's a poem by the Jewish writer Melanie Kaye/Kantrowitz called "Notes of an Immigrant Daughter" in which she says:

> *i can't go back*
> *where i came from was*
> *burned off the map*
>
> *i'm a jew*

While most Jews can probably relate to those lines, they've had particular meaning for me as a gay child of survivors. Growing up, I felt alienated in profound ways: from Americans as the son of immigrants; from other Jews as a child of secular, conflicted survivors; and from a world that was as far as I knew completely straight.

For me, writing has proven to be a catalyst, a laboratory, it has led to a deepened Jewish consciousness, profound connections with my people, building bridges between Jew and non-Jew, gay and straight. It has healed my own inner world and it has been *tikkun olam*. But most of all, it's been a map for someone who grew up lost to his people and himself.

ROBERT COHEN

Living, Loving, Temple-Going

> *Men resist the conclusion in the morning, but adopt it as the*
> *evening wears on, that temper prevails over everything of time,*
> *place, and condition, and is inconsumable in the flames of*
> *religion.*
>
> Emerson, "Experience"

In 1981 I moved to New York, with the idea of turning
myself into a writer. I was twenty-four. I had no job,
no money, no prospects, and only the most attenuated sense of my own identity. No flag to plant and
nowhere to plant it. Turning myself into a writer, as things
turned out, wasn't even the hard part; the hard part was
turning myself into a *self*. I had come to New York to
escape everything I was: my impressive catalogue of
doubts, longings, and confusions, my ongoing sense of
being not quite young, not quite grown up, not quite
American, not quite Jew, not quite anything in particular,
someone inadequately aligned and incompletely formed,

still in the process of becoming . . . what? The only thing I was good for, that I really cared about, was reading. Books were what moved me. They moved me more powerfully, sad to say, than that dubious and provisional sphere called the real world.

It didn't help matters that my girlfriend at the time, with whom I'd carefully planned this move to New York, bailed out at the last minute and flew to Israel instead, where she'd been born, and where not long after she married someone else. I didn't blame her either. I would have married someone else too, had I been her. In the four-hanky melodrama that comprised her life's narrative (her father escaped the Auschwitz infirmary, married her mother in a deportation camp, settled in Israel, then chased his wandering wife to San Francisco, where he died young), the entire American episode could be edited down to a rather silly if malign digression. America was the escape that was no escape, the comfort that was no comfort; the slow, second murder of the nearly murdered. Or so went her thinking. My own thinking, such as it was, offered little in the way of clarity. To my bookish, feverish mind, our whole affair could have been lifted straight from Roth's *The Ghost Writer*—assimilated young man at large meets Anne Frank, who carries the dead of Europe in the bags under her eyes.

But this is to turn her into a literary conceit, when believe me she was anything but. Not for her the tenement house of American Jewish literary culture. All those gabby grandpas, the Howes and Kazins and Bellows and Malamuds, sharing room in our heads with those stoned young night boarders, the Ginsbergs and Dylans and Leonard Cohens—the whole scene struck her as a clown show, both cause and consequence of the unbearable lightness of American being. Laughing at Portnoy offered no consolation; it was only an extension of the illness it sought to describe. All of which she undertook to explain to me with withering clarity in our very first conversation—and, come to think of it, in our last conversation too, as well as quite a few conversations in between.

I protested that to give Roth his due, this was in fact the point of Portnoy, and that moreover the duty of art was not to answer questions but to pose them. It appeared that literary conceits were the only kind I had.

Who cares about art? she wanted to know. All she cared about was getting out of this weightless, purposeless country, in order to live a coherent life, which for a Jew could of course only be managed in Israel.

I countered that this poster-child Zionism of hers was a backward and regressive impulse, a retreat into a kind of nationalism that our cushy lives in America, for better or okay, maybe for worse, had made obsolete. For enlightened beings like us, wasn't the narrow parochialism of religion an unnecessary, perhaps even irrelevant, worldview? Wasn't all this prosperity and tolerance and culture, all our Grouchos and Bellows and Rothkos, good for *something*, as legitimate a form of being—yes, dammit, *Jewish* being—as digging a ditch in the Negev? Oh, I spoke up for progressive humanism, all right. I too was a poster child, the Diaspora's favorite son. True, I did not convince her, but then I didn't have to, not yet—we were still young, newly launched. There would be plenty of time later to make harsh, tedious distinctions between this kind of Jew, that kind of Jew. That would come later. For now we were fellow travelers. And besides, I too was the real thing, wasn't I? Historically and genetically certifiable? After all, I had the nose, the one-generation-old name, the ironic, self-deprecating temperament. I had the face in which could be plainly seen, as I was often reminded, the entire map of Poland (a Jew, says Sartre, is someone others take as a Jew). Hence whatever I did was essentially and inevitably of Jewish consequence. Wasn't that how these things worked? I was pretty sure the rabbi had said something along those lines back in confirmation class, on those rare occasions when he wasn't addressing the subject of intermarriage.

And even if he hadn't, the great Russian poet Osip Mandelstam (whom I had not yet discovered, but would soon enough) had already captured my feeling on this subject more or less exactly: "As a little bit of musk fills an entire house, so the least influence of Judaism overflows all of one's life."

Try to explain this to someone with an El Al ticket and a haunted, lifelong sense of oedipal destiny. Mandelstam shmandelstam: there were Jews and there were Jews, and apparently I was one kind but not the other, not quite. So she flew off to Lod, and I dragged my diaspora ass and what was left of my heart to New York.

•••

I cocooned myself in a tiny one-room apartment on 110th Street, with an impressive cast of gargoyles out the window and, like Dostoyevsky's hell, spiders in every corner, and taught myself to write by the usual methods of trial, error, loneliness, and humiliation. It took a long time. It continues to take a long time. But I had settled into a purpose. I may have been without a woman and without a country, but I no longer lacked a cause—I'd turn myself into a writer, goddamn it. I'd make the library my temple, the desk my altar. There I'd daven over my humming

Selectric, beseeching powers I couldn't see for knowledge I didn't have. Fiction would be—would *have* to be—my default mode of coherence, the one way to make my lack of coherence cohere. True, I had no idea what kind of fiction I'd actually write, once I got started, but that seemed a minor issue; I did not let it deter me. If anything it impelled me forward. To be ignorant of my own intentions meant that I was free to stumble on blindly, to flounder and flail. To try to make of my not-knowing a hard, gemlike thing . . .

Would it be *Jewish* fiction, though? And did it matter? Already I'd read enough to see that I was only one more singer in the back row of the Diaspora chorus, fashioning our cunning little fugues of internal exile, turning Kafka's lament—"What have I in common with the Jews? I have nothing in common even with myself"—into our own (anti-) national anthem. Give me your tired, your poor, your S. J. Perelman, your Bruce Jay Friedman. Around this time, I read the Irving Howe anthology of Jewish American Stories, the bright yellow paperback edition. Talk about a noisy choir! Between Singer's eros, Bellow's learning, Elkin's rage, Paley's wit, Malamud's mournfulness, and Weidman's haunting Bartleby-like father, sitting in the dark . . . I could hardly hear myself think. On the other hand, I didn't *need* to think. Because at last I'd found a club I really did want to join, all those angry sons and daughters wrestling with their patriarchal angels, struggling—you could feel it in the nervous, visceral energies of the prose—to free themselves from, among other things, clubs in general, and anthologies too, with their glued bindings. ("The reason one becomes a poet," writes Mandelstam's own ex-girlfriend, Marina Tsvetaeva, "is to avoid being French, Russian, etc., in order to be everything.")

Every page in that Howe book felt electric to me, bump-
tious and heterodox, rocked by waves of fusion and fission,
as if the language itself, under the situational pressure of
the moment, was tearing loose and reassembling. Clearly
for the writers of that generation, the second side of the
hyphen, the American side, *mattered*. It had weight, consequence, shock value. In any case it was a Subject.

But to see it that way required an outsider's lens ("a
state of useful discontent," Howe calls it, though I prefer
Danilo Kis's phrase: "a troubling strangeness"), and I was
raised *inside*. No wonder my own prose seemed forced, my
material thin and elusive. My discontent was formless,
useless; I had never been shamed by immigrant parents or
chased in fear of my life down the mean streets. I was a
suburban Reform kid, New Jersey division. Like many of
my peers I'd been bred with a tenacious but sentimental
and also highly confused tribalism, a sense of the Chosen
as a kind of embattled small-market baseball team, one
whose fortunes, for all the media attention we generated,
were forever suspended precipitously over an abyss. Only
the financial and spiritual loyalty of the community kept
the franchise afloat. Hence our running game of Name
That Jew—*Go Tony Curtis* (Bernie Schwartz)! *You rule,
Kirk Douglas* (Issur Demsky)!—was perhaps a more serious business than we realized. As if by outing the stars, we
hoped to warm ourselves in their light, to certify our
betweenness and make of it a virtue. What else could we
do? We were two generations removed from a coherent
communal identity, from the bonds, and bondedness, of
the mitzvot. Sunday school was a joke, Hebrew school a
bad joke. And let's not go into the bar mitzvahs. After a
dozen years of study my comprehension of Judaic law was
a lamentable pastiche, a crazy quilt of slogans and exhorta-

tions, easily remembered, easily ignored—Never Again!
Next Year in Jerusalem! Paul Newman's Really Jewish!—
accompanied by a tentative understanding that somewhere in the coiled scrolls of the Torah was a mandate that
stipulated, on days of particular solemnity, the suspension
of alternate-side-of-the-street parking.

So much for background. This thin gruel neither
starved nor sustained; it did, however, provide just enough
to gain me summer employment during my college years
at Camp Swig—"an Institute for Living Judaism" in the
Santa Cruz Mountains. As camps go, Swig was not a particularly impressive facility. The lawns were feeble and
parched, there was no lake, and the massive trunks of the
redwood trees, for all their grandeur, provided little insu-
lation from the psychotic roar of motorcycles on Highway
9. Then too the Hayward Fault ran the length of the
place, an active and alarmingly subversive presence, forever moving the buildings around when we weren't
looking, threatening to topple the stilted, teetering, jerry-
rigged cabins where we slept, and providing, even for the
dimmest and most solipsistic among us, too obvious a
metaphor to ignore. *It could all end any second* . . .

Fortunately we were often stoned, so the prospect of
being crushed like bugs was more amusing than alarming.
"Living Judaism," I was gratified to discover, entailed not
only the usual Israeli dancing, kibbutz breakfasts, educational programming, and daily prayers, but also, may His
name be praised, an almost ridiculous quantity of recre-
ational drugs, drinking (we had our camp name to live up
to), and, oh yes, sex, at least among the staff, once the
lights were out. Living Judaism turned out to be a very
agreeable proposition indeed. Compared to, say, the tepid
and attenuated forms of worship I had practiced to that
point—I recalled, through a glassy nictitating membrane

of boredom, attending services at my suburban temple, with its admixture of pieties and vacuities, its High Holiday fashion parades, its pledge-envelope Zionism, its educational brunches sponsored by the Men's Club or Sisterhood, all those round trays of sponge cake and rugelach that were our reward for not screaming or weeping or punching someone or running off to play basketball, as we all, incessantly, fantasized doing whenever we set foot in the place—compared to that, this lively, sunshot, West Coast approach was extremely winning.

Then too it confirmed something I had begun to suspect about my religion, and took to be, in a sense, the key to its survival: its stubborn and enduring plasticity. Clearly one could be reckoned a serious Jew without submitting oneself every week, hatless before God, to the airless tedium of the synagogue. One could be a serious Jew and still be skeptical about religion and even snort a little coke on the side: look at Freud. One could grow a long beard and mouth off to impressionable youths about fascism and capitalism: look at Marx. One could sing nasty runic songs of alienation in a nasal, unsteady voice: look at Dylan. Most gratifyingly, one could be a serious Jew, do all these things, and still enjoy quick, groping outdoor sex with vegetarian girls from L.A. whose leg and armpit hair matched if not exceeded one's own, huffing away amid the shaded eruptions of the redwood trees (a fantasy right out of Malamud): look at—well, look at *me*.

There was only one problem with being a serious Jew, as I could figure it: I had virtually no idea what serious Judaism was.

This became increasingly evident to me in the years that followed, as our soft 1970s pieties were confronted with something much harder and more polarizing: the 1980s. I watched the composition of our camp faculty shift

from scraggly posthippies of a lefty, secularist, transgres-
sive bent to a cohort of bright, well-groomed rabbinical
students just back from Israel—driven and intelligent
young men and women who sat around the staff lounge
practicing their Hebrew and talking about Rashi (not, as
in the old days, *Rashomon*) as if the man were still alive, as
if there was something urgent and pressing and thoroughly, rigorously contemporary about whatever it was
(naturally I couldn't be bothered to read him) he had to
say. In short, they not only knew a great deal more than I
knew about the textual foundations of the religion we'd
been born into, they cared a great deal more than I cared.
For them, not just camp but life itself, the whole twelve
months of it, really *was* a matter of living Judaism. And,
regarding myself through their eyes, I came to see myself,
for all my cultural Jewish airs, as a dilettante, a fake, a
flyer—or rather, floater—on borrowed wings. A *luftmen-
sch* more *luft* than *mensch*.

Yes, the football coach's son in high school, an all-
state halfback, once called me a kike in the clubhouse, to
the amusement of the entire team. So what? Such garden
variety anti-Semitism was hardly rich enough soil from
which to harvest a worldview. For the most part the Jews I
knew, in the shade of our enormous houses, experienced
the lazy roar of lawn mowers on a summer afternoon not
as a reminder of the pogroms but as a benign, even cheer-
ful sort of applause. We weren't driven out of the Garden;
we were pampered and indulged. We had grown up inside
the leviathan's plush, capacious belly, under the spell of
the great American antimatter, staring into its particulate
frenzy, dazed but oddly buoyant, like a stoner watching
television. It was a more difficult prospect than we'd imagined, finding the will and energy to climb out.

If an unhappy childhood is, as Graham Greene said,

a writer's gold mine, then what ore can be dug from a happy one?

Even so: by the time I moved to New York, that happy childhood was fading fast. When it came to misery and alienation I seemed to be making up for lost time. My apartment was dingy, loveless; my desk an old door bereft of knobs, propped on two wobbly sawhorses. I'd set up my Selectric and hammer away at it like a prisoner, full of meanness and me-ness, as if by sheer willful industry I could make that door open up and lead me somewhere newer and better. Perhaps the stories I wrote would not be Jewish-American, strictly speaking, but American-Jewish instead. Or both. Or neither. Enough with the hyphens already! Enough with "minority" literature and its freight of grandiloquent pathos! I tried to banish all such considerations from my mind. After all, writers of my cohort may have been descended from Bellow, Roth, Malamud, Paley, but we also had a number of quirky and influential aunts and uncles from around the globe, Jorge and Italo, Tom, Flannery, the Dons, Gabe down in Colombia, jockeying for space at the family table. Besides, we knew that Bellow and Roth hadn't grown up reading Bellow and Roth—they'd read Dostoyevsky, James, Flaubert, Céline. The Jewishness of the great Jewish-American laureates was, as Leslie Fiedler has pointed out, more than a little vestigial to begin with. This made us vestiges of vestiges. So what use were hyphens to us? (*"Foo to all these categories!"* says Herzog.) Our task was not to revisit the material of the previous generation, but to write the truth of our own experience, such as it was. Our own singular reactions to our own singular reality.

Only what was there in our own singular reality to react *to*?

Was this, then, the American subject of our era, our

(middle) class: the difficulty—and necessity—of finding something out there in the addled blankness of the culture to react to? Trying to form a community of those-who-lack-community, a context of having-no-context? Was this what it meant to be "post-acculturated"—this flailing field of zero gravity, this choice between Nostalgia and Nothingness, between earnest "treatments" of the vanished world and frivolous satiric explorations of Western anomie, which was rapidly performing its own vanishing act right before our eyes?

•••

Of course such questions are easier to raise than to answer. Speaking for myself alone, I felt at once sheepish and exhilarated when I finally sat down to write what I conceived as my "Jewish" novel (*The Here and Now*); I couldn't decide, given my history of mixed feelings on the subject, if such a book signaled an advance or a retreat. All I knew was that I found it impossible to view the material without quotes around it, some mark of literary self-consciousness with which to contextualize it, ironize it, locate it as part of a tradition ("Tradition!") larger than—and perhaps more to the point, separate from—myself. Or was it separate? I had always wanted to belong to something, to be enfolded into a larger entity; wanted it, that is, almost as much as I *didn't* want it. Like my inept, unfocused narrator, I could not decide if I was bored by my Hasidic characters or stimulated by them a lot more than I wished to be. It was not a case of writing what you know, but writing what you don't know, what you'll never know, what you don't even quite *want* to know, about something you sort of already do know, or half-know, but can't express, or for that matter conceptualize, however much you try. This tedious, terminal, Beckett-like uncertainty perhaps underlies the composition of most novels, as well as the illegal substance intake of most novelists.

And yet, here's the thing: even in my attempt to tackle the subject of Jewishness more or less directly, I made the protagonist of my novel a *half*-Jew. How's *that* for direct? Oh, I was full of literary conceits, all right, symbolic strategies for distilling the vapor cloud of my own mixed feelings. But it gets worse. I grew more and more interested in the great generational cataclysm in American Jewry, one in which I was a full—not half—participant: the increasing prevalence of mixed marriages. The complication of the gene pool seemed an urgent matter to confront, because by then, despite if not because of all those values-clarification exercises in confirmation class, I'd gone off and raided the far side of the hyphen. I'd fallen in love with a shiksa. Moreover, she was blond, blue-eyed, and Midwestern—the whole shmeer. Moreover, she was pregnant. Which meant that in case I'd been in any doubt on the subject, I was now, officially, a walking stereotype of assimilation.

The realization fell like a blow: there's no getting free. In my effort to wriggle out of the grasp of reductive sociological oppositions, I had only gotten myself further ensnared. This was the other side of what it meant to be Chosen. *To be Chosen was to have no choice.* All I had wanted was what everyone wanted, and yet somehow as a consequence of this desire I was now highly visible both to myself and to what was left of my tribe as someone responsible (in responsibilities, perhaps, begin dreams . . .) for bringing into the world a little half-breed, a mongrel, a literal manifestation of the very aspect of my existence I most longed to transcend—my divided self.

Or could this in fact turn out to be the vehicle of that transcendence?

"There are questions we would never get over were we not delivered from them by the operations of nature." This wistful little aphorism of Kafka's went on the birth announcement. Arguably there were less pretentious ways to introduce one's son to the world. But the words appeared to be calling to us. Perhaps even choosing us, as we chose them.

•••

Around the same time I began work on the novel, I came across the great Donald Barthelme story "Chablis." It's five a.m. The narrator sits at his desk, smoking, worrying, sipping a glass of wine, looking out at the joggers "running towards rude red health" on the predawn streets, and wonders to himself, "What's the matter with me? Why can't I be a more natural person?" By natural he means someone more like the joggers and less like himself, someone free of writerly ambivalence, someone who's not *at* the window but *in* it. Someone, in short, with a nature and temperament that's not like the narrator's at all. Still, it seems more natural, even to him, to be out there running than to be inside watching and worrying. The "natural" thing, we sense in our animal bones, is to transcend the paralysis that attends the contemplative secular postmodern sensibility and actually lace up our sneakers and *do* something. But what?

For my book, I imagined a character, an American Tonio Kroger, his nose pressed to the window, watching with both reluctance and fascination the ruddy dancers inside. The familiar scenario would place the ethical, self-conscious Jew outside and the lusty, "natural" gentiles within. But I decided to reverse the equation. I wanted to make the *Jew*, just for a change, the joyous dancer, and have the marginal secularist be the worrier, and at the same time make them as similar to each other as they were different, and at the same time make the witness and jury of all this dancing and not dancing a rather sexy, obdurate, and mysterious young woman, one looking out an altogether different window of her own. I was curious about them all, but for personal reasons I was most curious about the narrator. I wondered what would happen if someone even more secular and divided than I was—a half in search of a whole, a car in search of a road, prodded by accidents of circumstance and desire—put down his wineglass and walked right through the window that separates, or appears to separate, Either from Or. What kind of noise would it make, all that shattered glass?

That's what I had in mind, anyway, with my little love triangle between a half-Jewish Manhattan fuck-up and two contentious Hasids from Brooklyn. After I began I ran across the great Chaim Grade story, "My Quarrel with Hersh Rasseyner," and was horrified though unsurprised to find that my little dialectic was nothing new. It had all been done before. No matter who you are, it has *always* all been done before. And yet, like the hunger artist, there is this gnawing and persistent problem of finding anything else to eat . . .

So I went ahead and wrote the damn thing. Even the voice I found for the novel turned out to be, all pretensions to the contrary, a rather familiar one, tinged by the same nervous ironical musical inflections I had once set out to escape. (Tsvetaeva again: "Yet every language has something that belongs to it alone, that *is* it.") And that became more and more the point. *No choice.* It so happens I was on a plane to Houston once with a Hasidic couple very much like the ones I based my novel on, though I remember little of the conversation and nothing came of it but an invitation to dinner to which I never responded. Or it may have been coffee. Maybe there was no invitation. Maybe there wasn't even a *plane*. But I had this half-Jewish son growing increasingly visible in my wife's belly, and every kick of his tiny foot set off a more or less inevitable chain of associations, and so I started to play around a bit with the what-ifs. I thought, for some reason, it would be fun. At the very least I figured it would help me work out some of my long-standing and by now quite tiresome ambivalence on the subject of religion.

As it happened, it wasn't fun, it took me eight drafts, and I never got very far in the way of resolving, or even defining, my own Jewish problem. In the end, no matter how much I researched and imagined, no matter how much Rashi and Buber and Scholem I read, nor how expectantly I listened for the click of that internal soul-lock, the one that would make it—me—spring open, and allow me to embrace and be embraced by a liturgy of wholeness for my characters and for myself . . . it never happened. What I wound up with instead was three years of labored attentiveness and five hundred pages of manuscript, more of an illustration than a transformation of the mixed feelings I'd set out with. It didn't seem like enough. On the other hand it didn't seem like nothing, either. Attentiveness of any kind was arguably a good thing. As for mixed feelings, weren't they better, in the end, than none at all? There was no choice but to think so, and to believe as well that mixed feelings were no less the province of living, serious Judaism—though we could debate this, and should, and will, again and again—than the other kind, on what remains, even now, the far side of the glass.

Meanwhile I'm still here looking.

BINNIE KIRSHENBAUM

Princess

U nder the rubric that there are no coincidences, Philip Roth wrote *Goodbye, Columbus* right around the same time—as the 1950s came to a close— that I was born. Fast-forward fifteen years and find me stretched out on my four-poster bed with white organdy spread and matching pillow shams, reading a tattered paperback edition of the story of Neil Klugman and Brenda Patimkin. True, in those intervening fifteen years, a whole lot happened—Vietnam, the Kennedy assassinations, the assassination of Martin Luther King, civil rights, feminism, Woodstock—but as I read, it seemed that not much had changed in the world because I fully recognized the Patimkins' landscape as my own. Except for the mores regarding sex. Had I been older, the same age Brenda was in the book, it's not likely my parents would have gone wiggy to discover a diaphragm in my drawer, which they wouldn't have found anyway because I came of age in the time of the Pill. But just because premarital sex wasn't the disgrace it once was didn't mean that nice Jewish girls such as Brenda, or I, put out for just anybody. There was also some debate among my friends as to the degree of pleasure we were supposed to derive from sex or was it simply a means to various ends. At age fifteen, I was well on my way to becoming something of a Brenda Patimkin myself.

It might not appear so at first glance, but American Jews are no less nomadic than were the Israelites. While we are not so much traversing the desert, we are in constant motion: an upward mobility from the shtetl to the ghetto of the Lower East Side to the Bronx to Westchester County. We, my family and the others like us, lived in big houses set on manicured lawns. We belonged to country clubs. We wore designer clothes. We, the junior Brendas of this world, were given Add-A-Pearl necklaces completed for Sweet Sixteens that were held at fancy catering halls just as were our brothers' bar mitzvahs. We were pampered and spoiled. Our hair was frosted with streaks of gold. Our fingernails were painted pearly pink. We were primed and prepped for really not a whole lot more than to get ourselves a husband, a mensch. A successful mensch, who did at least as well as our fathers did, if not better.

Get this: When I was fourteen, out shopping one afternoon with my mother in Lord & Taylor's, we ran into a classmate of mine, Deborah Silverman, and her boyfriend Robert, whom she introduced to my mother. "This is my Robert," Deborah said. "He's going to be a doctor." Robert's voice had not yet changed, his cheeks sported down, not stubble. But he was going to be a doctor. And why not? This was our due. This was our destiny. Deborah Silverman would not consort with a boy who was not planning on a medical practice. Yes, we girls were educated. We went to college because where else would we meet our future husbands? A professional man wasn't going to marry a girl with only a high school diploma. But we weren't really expected to *be* anything. Mostly we majored in education because teaching was a respectable job in case we did not get married immediately after college. Plus it was something we could always fall back on, if, G–d forbid . . . and it was proof that we were good with children.

Our mothers gave us Herman Wouk's *Marjorie Morningstar* to read. What we were supposed to take away from that novel was this: Okay, maybe you'll go through a rebellious phase, maybe you'll have some artsy leanings, but in the end, you'll be sensible. "Sensible" meant you'll return to the fold. "Fold," in this case, had to do not with faith but with fortune.

So who could blame Brenda Patimkin for not sticking by Neil Klugman in the end? Neil was a librarian. That was no kind of husband for Brenda. She could do so much better than a librarian. Brenda was destined to marry a doctor, a lawyer, a captain of industry, to continue on in the tradition of the good life, to live out, even more so than her own parents had, the American dream. And Neil? Neil would remain in Newark. But I wept not for Neil, the poor schnook who would never again spend a glorious summer swimming in the blue, chlorinated pool at the Green Lane Country Club. For reasons unfamiliar to me, country club banishment didn't seem all that terrible. Instead I wept for Brenda. And I wept for myself, because with reading *Goodbye, Columbus* came the realization that to be breathtakingly shallow was not the pinnacle of human achievement I'd cracked it up to be. My sky fell. My life would never be the same.

A colder eye cast on the Patimkin world in which I lived revealed us to be WASP wannabes. My parents were nonbelievers, and they referred to us as "secular Jews," which was not exactly denying that we were Jews. Oh, there were a few halfhearted attempts at Hanukkah, a couple of years there when we lit candles on a menorah, but we really celebrated Christmas (the key figure being Santa Claus, with Jesus neatly cropped from the picture). One year we had a seder, but it was no different from Thanksgiving except that it was April. We asked no questions, tasted no bitter herbs, and had apple pie for desert. My older brother was bar mitzvahed. My younger brother was not. I had a big Sweet Sixteen bash in a Hawaiian-themed restaurant.

We aspired to be fully assimilated, which meant to blend in with the Episcopalians, to be American without a hyphen. Because really, what were we, Jews, doing there, in this land of green hedges and golf courses? What did we want with tennis courts and packaged white bread from the A&P? How did it happen that Saturday became a day for shopping and Little League baseball? For synagogue to be nothing more than Hebrew School once a week and the Ladies' Auxiliary? How long did it take to get from the shtetl to the suburb? For us to become, as my father's Aunt Sadie called us, Yenkees? And that's what we were. Yenkees, which is almost a Yankee, but not quite. And sometimes I wondered if that wasn't the worst of it; not that we aspired to be WASPs but that we tried too hard and failed at it.

Still, it was a charmed life, the lap of luxury and free from care. So why then, did I weep for Brenda Patimkin, whose life was similarly charmed? Where did I get the idea that there was something sad about the way we lived? What led me to suspect that a bunny fur ski jacket was the fruit of a Faustian deal? How did I come to conclude that this life, this good life, this attainment of the American dream, could not, must not, be the life for me?

Books, maybe. I always read a lot. "Binnie's a reader," my mother would say, although I was never quite sure if she meant this as praise or was she expressing concern. It would still be several years until I read Tolstoy's *The Death of Ivan Ilych*, the book which revealed my shadowy hunches to be, for me, empirical truths (and also a book which, if I had my way, would be mandatory reading for all inhabitants of the Western world). Books were a likely culprit, at least as far as letting me know that there were other ways of being, other lives to lead. But it was *Goodbye, Columbus* which first got under my skin. And just like that my own skin no longer fit me, like a coat too small. Then there were the Jewish Princess jokes (What do Jewish women make for dinner? Reservations) and the coinage of the acronym JAP, which was decidedly not meant as a compliment. The Princess and all that was associated with her—spoiled, selfish, materialistic, and no more than an inch deep—filled me with a sense of shame.

My earliest fiction—short stories I wrote in high school that blessedly are nowhere to be found—featured girls named Lib and Bootsy who went to Vassar, where they suffered from nervous breakdowns; an attempt to dis-associate myself perhaps not so much from being a Jew as from being a Jewish American Princess. Aside from all the negative connotations associated with the title, I had not, at that point in my life, read or even heard of any Jewish writers who were women. (The one exception was Sylvia Plath, who clearly out-WASPed me.) The Jewish writers I knew of were men—Saul Bellow, Norman Mailer, Philip Roth, the beloved Chaim Potok, Joseph Heller, even *Marjorie Morningstar* was written by a man—thus confirming the misconception I had that Jewish women were incapable of a profound thought.

The way some genetic dispositions skip a generation, I yearned to wrest free of this golden yoke, the way my ancestors yearned to escape pogroms. And as my ancestors did, I too journeyed to the promised land: New York City. Unlike that of my forebears, however, my journey to New York took all of a half an hour by train, and on the commuter line, at that. Grand Central Station was my Ellis Island, the big clock was my Statue of Liberty. But no less than those immigrants had done, I came to New York to start a new life, to be something other than a Brenda.

Yes, first there was Edna Ferber (if only I had known) and Sydney Nyberg, among a handful of others, but it is arguable that Jewish American literature began in 1934 with Henry Roth's *Call It Sleep*, with the immigrant experience of *coming to America*, of being caught as if one foot were in the glue pot of the old world and the other in the new one. *Call It Sleep* then became the foundation for the post–World War II cohort of writers who addressed *becoming American*, the casting off, and the subsequent entanglement of, the embarrassment of riches bequeathed to them by their parents with the accents. They eschewed faith and ritual and superstition, and turned to writing about war and academia and sex like other, that is, real, red-blooded American writers, albeit often tinged with an angst particular to the Jews. Still, it was out of the shtetl and into the mainstream.

And bless New York for extending hope and home for the dispossessed, the foreign, the immigrant, the outcast, the artist, the writer, the displaced, the Jew, the oddball, the refugee. The way so many immigrants embraced the new land with ardor and fierce loyalty, so do I embrace my city. I will shout it from the rooftops: I love New York.

I can admire the majesty of American landscape; I could, if I wanted to, take a raft down the Mississippi or fish the Big Two-Hearted River. Still, it is deducible that Jews, even "secular Jews," are at home in cities. In all cities, in every and any city. In the asphalt diaspora we have not only survived, we have thrived against the odds. It is part of Jewish life to meet up with our landsmen in Shanghai, Buenos Aires, Quebec, Calcutta. To be scattered and yet to be contained, if no longer by ghetto walls, then by choice.

To love a city is not the same thing as to love a country. Although sometimes there is an elitism associated with urbanophilia, an arrogance as to the quality of museums, restaurants, symphonies, shopping, that is not the same thing as patriotism. To my mind, there is something about patriotism that is tainted with a whiff of fascism. The parades, the flag waving, the boasting of military hardware all convey a bellicosity. *Vive la France* and *God Save the Queen* and *America, Love It or Leave It* are dares, threats even, whereas no one ever died defending their *I Love New York* T-shirt.

In New York, that city of reinvention, I could shed my Brenda-ness. I could belong to that tribe of aspiring writers. What Jews and writers have in common is to be from every place and from no place. To be a part of, and yet outside of, a nation, a state. We are exiles. Outside a nation and a state but within city walls, we can stake a claim and be a part of a collective identity; the identity of the hodgepodge. In New York, I could become a writer, a writer without a hyphen. Yes, often my characters were Jews, but "secular Jews," simply because what I knew informed my work. I was not a Jewish American writer and no one took me for one.

But then, if it is our, the Jewish, destiny to wander,

where was there left for me to go? As the world is round, was I destined to walk in a circle? From *becoming American*, have I gone counterclockwise? From questions of identity to history to theology, Jewishness crept into my writing, just as Jewishness bit by bit revealed itself in my being. I got to abdicate the crown of Princess, and begin to discover what it means to me to be Jewish, which necessitates looking back. Which leads me to the question: Am I now a Jewish American writer?

It is a warm place to be, part of this group of Jewish American writers. It's cozy to belong to the club. I often feel as if I am being embraced, welcomed home into bubba's loving arms which smell of baked goods, even if my own bubba (who was called Grandma) bought Sara Lee and never baked a rugelach in her life.

Isaac Singer once said, "All writers must have an address." I think he meant not so much a roof overhead (although that too is a good thing) but rather a place where the soul resides. Perhaps we, this generation of Jewish American writers, are finding that our souls reside in Galicia and not in Fairfield County.

We seem to have, for the time being, left the quintessential American landscape to writers with stronger ties to America, with deeper roots, with Pilgrim ancestors, to writers such as Rick Moody, Richard Ford, Ann Beattie, Anne Tyler, Jonathan Franzen, David Gates.

And it is not only the writers who have gone in search of reminiscence, judging by the plethora of seder invitations I now annually receive. My friends are naming their babies Itzak and Rivka and Tziporah. The concept of the shiksa goddess, popularized by Philip Roth and Woody Allen so that every Jewish boy wanted one and Jewish girls were bobbing their noses and dying their hair blond in order to pass, has fallen out of favor. Jewish girls are, I'm pleased to say, once again considered hot. My generation is traveling to Prague and to Kraków and Berlin. Looking for what? we can ask. For what got lost along the way to America, what was lost on the way to becoming American? Has the shame of being "too Jewish" eased into a shame at having been self-loathing? And we are writing about that search, the longing. We're attaching ourselves to the world of our grandparents. The literary theme of alienation in America has taken a new (re)turn. Whether it be the Lower East Side of New York or back to Europe, it is decidedly east, into the bosom of yesterday.

But this warm embrace, as with all warm embraces, can be stifling. Too comforting and too comfortable. If writers and Jews are to both wander and question, how can we remain snug in a collective, a ghetto? Are we getting tangled in our roots?

To welcome only that which is familiar is to deny literature and to limit our world. There is the danger of complacency, of sliding into shtick, of shying away from the unknown. That I am Jewish informs my writing the same way that being a woman does and a New Yorker too. But is that the sum total of who I am and what I know? Do I not want to, need to, venture beyond those borders?

Had I not, earlier in my life, ventured beyond the lines of demarcation, where would I be? At the country club, sitting on the chaise longue next to Brenda Patimkin, who'd be munching on Valium like they were salted cashew nuts and going on about her decorator, her tennis lessons, and her memories of some guy who worked at a library.

It would seem this is the right place for me to end. But there is an addendum to my easterly travels. Along the way, I passed back through the Patimkin world, which was worth revisiting. The way French Communists believe fervently in liberty and luxury for all, I, by examining whence I came, grew to understand that "JAP" and "Writer" are not mutually exclusive. Somehow I'd been led to believe that to be an upper-middle-class Jewish girl was to be a vacuous one, whereas the well-to-do of other ethnic groups were entitled to complexities. I came to see that a materially comfortable life need not be an unexamined one, and surely the list of solvent writers, philosophers, humanitarians, is endless. So there. I confess I like pretty things. I like creature comforts and have even come to insist upon some of them (indoor plumbing, for example). Bourgeois trappings do not render me, or any other Jewish American Princess, selfish or mean or limited or breathtakingly shallow. For me to have had utter disdain for the Patimkin world was no different from how my parents had disdain for the Old World; it's a kind of rejection of self. And as rejection of self is flat out, it precludes exploration of, and examination of, self. So while it's true I still do not want to *be* Brenda Patimkin, I do now understand why Neil loved her.

PEARL ABRAHAM

Divinity School or Trusting
the Act of Writing

Arecent *Newsweek* magazine article reporting on a
field of study called neurotheology asks whether
our brain wiring creates the idea of God, or
whether God created our brain wiring. It's similar to the
question linguists have been asking about the structure of
language: Does language reflect the attributes of our
brains because it was designed by us, or do our brains
develop in childhood to accommodate linguistic structures? I suspect the answer, if there is one, is a mixed one,
that a little of both takes place. In my particular case,
whether or not I was born with religious wiring, certainly
by the time I was in my teens, I should have grown into a
fervent Hasidic woman, prepared to marry at eighteen,
give birth to eight to ten children, marry them off, await
dozens of grandchildren and great-grandchildren, and
consider this existence the happiest on earth. From every
angle, the circumstances of my life pointed me in the
direction of a devout religiosity, but this didn't happen. I
became a writer.

My mother believes that America is somehow to blame. After years of shrugging my shoulders, I'm beginning to understand that this country did have a great deal to do with who I became.

A singular episode in my life inspired in me an acute self-awareness. It happened when I was fourteen or fifteen, and my Aunt Rachel from Israel was visiting. We were in Brooklyn for the day, waiting in the car for my mother and sister, who had stepped out to run an errand. My father was in the driver's seat, reading from Psalms or Mishnah, as was his habit during such stops. Taking my cue from him, I immersed myself in a novel. Aunt Rachel, who must have been bored, tried to engage me in conversation, which I discouraged by keeping my eyes on the page. When my mother returned, Rachel informed her that I was a child who ought to be watched, that I was dangerous. My father was upset that this had been said in front of me, and called it nonsense. I was deeply thrilled because it confirmed for me what I had known all along, though perhaps not so clearly: that I would be someone different, dangerous somehow.

In his introduction to *Omens of Millennium*, Harold Bloom refers to what might be a universal childhood experience, when one feels with certainty that one is not after all the child of one's natural parents. Bloom calls this sensation curious and asks whether it isn't an awakening to the knowledge (Gnosis) of something in the self that's older than even one's parents. He goes on to write of the pleasurable experience of deep reading in childhood, which reveals an inner identity, a previously unknown self within the self.

Reconsidering the event of my awakening from this late, present-day perspective, various aspects stand out, for example, my father's awareness that Rachel's mere articulation of my difference was potentially damaging or empowering. More significantly, that it wasn't the act of reading that brought forth the criticism but rather my disdain for conventional social behavior, which any decent Israeli child, Rachel pointed out, understood perfectly. My sin: I had placed personal desire above the needs of the other, thereby rebelling against the familial institution. In other words, I had become an American.

The protagonist of E. L. Doctorow's *The Book of Daniel* describes this social responsibility in a sentence I liked enough to memorize: "And all my life I have been running from my family, and I have been intricate in my run, but one way or another, they are what you come upon around the corner and the Lord God who is so anxious for recognition says you must ask how they are, and would they like something to drink, and what is it you can do for them this time."

Recall how much is made of the biblical Abraham's generosity as a host and you'll understand the significance of offering your relatives a drink. Daniel of *The Book of Daniel* performs precisely the type of duty from which on that particular day I exempted myself, and Rachel was able to detect, in a way my parents weren't, the impudence in my refusal to respond to her. She also knew that in taking my father's example, I, a daughter (not a son) intended only for a domestic life, had in this one brazen act elevated myself to my father's level. Another detail that no one referred to that day was the disparity of the texts in question: by every rule I'd grown up with, my profane novel should not have been conflated with the holy book my father was reading. Though she might not have articulated it in just this way, Rachel knew something significant about institutions and the individual, namely that their interests run counter to one another, that the self-reliant individual is a threat to family and community, and most certainly to institutionalized religion.

At the time, I was living with my family in a small town near Suffern, New York, where Greyhound left off and Red & Tan buses picked up. Kids on their way up to Woodstock roamed the area, hitchhiking to get a mile up or down Route 59, and my father, who was new to driving and knew what it was to need a ride, made a habit of picking up anyone who needed one. At the dinner table he showed us their version of a handshake, the peace sign. To the kids my father must have seemed one of them, at least from a distance, a hippie with a beard. His perpetual slowness—he was never in too much of a hurry to listen to a story—must have been attractive.

The story of the hippies, like all stories my father told, had its didactic turn: the youth of America are searching for something their parents have neglected; they want more than houses and cars, they're seeking transcendence. We Jews are fortunate, we have the Torah.

I should perhaps explain that for various reasons, not least because of my father's antinomian sensibility, my family settled near, but on the outer edge of Jewish communities, and they weren't Hasidic. There were enough Orthodox, Reform, and Conservative Jews in the town; my teachers at school were members of these communities, which meant that I often felt I was on enemy territory, until my teens when I developed what one teacher called the proverbial chip on the shoulder. What actually happened was that I finally understood that American Jews looked down on my family, we who still dressed like the old Eastern European Jews, and spoke the old lan-

guage, and, though we lived in America, were quite uneducated in American ways. We remained unassimilated,
unlike other immigrants to the United States, not because
we were living in an isolated Hasidic community (we
weren't), but out of conviction. Our distinct way of dress-
ing and speaking made us unfortunately flamboyant,
which turned certain Jews apoplectic.

At the time, the accepted mode of life among American Jews was to accommodate in their lives both, "Torah
and the ways of the land," (this is a translation of a Hebrew
phrase). To this end, yeshiva students attended college at
night to study business or a professional trade. Reform
and Conservative Jews of America worked hard to fit in, to
melt into the great melting pot, grow prosperous, and
thereby prove their worthiness as Americans. This was the
1970s. I was coming of age, and just comprehending the
various messages. The contrast between the American
Jewish disposition toward accommodation and the Hasidic insistence on remaining distinctly themselves engaged my teenage sense of right and wrong. Fortified
probably by the era's leanings against the establishment, I
considered the idea of accommodation a dishonesty.

At the same time, a seemingly airborne idea that
appealed to me was the great possibility of who and what
one can be, in other words, of the tremendous potential of
the individual. It didn't seem to matter what family one
came from: I as an individual could become anything or
anyone, as if I'd sprung from nowhere, or simply from
within, a self-created self. Theoretically this idea of self-
creation isn't distant from the supreme task of the Hasid:
to achieve a measure of divinity. Having grown up charged
with this task of personal growth, I was familiar with the
dedication necessary to such pursuits. What I didn't know

then was how much these ideas resemble those of Emersonian self-reliance and rugged individualism, the foundation of what we might call, after Harold Bloom, the American religion. America, unlike other nations, including Israel, was able to provide for Hasidism a place to thrive precisely because it is the one country in the world that shares with the eighteenth-century movement this grounding in the idea of the individual as holy.

In *God and the American Writer*, Alfred Kazin writes that Emerson reimagined Jesus as himself. Kazin cites the words of Jesus Christ, which Ralph Waldo Emerson quoted in his Divinity School address: "I am divine. Through me, God acts; through me, speaks. Would you see God, see me; or, see thee, when thou also thinkest as I now think." Kazin explains Emerson's point of view. "In short, any of us can be as commanding a force as Jesus. Any of us, expanding to the full circle of the universe, may yet enjoy the jubilee of sublime emotion that Jesus knew in recognizing God in himself. God dwells in us, too."

The Hasidic Rabbi Nachman of Bratslav is another example of a messianic figure who believed in the divine potential of every individual. In his analysis of the rabbi's tales, Nachman's biographer, Arthur Green, writes that the mythic redeemer figure appears not to make a claim for himself, but to serve as the representative of the collective dream. If the potential to become this mythic figure resides within Everyman, then it is toward the self one must turn to find redemption.

That Emerson read and appropriated ideas from Jesus Christ is not news. But the parallels between Emersonian and Hasidic (Kabbalah) teachings, with their shared focus on individual divinity, are perhaps surprising. Even stranger are the similarities in the historical progression of the Old World ecstatic movement and the New World product of divinity schools, where they began and where they are today.

Jesus Christ's relationship with mystical Judaism is easy enough to establish, since his mentor was James the Just, who is believed to have been a member of the Essenes, a nonnormative Judaic mystical community that dates back to 150 B.C.E. Despite rabbinic censorship, strains of Judaic mysticism existed through the First and Second Temple periods, and continued developing in the Diaspora. After the Spanish crusades, Safed became a renowned mystic center. And in the 1600s, Shabbetai Zevi initiated a messianism that ended in disillusion. Less than one hundred years later, Hasidism arrived on the scene.

Contemporary rabbinic wisdom maintains that Hasidism was a heavenly time-bound gift granted the Jews when their need was at a peak. Indeed, the movement endured in its original state for less than one hundred years. Just as transcendentalism lost its ruggedness—the whole cult of the divine self descended into a therapeutic New Ageism with its vocabularies of the inner child, self-esteem, twelve-step programs, self-help books, and Oprah—so too, developing alongside in the Jewish world, is a radical Jewish revival culture. A recent article in *The New Republic* describes a New Age Passover seder on a beach in Israel, complete with New Age rituals. And in the summer of 2003, the Jewish Community Center in New York City held an event titled "Awakening, Yearning and Renewal: A Conference on the Chasidic Roots of Contemporary Jewish Spiritual Expression and Neo-Chasidic Shabbat Festival." Remarking in the *Forward* on the proclaimed inspiration for this conference—eighteenth-century Hasidism—Allan Nadler writes that, unlike the

Hasidim of Poland, who were immersed in Jewish law, ritual, and culture, these seekers are uninformed.

Of course, Hasidism survived, if in name only, by turning itself into a popular movement, with appealing features such as the royal courts in all their ritualized grandness. Along the way, the ascetic lifestyle, which could only attract a small elite, was much diminished. Contemporary Hasidic courts are no longer grand, nor is the lifestyle far from mainstream Jewish orthodoxy, which is also why they're more acceptable to established Judaism. Rabbinic, institutional Judaism was threatened by Hasidism only so long as it retained its nonnormative character, so long as charismatic individuals, such as Nachman of Bratslav, could hold sway over thousands.

Not surprisingly, Nachman or early Hasidism would not have found my modern project of self-development threatening. Indeed, they might have endorsed it; that is, if I weren't a woman. Though I have lost the humility necessary to subordinate myself to the religious institution, I am pursuing the ecstatic or higher way; the writing life (I am not the first to make this claim) is comparable to the ascetic lifestyle of the early mystics.

But I am a woman. And although I watched my father write and self-publish (the Hasidic way), and assisted in the mass mailings, I was never meant to be as much as a reader of his writings. Of course watching has its rewards. I loved everything about my father's writing requirements. The tools he used: the old, pale green, portable Olivettis, one with an English alphabet keyboard, the other a Hebrew one; the feather quill and ink he used to copy certain passages as they appeared in the original texts, complete with calligraphic crowns and sweeps; the dark wood credenza in which he kept it all; most significantly, his need for solitude, which was ever fleeting.

A formative experience that the revolutionary Hasidic Rabbi Nachman of Bratslav, author of thirteen tales, referred to in his later life was the move from his uncle's populous court to the solitude of Medvedevka, in the Ukraine, where he spent days alone, in his study room, in the woods, in his boat on the Dnieper River. Such solitude was and continues to be unusual, even suspect, in the Jewish religious world, where so many of the laws have a built-in need for community: the quorum of ten for prayer, the study partner, the wife, the multiple children. And yet it was in suspect solitude, studying alone and praying without a quorum, that Nachman grew as an individual, and probably also as a writer. A mark of the significance he placed on this experience was his demand, which would later become a requirement, of Bratslav disciples: that they spend time alone every day. To this day the Bratslavers' daily meditative hour of solitude remains a subject of ridicule among other Hasidic sects.

I found quiet time and space when I moved away from home. Away from my eight siblings, and from the constant company of women, I discovered loneliness. Sitting alone with a cup of coffee in the school cafeteria (I was attending Hunter College), I turned to the writer's journal required for a writing class and learned to appreciate the solitude both Rilke (*Letters to a Young Poet*) and Nachman of Bratslav recommend. With a pen in hand and my notebook in front of me, I attempted to do what my father had done before me. Also, under cover of my journal, I could more freely observe the other students, mostly women, mostly coupled with other women. I noted that lesbian mates often dressed alike—I recall in particular one punk pair, both young, both with long bleached-white hair, black jeans and belts, black jackets, black eyeliner—and their sameness made me feel more alone, more different.

Hunter College of the 1980s was probably a fortuitous landing for many a displaced young woman. I read, watched, listened, and felt twice, thrice, and four times removed. I'd arrived with a different language, culture, education; at Hunter College in the eighties my sexual preference also seemed in the minority. And I knew that even among Jews, my Judaism, based as it is in Hasidism, was nonnormative.

In a writing class I met a fellow student who'd grown up in Oregon, was raised in the Methodist Church, converted to Judaism, moved to Israel, served for a year in the army, and was dating a Jewish law student. She invited me to attend a Yom HaShoah remembrance event at the campus Hillel Center, where she worked part time. When I pointed out that she didn't have any Holocaust dead to remember and mourn, she informed me that the event was about communal rather than personal loss, and about remembering, an important Jewish principle. I was obnoxiously argumentative.

Just come, she said.

I received a warm welcome at Hillel; it didn't seem to matter what I ate, studied, or with whom I lived, which I appreciated, coming as I did from a world in which even the style of the boots I wore was a topic of contention. And although Hillel Jews were commemorating the dead, the event wasn't especially sad, nothing like the solemn lighting of the *yahrzeit* candles in my parents' home. Hillel was accepting of everything, I thought; the problem was I didn't want to be accepted. Having experienced at an early age both the comforts and discomforts of traditional institutions, I was unlikely to join another. Consider what happens to revolutionary movements. Nothing dissipates a revolution faster than institutional acceptance. I seem to have learned this early, mainly on a subconscious level, and remain in my adult life skeptical of institutions, untrusting of the group, the general.

And yet, though I have emancipated myself from institutional religion, it's not quite true to say that I live without belief. Writing every day requires trusting the act of writing, a belief in an inner knowledge. As it turns out this belief in inner knowledge or an inner God, call it what you will, is very close to the mystical (Kabbalist) belief that the divine resides within the individual. Since such personal belief isn't dependent on institutionalized religion, it doesn't have the usual constraints. What it does have, strangely enough, is a grounding in Emersonian ideas, which is to say that under the influence of American religion, I returned to an earlier Hasidism. You might say that embracing the New World, becoming anything I wanted to become, in my case a writer, I also became an Old World, antiestablishment Hasid.

THANE ROSENBAUM

Law and Legacy in the Post-Holocaust Imagination

In the running debate between nature and nurture, perhaps there is something we can learn about the way in which the world ultimately receives its writers. For instance, are writers born, or are they transformed by circumstance, directed by the very accidents of history and detours of life that derail some people while placing others firmly on the writer's track?

Certainly there may be something innate within the human DNA that harbors the writer gene, but it is often suppressed, activated only by other impulses and outside influences. Some writers may have been more naturally suited for other professions, but unkind fates and often unwanted destinies compelled them to reimagine, as writers, the world they have witnessed.

The Holocaust, among its various moral implications and unintended consequences, also produced men of letters, men and women who might have otherwise, quite comfortably, settled on science or theology as their chosen fields. They had once been interned inside concentration camps, but upon liberation, an entirely different form of unfreedom awaited them. They were now cruelly conscripted into the service of memory. And they had little choice in avoiding either of these destinies.

In strange, often mystical ways, as a child of Holocaust survivors I feel as though the forces of history had as much to do with my decision to become a writer as anything else. I wasn't necessarily interested in becoming a writer when I was younger. I read a great deal, and many Jewish writers—Babel, Kafka, Wiesel, Singer—were canonical in our home. These were great men, not only wise, but magical. Their professional pursuits didn't seem earthly to me, and neither did what they chose to write about. I couldn't imagine how one could actually build a career out of the creative imagination, or whether writing novels could ever possibly constitute a profession (I still wonder about that). My own imagined career choices would be less exotic. Ironically, given how things ultimately worked out, none of my early interests had anything to do with my being Jewish, nor did they have any connection to my legacy, nor could any be described as writerly.

But out of all that annihilation that was the Holocaust—the murderous vanishing of European Jewry—the aftermath has been marked by renewal, the furious moral and aesthetic imperative not only to remember, but also somehow to reinvigorate, as implausible and improbable as that sounds. Many children of survivors gravitated to the medical or mental health professions. Others chose social work or public service. Still others created art.

The parents were survivors of the most unimaginable experiment in mass death in human history. The children would forever fall short in their own claims to immortality. For them, everything would inexorably be second-hand. Given this legacy of loss—this backstory that would forever foreshadow the future—the children were required to find some way to comprehend their inheritance, to invest it so that it wouldn't become wasted, squandered like the profligate children of parents who had once been far too intimate with evil.

There is something about the Jewish condition—overly imperiled, plagued by one kind of suppression or another—that compels Jewish writing, and transforms what could have otherwise been a harmless hobby into a moral imperative. A tribal community always in exile demands a narrative that is declarative and expository. It is a writing fueled by history, and arising out of tragedy—a reclamation project, constructed by words alone. A people wandering in the Diaspora, worshiping the mobility of their Torah, homeless yet somehow anchored, as long as their story is being recorded.

In my case, I now realize that the burden of my parents' story—and their cameo role in Jewish history—drew me in the direction of two career paths, neither of which interested me very much when I was a child growing up in Miami Beach. I went from being a lawyer to a fiction writer for seemingly inscrutable reasons, other than the fact that it was fatefully necessary that I become a lifelong teller of stories. Lawyers are storytellers by trade. It is their job to convey the stories of their clients in the most favorable, sympathetic light. Novelists tell stories that are illuminated by imagination and defined by narrative and emotional complexity. The lawyer's stories are more restrained and narrow in vision, more formulaic, more quiet and controlled. But the nature of the lawyer's and the novelist's writerly task is the same: it is one of strategic and necessary storytelling, the apparent burden of all Jews.

I discovered this burden shortly after I turned twenty-one, when both of my parents died within two months of one another. I suddenly found myself an adult orphan with an innate sense of vulnerability deepened by the fact that I had been a child of Holocaust survivors. In the post-Holocaust world, survival seemed to be linked to financial security, and like other creatures of the 1980s, I knew where to find it.

I accepted a scholarship to law school and soon joined the newly minted and mass-produced legions of corporate yuppies—the first generation, in fact. Our incomes were already higher than that of our parents; and we spent our money with less conflict. We owned co-ops, but found time only to sleep in them. We developed careers, and yet remained unattached—often detached. Working late into the night, we traveled home in Lincoln Town cars that waited outside our office buildings. We were given an assigned number—posted on the passenger window—as a way to claim our rides. All of us were guided by the spin doctors of an imminently sick economy, and cynically manipulated by popular culture. Our marching orders came directly from the novel *Bonfire of the Vanities* and the movie *Wall Street*.

The seduction of money, though, could never quite compensate for all the damage done to the soul from all those days spent without purpose. Our clients were face-less corporate entities, behemoths of the Fortune 500 uni-verse, producers of very little other than complicated financial statements. The compromise I had made soon after my parents died no longer seemed acceptable. Per-haps the truest expression of my legacy was that I was destined ultimately to feel unsafe. Life was not meant to go smoothly, or safely; the same ghosts that haunted my past and feared for my future also seemed to insist that my life have meaning, as well.

The lessons of my childhood were suddenly in conflict. My parents had warned repeatedly that I should protect myself against the foreseen—and unforeseen—perils of life, the least of which was financial and professional uncertainty. But the depth of those warnings had led to a competing impulse to speak to the experience of having to hear doomsday prophesies restated so often as a child. Perhaps only as a writer could I begin the complex untangling of the fears that had once belonged to my parents but now had been passed on to me.

My apprenticeship on Wall Street would still take time to abandon. I had to muster the necessary courage, to feel confident that my desire to write was more than just a dream, that I might, in fact, have something to say. Meanwhile, I was beginning to send out subtle but unmistakable clues that the path to partnership was not a direction I was following. My afternoon gym workouts went from one hour to two. I made all efforts to dodge the larger cases, gravitating to the firm's pro bono work.

As time passed, I began to take on a far more daring look than you would expect to find on Wall Street. Fewer haircuts. I started wearing East Village urban shoes—the ones that had metal buckles attached to the heel and the toe—with an Armani suit. I was rebelling, expressing myself in ways even I couldn't fathom.

It was around this time that I began to feel, almost mystically, as though there was a book inside me—maybe even more than one. I didn't know the title of this book, or what it would be about. Indeed, while I believed that it would be a work of fiction, I had no conscious thought that it would contain Jewish characters, and that every move these characters made would pivot around the shadows, and haltingly trudge through the darkness, of the Holocaust. (Ironically, that book was eventually titled *Elijah Visible*.)

Who would give up a lucrative position at a New York corporate law firm to write fiction? That's what they all asked—the well-wishers and the generally dumbfounded ones, too. No one could seem to get over the fact that I once had the big salary, a recognizable business card, and a skyscraper view of the East River. Some regarded me as an alien—well, at least a cultural one.

Abandoning legal careers seems to run in my family. My father had also once been a lawyer—before the Holocaust. After the war and the concentration camps, he was never a lawyer again. The madness he had witnessed poisoned his faith in law. Justice was now understood as a mere abstraction, not something that the law could actually provide. The world, like the law itself, was easily corrupted, and corrupting. He came to America leaving everything else behind—including his profession.

Eventually, I, too, left the law. I decided that a corporate life was not for me. In fact, you could say that I experienced a midcareer crisis—even though I was still in my early thirties. I lived off savings during my first year. There were days when I awoke with the sickening feeling that I wasn't accomplishing anything, that I had made a terrible mistake. Unwisely I had given up my one chance at feeling safe, gone ahead and disconnected myself from a crowd that rejoiced in absolute privilege—people who never for a moment doubted their success or their entitlement to security.

But there were also the words that I started tapping out on the keyboard, fiction that spoke to an eternal truth about the legacy I had inherited, that I carried around with me, that wouldn't leave me alone. Without realizing it at the time, I was writing a book that gave new life to the world of my parents, and the way their experiences became processed in the mind of a small boy. I couldn't bring my parents back, but I could write something to remember them by, and perhaps allow their ghosts, and mine, some peace.

I suppose I still haven't gotten the impulse of imagined resurrection and repair out of my system. At this point I have written several Jewish-themed, Holocaust-inspired books, even though I decry being a Holocaust writer, and have no compunction writing about something else. So then why don't I? In some ways I imagine that I am continually seeking to comprehend my own connection to Jewish history, or perhaps, even more tellingly, to rewrite history altogether. And for this reason I am stuck between two seemingly contradictory worlds: the artist who places no restriction on the imagination and can therefore do whatever he wishes with history; and the child of Holocaust survivors, who owes everything to history, and whose writing is both an act of creation and of memory.

In this post-Holocaust age, we have a moral duty to remember, to honor, ritualize, and acknowledge our collective and individual losses and pain, and yet we can't go too far in our obsessions with memory, because to do so presents risks and obstacles to our ability to engage in and enjoy the fullness of life, even as we have been so mercilessly robbed of so much of that richness.

I am a post-Holocaust novelist, which means that I

rely on my imagination—my capacity to reinvent worlds and reveal emotional truths—in order to speak to the Holocaust and its aftermath, one generation removed from Auschwitz. I don't write about the years 1939–1945. I see that time period as holy ground, the last millennium's answer to Mount Sinai. Instead, I focus on the looming dark shadow of the Holocaust as a continuing, implacable event; how it, inexorably, is still with us, flashing its radioactive teeth, keeping us all on our toes, imprinting our memories with symbols of, and metaphors for, mass death.

Yes, there were survivors of the Holocaust, one out of every three Jews of Europe did inexplicably survive. Yet when we speak of survival and survivors, what do we mean? What are we talking about? What is the quality of a survivor's life? Are vital signs only measured in terms of pulse rates and heartbeats, or is there something even more vital, other signs of life that can't be measured solely by medical criteria? Sometimes a heart can be broken even though it beats just fine. Physical survival, alone, is not a satisfying victory. There were millions of lost lives. Yet those who were miraculously found were nonetheless insufficiently alive. Even among the survivors, there was unspeakable spiritual damage—dead souls—which inevitably is more long-lasting and far-reaching, since it invades the bloodstream and the DNA, infecting new generations, making it nearly impossible to engage fully, faithfully, in everyday life.

Survivors are first and foremost realists, and fatalists. The Nazis had robbed them of their faith in a normal, carefree, ordinary life. And yet the post-Holocaust world is invariably, and bizarrely, forced to live with faith; it depends on faith, almost as fossil fuel for man's continuing march away from the Stone Age. Though we all know that the very things in which we have placed our faith will eventually disappoint us, we go on with our faith anyway, because we are commanded to do so—not by a god, but by our instincts for moral survival.

That's my fictional landscape, where my characters live, what they face, what they know to be true, the secrets they possess but are afraid to share. There is something patently absurd about reentering the world of the living after so much collective loss. Just think about it: when everything that you once loved was taken away from you—murdered, stolen, gassed, and burned—and you are now left to the world all by yourself, what incentives and reasons do you have to start anew? Unlike Job, most people would not, and should not, accept replacement children for the ones that were taken away and murdered. And yet they did. Holocaust survivors started over. They rebuilt their lives. They packed their memories in ice. They somehow managed to focus entirely on a future that was improbably cast before them.

I am not a survivor and I have a full range of choices before me. Apparently, the laws of the physical universe and the artistic liberties of a free society inform me that I have all the freedom in the world to create whatever it is that I want. And yet I am seemingly trapped by history, and historical forces, that have made imperious claims on what it is that I can and should write.

My most recent book is *The Myth of Moral Justice: Why Our Legal System Fails to Do What's Right.* After three novels, it is my first book of nonfiction. The novels all deal with post-Holocaust themes. The new book is a moral critique of the legal system, holding the law's feet to the fire of moral inquiry: why is it that so much of what lawyers and judges do—even if their actions and judgments are legally correct—doesn't feel emotionally or morally right to the rest of us?

It is ironic that I would one day write such a book. For many years I had been in denial about once having been a practicing lawyer. Play acting. Pretending that I had no bar affiliations, that I couldn't tell you the difference between a contract and a will, that my sum total of legal knowledge came by way of Court TV, or the O.J. trial. My former colleagues would probably no longer recognize me. My law students (in addition to being a novelist and essayist, I'm also a law professor) regard me, I sometimes fear, guardedly.

And who can blame them? Even I sometimes wonder how this latest book, which is not a work of post-Holocaust imagination, but rather a moral, philosophical critique of the legal system, is connected to a literary journey that I somehow managed to make. *The Myth of Moral Justice*, after all, is without an explicit Jewish agenda or sensibility. Perhaps without even realizing it, I seemed to have returned to my father's prewar profession—not as a practitioner, but rather as an artist urging reform.

The aspiration in writing *The Myth of Moral Justice*, in many ways, was to introduce moral consciousness into legal decision making, to encourage warmth, decency, and dignity in a profession that more commonly provides, and luxuriates in, cold, methodical judgment. The artist in me, through my fiction, seeks renewed pathways to remembrance. But the former lawyer in me obviously longs for a kind of justice that feels just. Perhaps this, too, is not so surprising. It is a natural wish for our world that we would expect a child of Holocaust survivors to make. Perhaps more than anything else, the child of survivors in me longs mostly for justice—in whatever form it takes, in whatever manner it can be delivered, demanded, and experienced.

The legacy of loss that was the mystery of my childhood one day became the inspiration for my art and my other writings. I had and continue to have no idea of the specific horrors that my parents experienced and witnessed, and so I write entirely out of the imaginative realm. I feel compelled to write about what I don't actually know, as a way to at least participate in my family's story—if not as an eyewitness, then as a creative caretaker. Writing about Jewish themes is an extension of that impulse. In fact, I would have to say that I am functioning at my most Jewish when I am writing about Jewish art, culture, and society; that my faith is at its most devout when my books deal in everything that should give Jews reasons to renounce their faith, but in the true spirit of the covenant, does not.

We Jews are a complicated people, complicated even more so by our history, a history that in so many profound ways we did not choose. It is the tragic irony of being Chosen. Had we been given a choice, we might have picked an entirely different story. For this reason, it is inevitable that Jewish writers have been unable to resist rewriting some of the stories, reimagining the endings—and sometimes inserting finales that are indeed, and improbably, happy—recasting some of the grotesque portraiture, wishing for these lamentable tales to read more sanguinely, and hopefully. The imagined life of the Jew is no better than the one that he or she has actually lived. But it is a life that he or she at least had the chance to create. And so I have chosen to be a writer, to draw from the emotional inheritance that was given to me as an accident of my birth, and, through it, to imagine the world otherwise.

JONATHAN ROSEN

Forward and Back:
A Journey Between Worlds

"Forward and Back" is the name of the weekly column that I wrote for the English-language *Forward* for two years, beginning in 1990. I was fresh out of graduate school in English literature. I was new to journalism—especially Jewish journalism. And I was new to the *Forward*, which, to be honest, was new to me.

I must have heard something about the great Yiddish paper, the Jewish Daily *Forverts*, which I have since learned my mother's grandfather brandished—in rolled-up form—while chasing his children around the dining room table. But the *Forverts* was not part of the mythology of my home and it rang no real bells when Lucy Dawidowicz, a family friend, told me that Seth Lipsky was going to turn the Yiddish *Forverts* into an English-language newspaper and that I should go work for it.

If I'm really honest, I should probably add that the thought of working at a Jewish newspaper did not at first inspire me. If I were even more honest, I'd have to admit that it frightened and embarrassed me. It was one thing to leave off studying John Milton and quit the ivory tower. It was another thing to find myself washing up on the shores of Ellis Island, which my maternal great-grandparents had so eagerly left behind.

That, at least, is how I initially—and shamefully—thought of it. I had left graduate school to become a writer. Not to become a journalist. Certainly not a *Jewish* journalist.

My heroes, to be sure, were American Jewish writers—particularly Saul Bellow—but I assumed I would continue their ever-expanding journey into America. But for one thing, America itself was changing. There was no neutral heartland to be embraced. In the multicultural country that had taken shape since Bellow's Augie March set out on his journey, the rules were different. You discovered America by discovering yourself, your peculiar place in the country, rooted in your own religious or ethnic or cultural particularity.

Even without this change, I ought to have known that becoming a writer meant coming to terms with who you actually are. Nothing plunged me more quickly into contact with my ambivalent heritage as an American Jew than working at the *Forward*. Anxiety and embarrassment are often signs one is about to encounter oneself.

Which isn't to say that I wasn't also excited about my new job. I knew I wasn't about to take up residence in a rolled-up copy of the Yiddish *Forverts* clutched by my angry unknown forebear. I was going to work for an English-language newspaper created by a former foreign editor of *The Wall Street Journal*. It was not a nostalgic enterprise but an act of new creation. Or perhaps it was a little of both.

•••

My father, who was born in Vienna, took to calling the English-language *Forward* the *altneupaper*—the "old-new" paper. The name was an adaptation of Theodor Herzl's name for the land of Israel—Altneuland. The old-new land. It was a place that had a history and that would have a future as well. That description inspired me and made me feel the excitement of my own fin de siècle moment. "Old" didn't mean dead, and "new" didn't mean obliteration of the past. Why not have both together?

This in fact fit the accident of my own birth. Because while my mother's grandparents lived in this country, my father was, as I mentioned, born in Vienna. In fact, when my father arrived here, in 1940 via Scotland, where he had fled at fourteen, his picture was taken as he stepped off the boat. That picture was featured in the rotogravure section of the Sunday Jewish Daily *Forverts*. My own connection to the paper was turning out to be, as the Freudians like to say, "overdetermined."

The reality of my father's experience changed my relationship to the Jewish past. His parents and a great deal of his extended family had been killed in the Holocaust. Seeing the Jewish past through this terrible dark veil made me eager to draw close to that lost world. I believe an earlier generation of immigrant children was afraid of the world of their parents. They were afraid they might be sucked back into it. I was curious to learn about a world that didn't exist anymore.

In his "Letter to My Father," Franz Kafka imagines his father lying on a map of the world and, wherever his father's body touches, Kafka harshly declares that he himself could never live. He needed to define himself as the opposite of his father.

But the map *my* father lay on and that his experience

touched—Poland, where his parents came from, Jewish Vienna, where he grew up, refugee New York, where he spent most of the war—was not a world I was in danger of inhabiting because it didn't exist anymore. My father lay on the map of a vanished world. And I discovered myself drawn to the places his experience touched and that he was connected to.

And here he was, in the *Forverts*.

Of course my father hated the way he'd been portrayed in the *Forverts*—with a cutesy caption, in English and Yiddish—because at that point the paper was catering to the children of Yiddish speakers as much as to their parents. The caption read:

> JOURNEY'S END FOR A YOUNG WANDERER. An appealing study of a sixteen-year-old Viennese refugee, Samuel Rosen, made upon his recent arrival in this country after many hardships. Although he is mighty glad to be here, the pensive lad can't help thinking of the sad plight of his relatives and friends "back home."

The sentimental tone of the caption is what I think annoyed my father the most, since by 1940 most of the folks "back home" were in mortal peril or, like his father, already dead. He ripped the photograph and its caption in two, though he saved the paper. (I later found that very issue in the *Forward* archives and turned the page into a poster I have since framed and hung in my office.)

The *Forward* became a chance for me to knit myself together too. I was, on my mother's side, the great-grandchild of American citizens comfortably present in this country for many many years. And I was, on my father's side, the child of an immigrant ambivalent about America and keenly aware of a world left irretrievably behind. I'd inherited both phases of the Jewish American experience simultaneously. And the *Forward*, with its immigrant Yiddish roots and its contemporary English-language impulses, allowed me to explore and express both pieces of myself.

I've since come to feel that the immigrant experience isn't really a fleeting moment in Jewish American history that only recedes more and more into the past the farther American Jews move into the mainstream. I've since come to feel that we are all, metaphorically, immigrants. The assimilated, for example, are immigrants inside the Jewish world. I met many of these third-generation immigrants at the *Forward*—some were our readers, others worked alongside me at the paper, groping their way back to a sense of religious or ethnic or cultural belonging.

And like immigrants everywhere, they were zealous in their desire to master a new world they didn't always know much about.

"What's a dreidel?" our first news editor asked one day at a staff meeting during Hanukkah. This young man had been educated at a French lycée in Paris and had attended an Ivy League college. Jewishly, however, he was a total greenhorn. The English *Forward* taught him what a dreidel was the way the Yiddish *Forverts* might have taught his great-grandfather what a bowling ball was.

All of us are, metaphorically—or perhaps, metaphysically—immigrants of a spiritual sort. The Talmud tells us that in the womb we all study and master the Talmud, but that at birth an angel touches us and we forget everything we've learned. Which makes the womb a sort of shtetl, the Old Country we all pine for in every generation. No wonder actual immigrants have lent themselves to such mythologizing and are such potent metaphors for the human experience.

It may have taken having a child for me to realize this

fully. I was in my twenties when I started at the *Forward* and not even married. I was focused much more on the new than the old, or even on the way the old is carried forward inside the new. I wanted to impose that sense of the new on the paper I was helping to create.

•••

In my zeal to declare a new dispensation I may have gone a little overboard. The only thing I remember from my first "Forward and Back" column, which appeared in the first issue of the English-language *Forward*, was the phrase: "The fiddler has fallen off the roof—and a good thing, too, for we have all had enough violin music." I had actually played the violin for many years beginning when I was quite young, and it is of course possible that my dialogue with Jewish culture was in part a dialogue with myself.

In addition to writing a column, I was given permission by Seth Lipsky to create an "Arts and Letters" section. Like the little red hen, I immediately began running all over town trying to find people to help me bake my bread. That it was a challah I was in some sense baking, a Jewish braid of past and present, did not always help.

One of the first people I went to ask was Irving Howe. Howe seemed like an obvious choice. The fact that he was an eminent man of letters who had written a very good book about Faulkner, and was also the dean of Yiddish American culture, seemed ideal. It was, after all, to his great book about immigrant Jews and the culture they made, *World of Our Fathers*, that I ran for details about the Yiddish *Forverts*. Howe was a bridger of worlds and I hoped not only for his help but, in some sense, for his blessing.

But Howe did not want to meet with me. The notion of a reborn Jewish *Forward* did not excite him. Indeed, it seemed somehow to repel him. Nevertheless, I noodged him into it. "Who if not you?" I asked on the phone. "You taught a whole generation to care about Yiddish culture." I was in my twenties and was still technically enrolled in a Ph.D. program in English literature. I wasn't sure that I cared about a reborn *Forward*. But somehow it had become my job to care and the more I talked about it the more I believed in it.

Howe agreed to see me—more out of pity, I am sure, than enthusiasm. We met in a coffee shop on the Upper East Side. "Try the rice pudding," he instructed.

I laid out the ambitious plans I had begun hatching in my newfound enthusiasm. Here was an opportunity for a renaissance of Jewish American culture. The paper could build a bridge between the past and the future. Between popular culture and high culture. Between Israeli letters and American Jewish letters. The journey into American assimilation was complete. The time had come for the journey back. The Yiddish *Forward* had bound its readers together with a common language. A reborn *Forward* presented a subtle challenge of translation. Could we create a paper in English that nevertheless had about it a binding element that would hold its readers as Yiddish once had? I thought that Howe, a translator himself, would particularly appreciate this last point.

Howe listened very patiently. And when I was done talking he told me that if I did what I wanted, nobody would read the paper. And that if the paper did somehow manage to become a success, it would mean that I had sunk into hopeless mediocrity.

There was no malice in what he said. He was at the

end of his life, and I suspect that long before that he had developed the habit of saying what he believed. He seemed full of concern for me as a person. He wanted to know if I was being paid enough to live on. He wished me well and picked up the tab for my rice pudding (which was, in fact, delicious).

Like those blows on the head administered by Zen masters, the lesson Howe taught me was valuable and bracing: the guardians and chroniclers of immigrant Jewish culture did not always care about the Jewish culture that the grandchildren and great-grandchildren of those immigrants would produce. Howe had magisterially evoked the *World of Our Fathers*—but what about the world of the children? Couldn't that also be a Jewish world full of creativity and passion? And couldn't the exploration of that world be a continuation of the larger American story, and not a retreat from it?

Howe's rebuff in some sense strengthened my own resolve. I think again of my father's saying—that the paper was an *altneupaper*—and I think of a Zionist slogan the early pioneers used. One went to Israel to build the land and to be built by it. I was building a new *Forward* but I was being built by it as well, feeling the pull of my own partially hidden identity. I am amazed looking back at how quickly I came to take the project personally, to recognize in it an act of personal reconstruction. If Howe cared only about immigrant origins, then he was, in some sense, saying what Hegel had said about the Jews in general—they'd made their contribution and then fallen off the historical stage. I took this insult personally and set out to disprove it.

In the ten years I wound up working at the *Forward*, I went from feeling that nothing was stranger than my new career at a Jewish newspaper to feeling that nothing could be more obvious, even inevitable. It took me a long time to stop pining for the time Jewish writers made their escape from the smothering embrace of their immigrant origins and fled into the open arms of America. I was born into the accepting America to which these writers fled, and my story would have to be different. What I discovered is that there is romance and urgency to life in every generation and that every generation has its own story to tell.

In the end—and even at the beginning—I found a great many people, young and old, who did help me bake my bread. They turned up everywhere—in M.F.A. programs and on college campuses, even on the pages of *Raw Comics*, where Art Spiegelman—who gave me *Maus II* to serialize—introduced me to the brilliant Ben Katchor.

•••

In 1991, after I had been at the paper for a year, I got a letter, typed on an old manual typewriter, letters flying, that read:

> Dear Mr. Rosen,
> I am doing an autobiographical book, based on my lifetime journals. Some of this may interest you for the *Forward*. At the moment, describing the universalizing idealism of the Jewish labor movement in which I grew up many moons ago, I want to note a remarkable moment. Sometime—in the 1920s?—or earlier, a Black was lynched in Pennsylvania. The *Forward* had a banner headline, "POGROM IN PENNSYLVANIA."
> I have often thought of this, funny and touching as it was. . . .

The letter was from Alfred Kazin, the great literary critic and one of my heroes.

I treasure this letter for several reasons. There was first of all the simple fact that a critic I admired enormously actually sought me out at the *Forward*, called me "Mr. Rosen," and offered me a piece of his next book—take *that*, Irving Howe. But beyond that is the fact that Kazin, whose father read the Yiddish *Forverts* religiously, was haunted his whole life by something that was printed in a Jewish newspaper years and years and years before. And that Kazin, who devoted much of his distinguished career to interpreting American literature, knew he was nevertheless formed by the world the Jewish Daily *Forverts* represented.

And what stuck with Kazin was truly remarkable. "Pogrom in Pennsylvania," applied to the lynching of a black man, in a sense makes the whole world Jewish. Anyone who suffered was immediately admitted into the *Forward*'s family. Yiddish itself—like the use of the word "pogrom" for a lynching—may have had the mysterious power to link everything it described to Jewish culture and Jewish concerns.

Whether this is, as Kazin called it, a universalizing impulse, or actually its opposite, is for me another insoluble mystery. Perhaps calling a lynching a pogrom really reflects a Judaizing impulse. Assimilation itself can work both ways. We assimilate into a larger culture. But we assimilate that larger culture into ourselves and transform it in the process.

•••

Kazin's letter represented another transformation that happened while I was at the *Forward*. Busy as I was trying to knock the fiddler off his roof and tell everyone how different this *Forward* was from its Yiddish-speaking parent, I was discovering just how great its Yiddish parent had actually been.

The *Forverts* had covered everything in its pages—theater, literature, world politics, local politics. It ran a column by Bertrand Russell translated into Yiddish, it ran Flaubert in Yiddish. It turned letters from readers desperate for advice into a feature in its own right. It regularly serialized the work of I. B. Singer who had, after all, won the Nobel Prize for literature. The Jewish Daily *Forverts* had as broad a definition of "news" as a paper could have, including works of the imagination in that category.

Seth Lipsky, a great newspaperman, often made the point that the *Forverts* wasn't strictly speaking a Jewish newspaper. It was a general interest newspaper written in the language of the Jews. In some sense, that language imparted something Jewish to everything it touched. It was the young ivy leaguers at the English-language *Forward*, straining to define what constituted "Jewish" news and "Jewish" culture, who were the parochial ones. I think we ran three separate articles on a boxer who called himself "The Lion of Judah" simply because he was a boxer and, well, Jewish.

We were not only the parochial ones—we were the sentimental ones. In 1990, the Yiddish *Forverts* decided to switch production of the paper from Linotype machines to Macintosh computers because computers were more efficient. The heavy, hundred-year-old relics that had been brought over from the Lower East Side, with their wooden trays of movable type and heavy bars of zinc for melting into letters, were going to be chopped up and scrapped.

The staff of the English *Forward*—none of us, I believe, knew Yiddish—begged the managers of the Yiddish paper to keep one of the machines in operation as a display. But they were not in the museum business. Yiddish mattered—but if Yiddish on a Macintosh was more efficient, so be it. The English paper wouldn't have been caught dead using such dinosaurs, why should we expect it of them?

I remember running down to the basement and filling my pockets with Yiddish letters, like seeds I hoped someday to plant. I even got one of the typesetters to print my girlfriend's name in Yiddish—one of the last things printed on his machine. But these—the letters, my girlfriend's name—were mere souvenirs, and the people who ran the paper—who had memories of a daily circulation of 200,000—were not in the souvenir business.

I remember in a fevered moment of insane dreaming wondering if one of those behemoths could fit in my apartment. Fortunately, Aaron Lansky—it was the first time I had heard his name—drove down and rescued one lone machine, which has now become part of the Yiddish Book Center's permanent museum exhibition.

The basement of the *Forward* was turning out to be like the unconscious life of American Judaism itself. While down there I had another run-in with the anti-sentimental strain of Jewish tradition. One of the typesetters, with whom I had become friendly—the one, in fact, who'd printed my girlfriend's name in Yiddish—was reminiscing about I. B. Singer. This man couldn't stand Singer.

My typesetter was an Orthodox Jew—in one of the multiple ironies of life at the *Forward,* there were no longer enough secular Yiddishists to go around and they'd begun acquiring Orthodox and often Hasidic Jews. This man came from the *Tog,* which had once been the great rival of the Jewish Daily *Forverts.* In any case, to this man's

Orthodox sensibility, Singer was a pornographer—and he told me he used to take it upon himself to edit out the dirty stuff while he was setting Singer's stories.

More than that, when the Jewish Daily *Forverts* moved uptown from its home on East Broadway, he claimed to have found a manuscript of *Enemies, A Love Story* and thrown it in a Dumpster.

I was horrified, of course, but like the trashing of the Yiddish typesetting machines, there was something bracing about the story, a reminder that Jewish culture was a total world, with loves and hatreds. Singer, after all, knew what he was doing when he called his novel *Enemies, A Love Story*. Perhaps because Jews were loving and hating each other in their own language, there was an element of safety to the quarrels.

Among the many paradoxes I encountered at the *Forward* was this potent linguistic one that says so much about the translation of Jewish life out of Eastern Europe and into America. The Yiddish *Forverts*, though proudly, defiantly secular, was printed with the same alphabet King David used to write the psalms. And the English *Forward*, which actually called itself a Jewish newspaper, was printed with the same alphabet the Roman generals used when they ordered the destruction of the Second Temple.

The Yiddish *Forverts* didn't need to worry about whether or not what it covered and included was "Jewish." Was Flaubert Jewish? Was Bertrand Russell? Their words, rendered into Yiddish, were enough to qualify them for inclusion.

I often found myself wondering if it was possible to create that sense of community among English-language readers that the Yiddish paper's readers felt so deeply simply because the paper was in Yiddish. This is a question that continues to haunt me long after my departure from the paper, because it has less to do with creating an English *Forward* and more to do, in general, with the creation of Jewish American culture.

A great many things have carried over into my writing and thinking life from those early years spent hatching the "Arts and Letters" section of the *Forward*. I mentioned that the title of this piece—"Forward and Back"—is drawn from the column I wrote for the *Forward*. The subtitle, *A Journey Between Worlds*, is the subtitle of my book *The Talmud and the Internet*, which I published shortly after leaving the *Forward*.

I feel quite certain that my ten years at the paradoxical English-language *Forward*—really an oxymoron when you think about it, a Yiddish newspaper in English—shaped my appreciation for all the weird paradoxes of my own Jewish American experience. My time at the *Forward* helped attune me to historical contradictions Jews have been living with for a long time.

I never imagined that, as much as college and graduate school in English literature, my apprenticeship at a Jewish newspaper would play such a shaping role in determining the kind of writer I became.

The *Forward* even led me to the door of Saul Bellow—my literary hero. I interviewed him for the paper in 1991. Like Howe, he wasn't too keen to meet with me, but he had memories, he told me, of reading his father Sholem Aleichem from the pages of the Yiddish *Forverts*. (This may have been a false memory, since Sholem Aleichem wrote for the *Forverts*'s rival, the *Tog*, but what did I care?) For the sake of his father he agreed to meet with me.

Never in a million years, when I was in college dreaming my literary dreams, would I have believed that what would win me an audience with the greatest American writer since Faulkner was employment at the Jewish *Forward*. I flew to Chicago and met Bellow in Hyde Park. We sat under a tree on a bench talking while his young wife, Janice, brought us back slices of pizza. At the end of a long and satisfying rambling conversation I asked Bellow if there was anything about his career that he regretted. It was a stupid question to my mind—what could he possibly have to regret?—but I asked out of journalistic obligation. His answer surprised me. He told me that he regretted paying too little attention to the Holocaust.

Bellow had worked on *The Adventures of Augie March* in Paris in the late 1940s. That book is his wildest, freest adventure. But while he was working on it he was keenly aware of the Holocaust survivors all around him. He told me he blotted them out of his imagination because, in his words, he wanted to have his American seven-layer cake. He wanted his freewheeling adventure.

I wonder how Bellow would have written had he lived in an America that was less of an either/or culture. Where would Augie March have gone, what would he have done, if Bellow had introduced a few of those survivors into his novel? But Bellow—at that point in his career—saw America as antithetical to the grim European reality whose evidence was all around him.

What I came away feeling was that the pull of contradictory impulses was in itself a great subject. I knew from my own experience what it meant to be connected on one side to overwhelming tragedy and on the other side to easy prosperity. Why not accept the irreconcilable nature of the dilemma? Why not write about the tension of living between worlds?

The *Forward* equipped me to do that. The world of

the *Forverts* was steeped in Yiddishkeit and yearning for American freedoms. The world of the English paper was steeped in American freedoms, yearning for Yiddishkeit.

Jews have had a lot of practice, it seems to me, living between worlds. One of the things I wanted to write about in *The Talmud and the Internet* was the way Jews took up a kind of metaphysical residence inside the Talmud after the destruction of the Temple. They packed their culture into words and took it on the road. And the Talmud became a kind of virtual Temple, an intermediate space on the journey between exile and return.

Jews lost their home so long ago that a remarkable amount of Jewish culture evolved to mediate between our different homes and the contrary impulses and associations these places evoked. Jerusalem is our home and God's home, one body of religious texts asserts, while another explores the fact that exile is where we live—and even where God lives.

The powerful and opposing forces of exile and return rule a great deal of Jewish life. For me this makes it both harder and easier to feel at home. In my book, the Internet operates as a metaphor for people—Jews and non-Jews—who are at home everywhere and nowhere. We are linked, on line, to vast libraries and infinite communities. But we are also disembodied and adrift. Where else but in exile do you need a home page?

It's possible that, like the *Forverts* article that called a lynching a pogrom, I have a universalizing desire to project my own immediate Jewish heritage onto the rest of Jewish culture and even onto the world. But it is also possible that we all grapple with multiple worlds in our daily lives, toggling between contradictory realities.

My book is really a series of comparisons and unlikely

juxtapositions. Some of the stories I tell in it have to do with putting the ancient world side by side with the modern world. Some have to do with putting my own life beside historical figures or pitting the religious world against the secular world, the world of ancient religious impulses against contemporary secular technological society. I feel I am related to all these worlds and I am constantly looking for ways to knit these worlds together.

The human heart of my book is the story of my two grandmothers. My mother's mother, as I mentioned, was born in this country. It was her father who used to chase his children with a rolled-up copy of the *Forverts*. I was very close to this grandmother, who lived a long and prosperous American life and died a few years ago at the age of ninety-five. Her death set *The Talmud and the Internet* in motion, even though she didn't care much about either the Talmud or the Internet.

Alongside this grandmother I write about my father's mother. I never knew my paternal grandmother, who was born in Poland but fled to Vienna after the First World War, where she raised a family. She was shot after transport to the East more than fifty years ago.

What I came to realize was that the lives—and deaths—of these two women led me to radically different conclusions about the Jewish experience and, beyond that, about the human experience. In a book about reconciling opposing elements, nothing challenged me more than my own contradictory inheritance. The best I could do was put my grandmothers side by side and, in the manner of the Talmud, let them each stand as point and counterpoint, neither dissolving into the other.

I was fully aware that writing about the metaphorical journey between worlds was hardly a radical notion on my part. *The Dybbuk*, perhaps the most famous Yiddish play, is itself subtitled *Between Two Worlds*.

S. Ansky's subtitle, like my father's notion of an *alt-neupaper*, often seems like an apt description of the reborn *Forward*. The two worlds Ansky meant to suggest were the world of the living and the world of the dead—since *The Dybbuk* is about a dead lover who inhabits the body of his beloved. But the play, written as Yiddish culture in Europe was breaking down, was already a sort of parable about conjuring the spirit of a departed culture. After the Nazi destruction of European Jewry, that longing to summon the dead—that desire for possession—is even stronger, and even more painful.

We are always hoping that the past will speak through us. Of course we cannot live wholly possessed by the past or, like the young woman in *The Dybbuk*, we risk losing our lives. But we cannot live wholly possessed by the present—or we risk losing our souls.

ALLEGRA GOODMAN

Writing with a Return Address

A year ago I was sitting next to Cynthia Ozick at a dinner in her honor at Stanford University. We began to talk about the term "Jewish American writer," and she told me how much she resented the label. It is derogatory, she said, it is simplistic and reductive. It reduces art and ideas to ethnic commodities. The very word *ethnic*, she said, is a hateful term; it is really a slur, a term of alienation, with its root word *ethnos* connoting foreign and heathen. To label fiction as Jewish American, to think of it as ethnic, is not merely to categorize it but to attack it. Then she leaned over and asked, "What do you think?"

It is a difficult question for me: how to gauge my identity as a Jewish American writer. I fully understand Ozick's resentment at being labeled, and I share her mistrust for the trivializing and reductive capacity of labels. I certainly don't want my work stereotyped or ghettoized. When asked what I do, I say first that I am a writer; when pressed about what kind of writer, I say that I am a fiction writer, and yes, I often write about Jewish people. I do not

immediately say I am a Jewish American woman fiction
writer. But at the same time I understand that my most
intimate and immediate audience comes from the American Jewish community, that in many ways when I write
fiction I am writing not only about them but also for them.
This more specialized audience overlaps but also extends
my audience of general readers. The label *Jewish American*
is a way of pigeonholing me, of packaging and selling my
work, but it is also a symbol of an essential resource: a
community of passionate readers in an increasingly difficult world for serious fiction. My parents tell me that at
their synagogue in Nashville, people ask them if they are
related to Allegra Goodman the fiction writer. My parents—proud Jewish parents that they are—immediately
say, "Oh, you've read her book? You've seen her work in
The New Yorker?"

"No, no, we don't get *The New Yorker*" is the reply,
"We read her stories in *Commentary*."

I have come to think that a writer cannot have enough
labels if they are keys to new audiences, if they are combined and subverted imaginatively. I work with as many as
I can—Jewish writer, woman writer, Generation X. Each
provides a different opportunity.

And yet I take Ozick's critique seriously when she
speaks bitterly of the label "Jewish American writer." Jewish fiction has a complex and troubling position in the
United States. The Jewish writers of my generation are
the inheritors of two traditions of Jewish fiction. One is
the tradition of writers such as Chaim Grade, Sholem
Aleichem, and I. B. Singer. They wrote in Yiddish, and
their work must overcome the barrier of translation.
These are writers whose aesthetic qualities and achievements are rarely isolated from their subject matter. Always

they are the recorders of a lost culture and a lost language. Sholem Aleichem is always a great Jewish humorist, rather than a great writer. His texts suffer from the burden of thousands of productions of *Fiddler on the Roof* and bad artwork depicting shtetl life in the Old Country. Chaim Grade's work is always the elegiac record of times past. Even Grade's prewar work bears the shadow of the Holocaust. His texts are as haunting and tragic as the photographs of Roman Vishniac, images of a fragile, vanished world. The visions of Sholem Aleichem, Grade, and even the laureate Singer become in the public imagination records of an ethnic experience that truly is foreign and strange, rendered humorously by Sholem Aleichem, elegiacally by Grade, and with a piquant semierotic spice by Singer. These writers' books are marginalized as artifacts rather than read consistently as artworks.

The other tradition that comes down to us is that of Jewish American writers such as Roth and Bellow, who develop and project their self-consciousness, ambivalence, and guilt about the Jewish tradition into mainstream American fiction. If the translated Yiddish writers are marginalized as parochial, the great Jewish American writers are read as institutional. This institutional identity is in its way as limiting as that of the ethnic writer, for in the age of multiculturalism, it alienates these writers from their intimate constituency; it denies them their role as artists of the Jewish community. It is difficult to be a literary giant in the global village, to be ambassador without portfolio. Roth and Bellow have arrived and become great twentieth-century writers, and in a sense their fame makes it hard to hear them as ethnic voices. The biographical notes in *The Norton Anthology of Short Fiction* provide a fascinating index to this phenomenon. Bernard Malamud is described as being "recognized as one of the best of the writers who have portrayed Jewish life and sensibility in American fiction." But when it comes to Philip Roth, it is his "mastery of form" that the Norton editors mention, and his "gift for ribald, acid comedy." Nowhere in the entry on Roth and his work is his Jewishness or Jewish themes mentioned. Describing Isaac Bashevis Singer's work, the editors write, "Flavored with the colorful residue of folk tales, his explorations of Jewish life, past and present, are haunted allegories of the irrationality of history." But when it comes to Saul Bellow, it is impossible to tell from the biographical entry that this is a Jewish writer. In fact, the editors locate Bellow and his themes firmly in the Midwest; strangely enough he is endowed with a Midwestern ethos: "He has lived in Chicago for most of his later life, teaching and writing there, and this mid-American location seems to be reflected by the spirit and subject matter of his fiction, with its discoveries of eccentrics who wrestle with the quandaries of the individual destiny in a variety of American settings." These capsule discussions of Malamud, Roth, Singer, and Bellow reveal the divide between those writers read as Jewish and those who have moved on, and perhaps up, in the world to be read as masters of form or discoverers of the quandaries of the individual. On each side of the divide Jewish writers are read, described, and introduced to students in reductive terms.

The irony is that Jewish American writers are in many ways victims of their own success. Writers like Sholem Aleichem and Singer not only record and express Jewish values, but they also have become emblems of Old World Judaism, while such ambivalent assimilationists as Bellow and Roth have in fact become assimilated into the larger mainstream tradition. So, as a working Jewish American writer, where do I stand as I look for strategies and models? I write about Jewish culture, but not merely Jewish culture. I write about religion as well. Therefore, my models are the older writers like Grade and Sholem Aleichem, who wrote of a living unself-conscious tradition. I write from the inside, taking, as they did, an idiom in which ritual and liturgy are a natural part of my fictional world, and not anthropological objects to be translated and constantly explained. From the beginning of my career I have chosen this insider's perspective. My choice was influenced not only by my reading of Jewish literature, but also by my background as a child growing up in Hawaii. I was familiar with a place that seemed exotic to others, and in my writing I chose to present the exotic as familiar.

The first story I wrote, published in my 1989 collection, *Total Immersion*, is about a Yom Kippur service that takes place on the lanai of a family in Honolulu. The whole story occurs inside the service, with dialogue, fights, speeches, and exhortations whispered between prayers and songs. Another story in the collection focuses on a strictly Orthodox scholar named Cecil Birnbaum, who lives in Oxford. The plot hinges on Birnbaum's horror that one of his fellow congregants has pushed a stroller to synagogue, thus violating the injunction against carrying or pushing loads on the Sabbath. I used a glossary at the end of my book to explain Hebrew and Yiddish words, but I did not interrupt stories such as these to explain or translate religious terms or rituals. I found that readers relished a feeling of total immersion. I was not trying to be obscure; I worked for clarity, but at the same time I was not apologetic about my characters and their activities. In much of my work I use ritual as both structural tool and subject. In doing so I look not only to the translated Jewish writers, but also to Chaim Potok and Cynthia Ozick, who treat not merely the ethnic but also the religious dimension of Judaism. I also find inspiration in the work of writers like Maxine Hong Kingston, another writer who lived for many years in Hawaii. Kingston developed fiction out of the interior of Chinese culture in *Woman Warrior*—an interior that she believed could speak in its own terms, without guilty nostalgia and anger or condescending bemusement.

Since *Total Immersion* I have focused primarily on characters who are far more assimilated than those of my earliest stories. There is guilt, there is ambivalence and confusion about Judaism, about Israel, about synagogues in the stories of my new collection, *The Family Markowitz*. And yet I view my characters' guilt and ambivalence with some perspective. Their guilt is not my own. I am interested in drawing on my heritage and my history, but I do not feel I must dramatize only one perspective on Judaism—or that I must take that perspective seriously all the time.

I practice this kind of writing—a fiction that is unapologetic and energetically ethnic, but like Ozick I bridle at the thought that this is all that I am about. What joy I felt, when after sending my new story about Rose Markowitz to Chip McGrath at *The New Yorker*, he called me to say it was a great piece of writing about—old age. It was not Rose Markowitz with her rent-controlled apartment in Washington Heights and her stepdaughter from Israel, but old age itself that he saw as the subject. And at a deep level that was the subject of the story for me as well. Of course, it is the particulars that sustain a story, the sense of place, the idiosyncrasies of speech and character. And it is the social, political, material, biographical, literary context of a story that scholars study and discuss. But I think that few writers can hide their longing to convey the universal.

My character Sarah Markowitz suffers from this longing. She is a fifty-year-old creative-writing teacher, a would-be poet and novelist, but she has not been recognized by the world. I describe her in my story "Sarah" as she sits at her desk, thinking:

> It has been difficult for her as a poet, to be influenced by Donne, Marvell, and Herbert, but to write about giving birth, a son's bar mitzvah, Yom Kippur. . . . She has pined to have a literary career, to have her work discovered by the world. This has been her dream since her school days, when she discovered John Donne and felt suddenly and secretly clever, as if, like a safecracker, she could find the puns and hidden springs in his poetry. And when she wrote her essays in college about this image and that metaphor, what she was really wondering was how to become like Shakespeare—without seeming to imitate him, of course. When would she be called into that shining multitude of poets and playwrights, mainly Elizabethan, who rose in shimmering waves before her at Queens College? She wrote her M.A. thesis in English Literature about Emma Lazarus—not about the poem on the Statue of Liberty but about her major and forgotten works, the verse plays and poems.

Many ideas passed through my mind as I wrote that passage, among them the difficulties for women Sarah's age, would-be literary women, and the difficulties for Jewish readers and writers of every age who discover the grandeur of English and American literature and then with experience come to feel that in subtle ways they are excluded from the grand tradition. Sarah has been educated by the poets of the Protestant religious experience, Donne, Herbert, Milton, but as she writes her own poetry she finds that she will not become a literary star by writing about her Jewish experience. And it is not just that she will not be a literary lion in the eyes of the world, it is that she will not be a literary star in her own terms. She has internalized the standards and the aesthetic of Protestant England's seventeenth-century poetry. At a deep level Sarah herself believes that the language of the Protestant religious experience is profound and universal, whereas the Jewish religious experience is obscure or even earthy—somehow not as well suited to the poetic, somehow neither universal nor spiritual. As I wrote about Sarah and took her point of view, I recognized how much I share with the character, how much I sympathize with her wistful aspirations. At the same time, creating Sarah's character gave me a chance to look objectively at her ideas, to examine her from the outside, and to draw boundaries between her ideas and my own. As I wrote "Sarah," I indulged my misgivings about Jewish American fiction, about women's fiction—and then, after I finished writing the story, I felt much better. I tossed aside all of Sarah's musings and I was ready to move on.

Where should Jewish American writing move? I believe that Jewish American writers must recapture the spiritual and the religious dimension of Judaism. Ted Solotaroff goes so far as to say that only by moving into this new territory, into the post-assimilated realm of tradition, can Jewish American fiction resuscitate and sustain itself. He wrote in a 1988 *New York Times Book Review* article that "As assimilation continues to practice its diluting and dimming ways, it seems evident that the interesting

Jewish bargain or edge in American fiction will be more
and more in the keeping of writers . . . who are anchored
in the present-day observant Jewish community and who
are drawn to the intense and growing dialogue between
Judaism and modernity under the impact of feminism, the
sexual revolution, and the Holocaust." Solotaroff put it in
darker terms in a 1991 interview with the Baltimore *Jewish
Times*, prophesying of Jewish American literature, "Only
those writers steeped in Judaism will survive." I think it is
a hundred years too early to tell who will survive and who
will not, but I agree wholeheartedly with Solotaroff that it
is time for Jewish American writers to use the Jewish religion as more than "shtick," to borrow Solotaroff's term. If
literary images of Judaism are to be read seriously and not
satirically or sentimentally or dismissively, they must be
written that way. There must be Jewish wedding scenes
other than that of *Goodbye, Columbus;* there must be alter-
natives to the self-deprecating rhythms of Woody Allen
and the one-liners of Neil Simon. Allen and Simon seem
to recognize this themselves. In *Crimes and Misdemeanors*,
Allen uses the family seder, not as a raucous emblem of an
overheated, distraught childhood, but as a forum for a
serious discussion of good and evil. In his autobiographical trilogy, Neil Simon moves far beyond jokes as he interprets and dramatizes life in his Jewish family.

Yes, Jewish American writers have a difficult position
in the multicultural context, but they are also confronting
an old problem—the problem of every artist. Ultimately, I
believe, all writing is ethnic writing, and all writers are
ethnic writers grappling with great ambitions and a particular language and culture. Milton dared to confront the
classical tradition in English. Faulkner used Shakespeare
and Southern dialect together. Shakespeare himself faced

the formidable tradition of the Petrarchan sonnet, dismantled it, tinkered with it, mocked it, and made it new. Every writer works to develop and express ideas and emotions in the language of the particular and the mundane, to say something new and use what is old. Each strives to make a specific cultural experience an asset instead of a liability. I look at this as an old problem, and I turn to old resources—the deep Jewish tradition beneath the self-deprecating Jewish jokes, the biblical language and the poetry welling up beneath layers of satire.

RACHEL KADISH

The Davka Method

In my childhood two conversations stand out like sur-
veying poles, marking the parameters of my cultural
upbringing.

The first was with my mother's father, an educated,
didactic refugee who just barely escaped Hitler's Poland.
He, along with my grandmother and a handful of other
family members, had survived bombardments, illegal border crossings, imprisonment in a Russian camp, and
FDR's immigration policies, rooting themselves in America for a few decades but always with an eye toward moving to Israel. My grandfather, who moved to Jerusalem the
year I was nine, was among the last to leave the United
States.

You're not safe in America, he told me. We thought
we were safe in Poland. Our non-Jewish friends turned on
us. You only *think* you can trust your non-Jewish friends.

The second conversation was with my father, whose
family has been in the United States since the turn of the
twentieth century. In 1970, when I was a baby and the
Vietnam War was at its height, my father left for a year-

long posting as a surgeon with the U.S. Air Force in Thailand. Once, when I was perhaps six years old, he made a brief reference to the pain of the separation. I asked him why he'd gone. He explained that he'd been drafted.

But couldn't he have said no?

I could have gone to Canada, he said. But I had skills that were needed, so I served my country. I believe the United States is the best country in the world to live in.

•••

My American grandmother is the only person I know who read *Moby-Dick*, in her seventies, for pleasure. Continuing her education was a lifelong habit; she, like her husband, who ran a cleaning-powder factory in Newark, had ended her formal education early to help support her family during the Depression. Her first question upon seeing me was always *Have you read anything good?* She was thoughtful, loyal, modest in her ambitions. Her house was a place of order and sense, where a visiting adult could take a long, quiet afternoon nap and wake to the smells of kitchen industry. My grandmother kept twenty-dollar bills in the sugar bowl. When the orange juice container was two-thirds full she would transfer its contents to an old mayonnaise jar, so it would take up less space in the refrigerator. She practiced the American virtue of thrift—a habit dating from back when thrift was an American virtue. She practiced the Jewish virtues of bagels and bridge. She believed in beauty parlors and saran wrap. She went to synagogue on High Holidays, took care of her family, lived right. To my grandmother, people were "good citizens" or "bad neighbors," the latter category encompassing the full range from someone who took your parking spot to Stalin. People did not blow up at one another; they simply stopped speaking. When she said someone was having an affair, she meant the catered kind.

I once described my father's family as Jewish Calvinists who take their baseball seriously. The Calvinist fire-and-brimstone attitude may not have been the right comparison, but the work ethic was. My father's family prized honest work and the American dream. They had names like Frankie and Walter, Sadie and Joe. They had football injuries. My father taught me how to fish. He taught me about being a proud American. He taught me the infield fly rule, and that peculiarly American wryness toward anyone who takes high culture too seriously.

•••

My mother's relatives had names like Bubash, Moniek, Bala, and Bezu. Before World War II, they were involved in Zionist congresses in Europe. By the time I was ten most of them were living in Israel; the rest visited often. They had lost almost every friend and loved one from prewar Poland. Itzik Stern—the character played by Ben Kingsley in *Schindler's List*—was my grandmother's cousin. The fate of the Kraków community in that film was the fate of their world.

In my childhood, my grandfather discussed politics, the Holocaust, anti-Semitism, and the state of the State of Israel on as little provocation as most Americans need to discuss the weather. For him, argument was an automatic and necessary form of intellectual calisthenics. He had a forceful opinion about everything that had to do with Jews, and much that did not. Life was not for the faint of heart; a person needed to be willing to defend his beliefs.

My mother's family were educated, proud, multilingual, voluble—capable of shouting and forgetting the outburst ten minutes later. They took ideas seriously; were dubious about a culture in which youth did not study Latin and Greek; remained profoundly Jewish even when disagreeing with everything Jewish. Education was paramount, ignorance inexcusable. An old friend of mine, who has abandoned much of his own early religious training, was recently discussing his desire for his young daughter to have a strong Jewish education. With a wink, he perfectly summarized my mother's family's worldview. *That she should be an* apikores, *but* never *an* am ha'aretz.

A heretic, but never an ignoramus.

For breakfast my mother's family ate dark crusty rye—the kind that requires you to work for every bite. The unschooled jaw aches after the encounter, but you know you've eaten *bread.*

...

My parents sent me to a Jewish day school to become a Hebrew-fluent *apikores.* My mother, whose family by this time lived almost entirely in Israel, was insistent that her three children gain some measure of fluency; my father acceded, though he worried about the impact of a religious education. Fortunately there was enough Yankee skeptic in each of us to allay his fears—none of us ended up glassy-eyed.

To this day I draw regularly on what I learned in those nine years of Jewish education. I turn to my day school background for ethical language, poetic language, comfort. Yes, there were some bad eggs—there were some small-minded people, bigots, people who walked through the world with "Is it good for the Jews?" blinders on. But they were in the minority. Judaism was, as I encountered it, a beautiful and all-encompassing system. We were taught the highest possible form of charity; the poetry of Nach-

man Bialik; the proper way to light a menorah; to write in
Rashi script; to address a letter to a Russian refusenik.

I was the only child in my class who would admit her
family did not keep kosher, but this seemed a small matter.
True: I realized with a jolt one day that despite what I'd
just parroted in my homework, I didn't believe God had
specified His will regarding the building of the Tabernacle
down to the cubit. But religion could be a parable, and
there was enough magic and wisdom and strangeness in
the Bible to absorb my curiosity. It didn't, ultimately, matter to me who had pelted the Jews with such a wealth of
story and wisdom—God or long-lost forebears.

Over every assembly hung two flags: American and
Israeli. Most of the time this seemed to pose no contradiction. But every now and then an Israeli teacher would
offer up the question, to much collective angst: Which are
you first, an American or a Jew? If there was one schizophrenia in my Jewish education, it was the matter of one's
home address. Israeli teachers schooled us in the truth
that the only authentically Jewish life was one lived in
Israel; that all Jews needed to make aliyah; that Israel
needed *people*, This Means You. I cannot recall any one of
these teachers ever explaining what he or she was doing in
the United States.

Israel was the source of our pride, the lift in our collective chin. One of my teachers had fought in the
Haganah. Another was rumored to have saved Moshe
Dayan's other eye. Israel was *real;* was in the news; was on
produce labels in the supermarket. Jews, even in the 1970s
of my childhood, couldn't quite get over this fact—had to
run their tongues over it again and again like a new tooth.
You see these shoes? They were made in Israel. Look, see
how durable. You see this cheese? It's from Israel. It's the
best cheese in the world.

Years later, a Palestinian friend would tell me she'd grown up hearing a similar litany, albeit suffused with more sorrowful emotions, from her own refugee family. You children have not seen oranges. In Jaffa there are oranges like you have never tasted. Oranges the size of basketballs.

By thirteen, when I graduated, my thoughts skipped readily between two languages. Most of the songs I knew were not in English. I could speak comfortably about the martyrdom of generations of Jews, the proper posture for saying the *amidah*, the classical music I'd studied since the age of five. I contemplated, with varying degrees of seriousness, moving to Israel.

A few months later I was in a public school with gangs and knife fights; A.P. courses and math clubs; hallways patrolled by security guards with walkie-talkies (one of the guards would soon be arrested for selling drugs to students). The talk was trashy, the hair was big, and the instruction ranged from vocational training to college-level classes. My classmates and my teachers were Chinese and Italian and Irish and African American and fill-in-the-blank. The only minority not represented in abundance was white Anglo-Saxon Protestants. Every walk of life walked those corridors.

I'd never even considered attending a Jewish high school; I'd wanted out, into the big broad world, and here I was. More than half my fellow students weren't going to college. Students showed up at school swaddling their own babies. Our athletes won trophies and got arrested, and you did not want to pick a fight with our cheerleaders. I had arrived in urban America, and I was in heaven.

I didn't know the pop singers on the radio. I didn't know the difference between Catholics and Protestants, or the name of the state's hockey team, or that "ribs" were pork. That first December I actually asked someone: What date does Christmas fall on this year?

New acquaintances drew breath, hesitating between finding my ignorance endearing or appalling. I told them to pretend I was from another planet.

•••

My maternal grandfather was the self-appointed pillar of memory, the family's teller of tales. His were stories of improbable survival. (He did not, ever, talk about the loved ones he had lost.) He counseled me, endlessly, to remember the stories of the Holocaust, stories of flight and betrayal and individual choice. If we grandchildren did not remember these stories, no one would. He charged us—a charge that was solemnly echoed in my Jewish school and summer camps—never to forget the stories of what had happened in Europe. To forget was to let the survivors' experiences wither away. To forget was to let Hitler's victims die all over again. To remember, to remember actively, was to ensure that these things could not happen again.

I have never stopped taking this message seriously. I knew the names of concentration camps when my peers were learning the names of movie stars. I knew how and where my family hid; who supported them and who failed to. I knew the unlikely path of their flight by heart—knew it so well I sometimes forgot whether it was my mother or I who was born on the run in Mexico City. When people asked where I was born, I had to stop and think.

I knew the warning signs of Hitler's rise, which my grandfather and his brother read with alarm in 1930s Kraków in the pages of *Mein Kampf.* I knew the thousand small clevernesses that had enabled my family to escape. Yes: my family had been clever, and vigilant. This was, in my grandfather's version of events, why they survived. It was not chance. Nothing so frightening as chance.

When I asserted that we were safe in America, my grandfather dug into the argument with relish. He told me stories of the Catholic colleagues with whom he had studied and worked, who had turned blank and stony faces to him when he tried to ride in their wagon while fleeing the German attack: he was not to be allowed a seat; he was a Jew.

I hate the Germans, my grandfather said to me once. I will never let go of that hate. It's all I have left.

Lying in bed at night, a child sees scenarios of the world ahead. Preparing herself is the only natural thing to do. My childhood ruminations were matter-of-fact. I kept a ranked list in my head of the countries I would flee to *If.* I speculated idly about which non-Jewish friends would help me hide. I asked myself: If I were in Amsterdam like Anne Frank, would I wear my yellow star or try to take it off? If I were in a gas chamber, would I stay high or crouch low? Should I try to put something over my mouth?

In those raw years before Spielberg put the Holocaust on a worldwide canvas, before universities offered Holocaust Studies programs and middle-school curricula had Holocaust units, my teachers and camp counselors didn't appear to linger over fine points of how to transmit history's lessons. In school we were given selections of Holocaust literature to read, then instructed to create board games involving these books' moral dilemmas, with players' fates decided by a combination of their own choices and rolls of the dice.

Night: The Board Game.

On the day appointed as Yom HaShoah (Holocaust

Remembrance Day) by my Jewish summer camp, we were divided into groups. We had to pretend to be Danish children hiding from the Nazis. We had to find ways to survive. We hid under the cabins. We ran from shelter to shelter, trying not to be caught by the guards.

I ran from shelter to shelter without being caught. Crouching alone under cabins, peering around corners. Running.

When my Jewish elementary school was spraypainted with swastikas one night, when non-Jewish neighbors threw rocks at a classmate while she and her family walked to synagogue, I knew better than to differentiate between these events and my grandfather's stories of anti-Semitism in Poland. Anti-Semitism was anti-Semitism.

Yet even then I thought: I refuse not to trust the people around me.

This was the seventies. America was tuning in to *Grease*, the Bee Gees, *Close Encounters of the Third Kind*. My generation of kids would grow up to be Generation X: cynicism-cured, immune to scandal, immune to history. Rootless and comfortably numb.

I, on the other hand, was educated to remember history. To be perennially out of step with my American generation. To keep an ear to the ground for the least tremor of anti-Semitism. To run first and ask questions later. To rent rather than buy. And never to exaggerate my own sense of safety, in light of my people's history.

Eddie Murphy used to do a routine on why no one bothers to make horror movies starring black people. It went, in paraphrase, like this:

Black man (moving his family into new home): Nice house—
Disembodied voice: *Get out.*
Black man: —too bad we can't stay.

I grew up with two paths stretched before me: the life I would live in the United States, and the life I would live if I had to flee.

•••

"How can I tell what I think," wrote E. M. Forster, "till I see what I say?" Somewhere along the line, I began to write. Somewhere along the line, I realized that writing was how I metabolized life.

Writing was the opposite of confinement—the opposite of a predetermined fate. It led me into different ways of seeing the world, let me shed my own skin and view others' experiences with empathy. It allowed me to be compassionate toward people I needed to defend against in real life. It allowed me to declare opinions I wasn't sure I believed in, and sit back and watch how they panned out.

In life I might walk with a lopsided gait between the two sides of my upbringing; in fiction, the contradictions began to seem a curiously vibrant whole.

"I've lived long among those I've invented," wrote Bernard Malamud. "Working alone to create stories, despite serious inconveniences, is not a bad way to live our human loneliness."

Using the implements available to us, we make meaning. Writing was the tool in my hand. If it had been a hammer, I would have hammered. It was a pen.

•••

The Hebrew word "davka" has no satisfactory English equivalent. "Davka" can be translated as "in spite of everything," or "wouldn't you just know it." Or "as if to spite us." Or "of all things."

I never pick up the phone in the late evening. Last night, for no particular reason, I did. And it was davka the one person in the world I did not want to talk to.

There is a drought this summer. So why davka does it have to rain on the one night we have baseball tickets?

"Davka" can also be a complete sentence. *Why did he do it? Davka.* (Translation: No reason . . . he simply did it . . . probably just to irk us.) In Hebrew, playwright-lyricist Tom Jones could have saved himself ink. *Why did the kids put beans in their ears? Davka.*

Davka is a measure of the perversity of fate. It is a measure of the universe's sense of humor, generally at our expense. It is also a measure of human stubbornness—the unaccountable will that prompts a person to set his teeth against the world, contrary to all reason.

After his strokes, my grandfather would say that he lived by what he called the davka method. So it was harder for him to go for walks now? He was davka going to go for a walk every morning. It was harder to type? He would davka undertake his memoirs.

•••

I davka trust. I assume the full humanity of the characters I write about—American, Jewish, female, or none of the above; characters seared by the Holocaust, and characters who have never heard of it. And I davka assume that readers, Jewish and otherwise, can see their humanity as well. This trust comes not out of naïveté, but its opposite. I chose, a long time ago, to believe stories can be emissaries sent to map out new possibilities for understanding. Stories are doves sent out from the ark to test whether the storm waters have receded. A world without them would be not only a less beautiful place but also a profoundly hazardous one. Writing is, I believe, a way to know others with an honesty adults usually deny each other; it is the most hopeful thing I know how to do.

In college my adviser was Toni Morrison. She was the first person who encouraged me to write about the particular themes and experiences that had shaped me. She gave me "permission" to write at an age when I felt my own voice couldn't possibly measure up to the gravity of the subject. I had the unforgettable experience of writing my senior thesis, a novel set in pre–World War II Poland, under her eye. At the time, there was heated scholarly debate about how one discussed slavery and the Holocaust—and whether these two catastrophes could possibly be compared, or whether one side's suffering was so vast it could be neither comprehended nor touched by the other.

In my meetings with my adviser, this was irrelevant. She talked about her experience researching slavery for *Beloved*; she talked about history and memory, and also warned of the seductions of tragedy. She said: You have to find something to love about every character in your fiction. Hate is too narrow a place to write from. And an avalanche of historical fact is less important, in the long run, than a clear vision of a human truth. (If a story is a dove, I soon learned, it is important not to freight it with so much History and Meaning that it cannot do what it was born to do: fly.)

In my early twenties, every line I wrote seemed to lead back to the Holocaust. I would begin a story with other things in mind, then a Holocaust survivor would politely part the curtains and enter stage left. (In the collection *The Missing Jew*, Rodger Kamenetz titles one poem "Jews Do Not Come from Heaven," and a complementary one, "They Come from Russia. . . ." In my case, Poland.) While I've yet to see this documented, I believe this to be a phenomenon of the grandchildren of Holocaust survivors: We are compulsive story gatherers. Many of our grandparents, who in the decades after the war focused on building new lives, are now facing life's end. They tell their grandchildren the stories they didn't want to impose on their own children, but don't now wish to take to the grave. And we grandchildren, freed from our parents' need to protect their own parents in those immediate postwar years, ask and ask and ask.

And then we tell those stories—relentlessly.

As I continued to write and to meet other writers, though—as I distilled family stories and brewed fiction, and helped two close non-Jewish friends research novels related to Judaism and the Holocaust (a process that felt blessedly like shifting some small portion of my own burden of memory onto trusted shoulders)—I noticed that my own writing began to alter. No longer did all roads lead to Poland. Some led to Cleveland. Some to Newark, or London. I moved on to writing about an eclectic set of subjects.

Most of what I write these days has to do with Jews, but some of it doesn't. Some of it is set in Israel, some in the United States, some elsewhere. Though I know the question is well intended, I can't help bristling a bit when asked: Are you a Jewish writer? I mistrust the question because I am not certain what the asker wants to know. *Nu*, the answer is yes: I'm Jewish. But there's something else at issue in this question—something perhaps to do with the way a writer's output is interpreted, or who has proprietary rights to an author. . . . I don't know exactly, because no one has ever explained it to my satisfaction. All I know is I respond to this question cagily, unwilling to sign up for a label that limits the range of what I am expected to write—or that urges a reader toward a narrow interpretation of my writing. Gender, too, predisposes me to resist labels. Even now, in 2005, when someone praises a novelist as a "wonderful woman writer," it is praise with an asterisk: special-interest praise, a track record set on a day with high winds. "Women's literature" is often code for "treacle." And labels can slight or misroute a writer's work. More than once I've felt compelled to approach bookstore owners who shelve Toni Morrison's novels solely in "African American literature," and gently inquire why they don't put her work on the mainstream literature shelves as well. I recognize that categories are important to scholars and students of literature, but that does not ease my discomfort when they're aimed in my direction. I am not convinced they mean me any good. So call me a Jewish writer, and I will start to pontificate (pontificate!) about artistic freedom. I will davka write about Catholic boys skipping church to go fishing.

Every writer, said Isaac Bashevis Singer, needs to have an address. But an address is simply that: an address. Not destiny, not a cage. As a writer, I glean material from what I see and read and think. In order to tell the story of one elderly Holocaust survivor, I found myself drawing on the language of the Psalms—the only language I knew that was powerful enough to convey her experiences. But the stories of a besieged Chicago schoolteacher and a burnt-out Midwestern orchestra conductor required entering worlds that were anything but Jewish. The novel I'm currently finishing is narrated by a young woman whose family connection to Judaism is so atrophied that she grew up wondering why her superstitious grandmother used to invoke the name of an Irishman: Ken O'Hara (only later does someone explain to her the meaning of *keyn eyin ha'roh*). The book is a romantic comedy of a sort, whose grist is love and feminism and the intellectual life, with Jewish themes decidedly on the back burner. When that's done, I'll return to a nonfiction book I've been researching: a book, inspired by my relatives' recent experiences, about Holocaust reparation claims and the question of what, if anything, a reparation claim repairs.

Dancing between subjects, between cultures and continents and past and present, suits me. Popular wisdom says *Write what you know*, but I can sign on to that dictum only in its broadest interpretation: *Write about the human spirit*. I've heard people assert that a man cannot successfully write about a woman, or a young person about an old one, someone African about someone Asian, and so on. To me, saying that we cannot cross these lines is equivalent to saying we cannot love across these lines—because fiction and love are predicated on the very same quality of empathy. And this is not only an unhopeful statement, but, to my mind, a dangerous one.

•••

My Polish grandfather died a decade ago. My American grandmother has receded, after a long, sad decline, into the final stages of Alzheimer's. It's arrived, of course, too soon: that juncture in adulthood when the upper generation begins to disappear, leaving one to carry all sides of an argument oneself.

I write these words, now, in a time of war, when Israel is deeply isolated and my chosen America seems profoundly off course. A time when it is difficult to feel optimism about what Mark Twain called the "damned human race."

One does not pass intact through a childhood amid

beloved Holocaust survivors without formulating some kind of a stance. I shape mine, such as it is, through a slim line of words on paper. In its refusal to simplify, sloganize, or traffic in stereotypes, in its disregard for boundaries, fiction writing is the opposite of resolving an argument. It is, at its best, the argument itself. And I, like my grandfather, argue as though argument were a somatic response to existence—like breathing, like my heartbeat. Fiction writing's grace, I think, is to embrace and sift the whole crazed picture—the American and Jewish and Israeli and Other, the refugee or the patriot, the whimsical and dark and lovely and uproarious et cetera ad infinitum. But perhaps more fundamentally, writing helps me enact this basic stubbornness: Because the world is treacherous, I davka trust that there are people of conscience, people willing to listen and care and act. I davka refuse to choose between being the granddaughter of survivors and being American. I treasure—and insist on—a freedom we too often deny ourselves: the freedom to let the world be as complicated and broken and davka beautiful as it really is.

LARA VAPNYAR

On Becoming a
Russian Jewish American

How does one know that one is Jewish?
Especially, how did one know if one was
growing up in the Soviet Union, where the
word "Jewish" was never used on television, in the newspaper, or in conversations with children, where Russian
folktales and Pushkin poems were read as bedtime stories,
where nobody practiced any kind of religion, and where
everybody decorated a New Year's tree on New Year's Eve
and expected presents from Grandpa Frost?

One usually knew when somebody told one. Most often somebody non-Jewish, and most often not in a kind way.

"I know something about you. You're a Jewess," my
classmate told me when I was six, shattering my happy
assumption that since my family lived in Moscow and
spoke Russian, we were Russians. Russians like everybody
else.

Even though I had no idea what Jewish or Jewess was,
from the tone in which my classmate spoke, I knew that it
meant to be something different, and most definitely
something inferior.

Over the years, more concrete signs of Jewishness accumulated, most acquired from non-Jewish neighbors' and classmates' remarks.

Being Jewish meant having wrong (frizzy) hair, wrong (long) nose, and wrong (thin) ankles and forearms.

It meant eating different food. Pale and bland, easy on fat and meats. "I don't want this Jewish *soupchik*," my half-Russian cousin often said.

It meant being devious. "Stop your Jewish tricks!" a salesperson yelled, when my mother sneakily tried to pick the good tomatoes from the pile.

It meant lacking the generosity and wideness of the Russian nature, the mysteriousness of the Russian soul. It meant being disgustingly timid, practical, and cautious. It meant NOT squandering all your money for vodka on your payday. As a child, I harbored a secret pride that my grandfather, unlike the other Jews we knew, drank, engaged in fights, and loved to give away family belongings when drunk. He was known to give away a kettle, a pillow, and his own reading glasses.

It meant hearing from your grandmother that even though Jewish boys made the best husbands (except possibly for my grandfather), they would marry anybody rather than a Jewish girl.

The worst was that it meant being stuck with your nationality, even if you resented it, hated it, wished that you could be anything but Jewish. "If we have to be something bad," I pleaded to my mother, "why can't we be Uzbeks or Tadzhiks? Why Jews? Why the worst?" Yet the word "Jewish" was clearly printed in all of our identification documents. It was required on all application forms, and on the class roster in school, so that even if you didn't have distinctly Jewish features or character traits, you still couldn't conceal your nationality from your teachers or classmates.

It meant, once you knew that you were stuck with being Jewish, that you learned to hate and resent people who hated and resented Jews.

The tragic part came if you happened to fall in love, as I did at an early age, with Russian literature. You were destined to have a one-sided, troubled, humiliating, torturous experience for life.

I read Gogol, Dostoyevsky, Chekhov, engrossed in the beauty of the language, captivated by the intricacy of the psychology, moved to tears by the power of emotions, longing to identify with those mysterious, beautiful, tragic, complex characters, yet feeling that those characters refused to identify with me. Here and there on the pages of my favorite authors emerged the little, dirty, smelly, devious, disgusting people incapable of beauty and grandeur. Those people were Jews. Those people were me.

I wished I could hate or disregard Chekhov and Dostoyevsky, the way I hated or disregarded my neighbors who squandered their money on the first day of the month, or classmates who failed their math tests and couldn't spell in their own dear Russian language. They whispered "the dirty Jew" behind my back because they were stupid. I could live with their hatred and repulsion. I couldn't live with Chekhov's! Yet, once I was hooked on him, I couldn't exist without reading him either. Again and again I would pick a book and lose myself in the beauty and subtlety of his stories, then invariably cringe in pain at another of his references to Jews. I behaved just like a scorned lover who couldn't help but try to be near the object of her love, no matter how painful it was for her.

Then at the age of thirteen I had a revelation. I read *Ivanhoe* and realized that it was Rebecca who really won Ivanhoe's heart, not Lady Rowena. Like most Soviet teenagers, I'd been familiar with the plot of *Ivanhoe* from the popular Russian movie loosely based on Walter Scott's novel. In the movie, both Ivanhoe and the bad guy (whatever his name was) were in love with Lady Rowena. They fought over Rowena. Rebecca was just a minor character with a couple of minutes of screen time. The moviemakers lied! They wanted to conceal the power of a Jewish beauty.

Shortly afterward, I read in some biographical book that Chekhov was powerfully drawn to Jewish women, was afraid of them, and hated them for that. The answer was right there. We were superior. They were afraid of us, and that's why they hated us. Ivanhoe and Chekhov showed me a way to deal with my Jewish identity.

"You know what I want to become when I grow up?" I asked my Jewish girlfriend. "I want to become a great Jewish beauty and defeat all the men." My friend looked at me doubtfully, but I firmly believed that it was the spirit, not physical attributes, that made Great Jewish Beauties.

A terrible fate might have struck men of the Soviet Union if, in a few years, either doubtful of my seductive powers or for some other reason, I hadn't swerved from my chosen direction. My new goal was to leave Russia for the United States. Perestroika was in bloom at that time, emigration stopped being a horrible ordeal, and every Jew who could afford to leave was leaving. I no longer believed that Jewish people were all that superior and that love was the only field in which a Jewish person could thrive. There were others, more exciting fields such as science, art, literature, and I was sure that as an American Jew, I'd have no trouble in finding out which one was for me.

But once in the United States, I realized that I couldn't be either American or Jewish. My Jewish identity, which I used to loathe and which I'd learned to embrace only a few years earlier, seemed to have existed only in the eyes of my Russian compatriots. Compared to American Jews, I felt no right to be called Jewish at all. What exactly was it that was Jewish about me? My nose? My hair? The nationality in my abandoned Soviet passport? Suddenly the designation seemed too small, too insignificant, ridiculous even, in light of my complete lack of knowledge of Jewish history and my ignorance of most Jewish writers, philosophers, and artists. I knew that with my atheist upbringing, I would never be able to accept any kind of religion, including Judaism. I once walked up the steps to the heavy door of a Brooklyn synagogue, but I froze with my hand on the knob, unable to go farther. I felt like an impostor.

I wasn't an American either. For one thing I didn't speak the language with the necessary fluency. More than that, I knew that I would never speak the language without sounding like a foreigner. I didn't know American history or understand American culture. I didn't get American jokes. Worse than that, all the Americans I met in New York seemed so different that I couldn't find unifying features to define them, couldn't determine what it was that made them Americans. The Americans, on the other hand, defined me easily. They defined me as a Russian.

In the United States, I was effortlessly granted the identity I had been so viciously denied before. I became a Russian. And regardless of whether I liked it or not, I realized that I probably was Russian. I was definitely more Russian than anything else. I had a degree in Russian. Russian was the only language I spoke fluently, Russian literature and history were the only ones I had a passable knowledge of. I had a strong liking for familiar Russian food, Russian customs, and Russian scenery. Of course, I was Russian in the eyes of others, but not in my own eyes. I couldn't possibly accept the identity of a people who had called me a dirty Jew. I would rather be a nobody, a rootless immigrant adrift in a foreign land.

Then, miraculously, I gained all three seemingly unattainable identities (Russian Jewish American) by acquiring a new and most unexpected identity—that of a writer. My book of short stories is listed in each of three categories: American first novelists; Russia—social customs; and Jews—history. In reviews I'm now called a Russian American, a Jewish American, a Russian Jew, or— if the reviewer is not afraid of excess—a Russian Jewish American writer.

Some people can pinpoint a moment when they decided to become writers, but it is easier to find a moment when a certain book or a story was conceived. "There Are Jews in My House" came to me in one of the dark rooms of the Holocaust Museum in Washington, D.C. I was gazing at a picture of a crowd of people at some train station on the threshold of a concentration camp. They were all so different, city dwellers and peasants, educated and uneducated, rich and poor, believers and nonbelievers. Yet there was something unifying about them that allowed Nazis to identify them as Jews, annihilate them, and put them all in one pile of bodies. I would have been in that pile, if I was there, regardless of my upbringing, regardless of whether other Jews accepted me or not. That moment I knew with the utmost certainty that I was Jewish, whatever that meant. I also knew that one day I would have to write a story about the Holocaust.

I wrote "There Are Jews in My House," the story about the historical tragedy of anti-Semitism, and then another story about my personal trauma of being Jewish in Russia. I wrote them the only way I knew how, as a Russian greatly influenced by Russian writers, who are still my painful favorites. I wrote them in English, the language I feel the most comfortable with, even though I often struggle with grammar and vocabulary. I would even say that I wrote in American, which for me became the language of immigrants, who come from all over the world bringing their stories, their cultures, and their pain.

Recently I got the news that *There Are Jews in My House* would be translated into Hebrew. I'm always overjoyed when my book gets translated into another language. But only the news of Hebrew made me cry. Somehow, it felt like my book, full of Jewish emotions, conceived through the Russian culture, and realized in American English, had come full circle.

TOVA MIRVIS

Writing Between Worlds

I do some of my best writing in shul. Not with pen and paper, not with my computer, all of which are forbidden on the Sabbath, but in my head. What moves me to write is the gap created in shul, the contrast between worlds: the public and the personal, the holy and the prosaic. People sit in rows, their siddurs open to the same page, and recite the prescribed prayers. They stand when the ark is opened, kiss the Torah scroll's velvet cover as it is carried past, bow at the knee as they begin the silent *Shemoneh Esrei.* These prayers ask for cohesion, everyone saying the same thing at the same time. The words are scripted, claiming to articulate what is in the heart.

Spliced seamlessly into these sacred words is another more human, more interesting world. Here, alternate, private prayers are formed. Here, minds wander. People glance at their watches. They daydream and whisper. Silent, inner words coexist with the outer public ones. Underneath the beauty of the prayers, inside the appearance of shared ideology and practice, I wonder who believes and who doesn't, and who is here because they want to be and who because they have been forced to come. In shul, the gap between the words we say and who we are becomes more pronounced. Lofty moments of yearning commingle with mundane moments. Both exist simultaneously, so richly, so exquisitely.

It isn't just in others that I wonder about this gap. I feel it in myself all too well. I know that I'm not really praying, at least not usually, at least not very well. I practically grew up in shul. Every Shabbos, in Memphis, Tennessee, in a purple-and-silver Orthodox shul resembling a disco, I sat in the women's section, next to my mother, one row behind my grandmother, my view obfuscated by the domes and decorations of grand hats and the *mechitza* that separates the men from the women. Now, I still daven in an Orthodox shul. The words of the prayers still come naturally. But it's harder to feel moved by them. I am still part of this Orthodox world but at the edge, looking outward. I have one foot inside and one foot stepping out. This dangling act, this living between worlds, is unresolved and probably unsustainable. It's not a comfortable place to live. But it's a very fertile place from which to write.

...

Orthodox Judaism has so many rules: what to eat, when to eat, what to wear, when to pray. The great works of traditional Judaism are not narrative; they are codes of law, the Mishnah, the Shulchan Aruch, the Mishnah Brurah. Here, every moment of life is categorized and examined. Creating categories is crucial to Jewish law. Underlying much of halacha is the need to make distinctions, to separate between holy and secular, between night and day, between Israel and the other nations. There are divisions in space, in time. The Sabbath is holiness in time; the land of Israel, the holy temple, are holiness in space. There are divisions between men and women, between the priestly caste and the rest of the people. There are commandments not to mix species, for men not to wear women's clothing. The laws draw clear lines; they create and enforce strict borders.

But in day-to-day life, the borders aren't demarcated with the grand strokes of theology. They are constructed from thousands of tiny details. Orthodoxy is about minutiae; the law resides in the smallest particulars of domestic life. Clothing, food, and furnishings are never incidental. They have become the stuff of God. Seemingly unimportant details, with no clear theological origin, bespeak major statements and have taken on the force of law. "There, nothing goes and everything matters—here everything goes and nothing matters," Philip Roth wrote, comparing the old Eastern Europe and America. The Orthodox world bears great resemblance to that Eastern Europe. Everything matters. Everything means something. Ideology can be determined from the tilt of a hat. Marriage prospects are decided, and a whole world is transmitted, in the absence or presence of a seam down the back of a stocking.

All these details, these rules, do more than just restrict behavior. They hold people tightly together, creating a hotbed of community. Every individual action has an echo in a communal forest. With eyes and ears lurking everywhere, nothing goes unseen or unheard. For me, as a writer, community is always primary. Both of my novels have been set within the Orthodox world. My first novel was about an outsider longing for community and trying to become part of an insular Orthodox community in Memphis. But it is narrated by the insiders, and ultimately, it is about them. My second novel is about the confrontation between tradition and modernity, about doubt and tolerance, about wanting to be inside this world and wanting to be outside it.

Happily for the fiction writer, communities bestow more than just rules. They offer the possibility for rebellion. Flannery O'Connor said, "Whenever I'm asked why Southern writers particularly have a penchant for writing about freaks, I say it is because we are still able to recognize one." In a well-ordered, tightly constructed community there are always insiders. And only when there are insiders can there be outsiders, strangers and freaks, this rich cast of characters that a fiction writer longs for.

I learned about community as much from my Southern background as from my Jewish one. In the South, where you're from and who you're related to are the first questions asked of someone. I am a sixth-generation Memphian and am related, one way or another, to practically everyone. More than anything, growing up in Memphis taught me how to listen to the voices of a community, to hear its unsaid but certain opinions. I learned, though, that this communal voice speaks not in its highest moments, not through its most learned, important members. Rather, a community speaks most honestly through its gossip, this supposedly trivial activity taking place off to the side—in the women's section of the shul, in the aisles of a grocery store, under the hair dryers of a beauty parlor. But in a community where the details are domestic and all-important, the largest issues are played out in these seemingly small, often female spaces. Gossip is the animating voice of these spaces, and through what is talked about and what is not, it reveals most clearly what a community values and fears.

Though O'Connor's Mississippi was just a short drive from my house, it was supposedly worlds away from my Orthodox Memphis. But I recognized the voices of her characters. This was true of Eudora Welty and William Faulkner as well. In their rich, complex evocations of community, I saw my own world clearer. I cannot imagine Eudora Welty's characters without community surrounding them, without these whispering, gossiping, all-seeing and all-knowing voices. The communities in which she places her characters, plots, and themes are not merely the side story of "setting." They are equal to her characters and plots and themes. In *The Golden Apples*, a member of the community comments that "In Morgana, most destinies were known to everybody and seemed to go without saying." Communities serve as measuring sticks; there is always a norm from which to deviate. For Faulkner, community is equally pervasive and inescapable. In "A Rose for Emily," an old woman presumably murders a lover and then keeps his body in her house. Faulkner tells this story from the communal perspective, in the first person plural, a voice which inspired the narrative choice in my first novel. In his short story, murdered lovers are interesting, but not as interesting as the community's take on this. The presence of a community observing and wondering magnifies every individual action. Without the question of What will they think? the fictional world becomes so much thinner.

•••

The writer wrestles with her own question of What will they think? In order to write about a community, you have to hear their voices, this ubiquitous "they" of public opinion. You have to know what they are proud of and afraid of, what they wish you would say, what they fear you will say. You have to know your subject matter so well that you can narrate a story from their perspective, until you could almost, almost quiet your objections, quell your restlessness, and become one of them again.

But for a writer, this is impossible. The official communal point of view always, eventually, must be pushed aside in favor of the individual voices that bubble up underneath. Fiction reveals what people might think but don't say, or what they won't let themselves think or don't notice or simply don't believe. The goal can't be to protect or affirm, which it inevitably becomes when you live fully, deeply, wholeheartedly inside the borders. To see a community clearly, you have to be willing to expose, to look not only from up close but from a distance. You can live within but need to make forays, imaginative and otherwise. The writer is a spy, slinking back and forth over well-delineated borders. The spy is essentially an outsider everywhere. But he or she is also an insider. By moving back and forth, the spy has the clearest sense of exactly where the border lies.

In the Torah, the spies Moses sends out to survey the land are guilty of the sin of *lashon harah:* they speak evil of the land. They are not accused of lying. Rather, they are guilty of telling the truth, for seeing the land as it actually is as opposed to how it ideally can be. Indeed, little has changed. Often, in tight-knit communities—and for me, most notably, in the Orthodox community where I've set my two novels—the worst crime a writer can commit is airing the dirty laundry in public. The dispute is rarely with the veracity of the portrayal. It is with the very act of telling. The writing is judged by whether it's "positive," whether it's "nice." Inside the protest of "negative" is, I think, the wish to believe that there is no story. The only acceptable discovery is that—what a relief!—nothing lies underneath, except for more sameness, more Orthodoxy.

But there is always a story. In the inner life, there are no orthodoxies. It is the writer's job to chip away at any insistence otherwise. Peer under a yarmulke, and what's there? Flip back a wig, lift one long skirt, and what do you find? This is not to say, of course, that the narrative of Orthodoxy must always be one of rebellion, that this is the only story that can emerge from such a world. But it is a useful and telling narrative because it explores not just what is outside but what is inside as well. By putting pressure on a world, by crossing lines, you can see both sides— what is rejected and what is valued—more clearly.

Here's a true story that gets me thinking in the middle of the night and writing early in the morning: Two girls from Borough Park, Frumchy and Elky, ran away from their ultra-Orthodox homes. Swearing they'd never come back, looking for the farthest place from Brooklyn they could find, they took a bus to Arizona, lived in a rundown neighborhood, lied about their ages, and tried to get jobs. Here it is, the potboiler novel of outsized rebellion, the coming-of-age story, the frum girls' novel of high adventure. The writer's mind begins to thrum. Which temptations of the outside world beckon first? Where do they begin? How do they end?

But in order to qualify as heroines, Frumchy and Elky don't have to cast off their long skirts and step happily into an unshackled modern life. Even fictional narratives about rebellion need not follow the path of entropy, from order to disorder, from belief to disbelief. I don't need large rebellions. Small acts of transgression will suffice. Give me the stirring of a forbidden thought, a quiet chafing against a rule. In religious literature, lots of stories tell of the way in. In secular literature, lots of stories tell of the way out. But the streets don't have to run only in one direction. They can double back and wind around in complicated, paradoxical patterns. Stories come from the tensions, the oscillations, the struggles, and the compromises. Without ambivalence in either direction, the intersections are gone, the conflicts are blanched, and in its place everything is parve.

In this case of Frumchy and Elky, life supplies the most resonant plot line, and also the quietest. In Arizona, the two girls spent most of their time shopping for blue jeans. They eventually were persuaded by their families to come home, but they returned clutching their shopping bags. Now the story seemingly shrinks and becomes less sensational: from grand adventure and high rebellion to sheepish return. Suddenly the story is about something so mundane as clothing. But Frumchy and Elky know, and the knowledgeable observer knows too, that their story is still large and subversive, maybe more so. In their shopping bags the girls carry more than jeans. They bring home pop culture and America and adolescence and sex. With one seemingly small action, they challenge their whole world.

•••

But Frumchy and Elky's jeans are the perfect ending to their story only when the desire for jeans is recognized as forbidden, only when this seemingly ordinary attire is imbued with religious and cultural overtones. When all this must be explained, the implicit power is diminished. In writing about traditional Judaism, there is a continual problem of language, of invoking words or concepts or rituals beyond Shabbos and challah, beyond shul. How can these be incorporated into a novel without italics, without a glossary? To use the actual language is crucial for any true rendering of this world. In deleting potentially incomprehensible words, the rhythms and authentic voice of a novel are put at risk. To write with this dilemma is to write in your native language yet be writing in translation.

But perhaps that is the most fitting way to write about the traditional world when it is transplanted to America. Because that world is lived in translation too. A Jew steeped in ritual or texts is always something of an immigrant, in time, not just in space. No matter how many generations one's family has lived in America, to live according to Jewish law is to live knowingly out of step with the outside world. It is to live in the suburbs, in Teaneck or New Rochelle or Memphis, but to cast a glance back over the shoulder at Babylonia and Yavneh, Vilna and Lublin. Sixteenth-century texts are not history, not legend, not myth. They are alive and binding, a means of deciding what may be eaten, what may be thought, what may be worn, during every minute, every day.

And yet, while heart and mind may be in the holy temple of Jerusalem and the great yeshivas of Babylonia and the shtetls of Eastern Europe, the rest of the body is still very much in twenty-first-century America. Despite its protests to the contrary, Orthodoxy has become thoroughly American. Yarmulkes are emblazoned with Yankees slogans and Nike insignias. Sushi is certified kosher and served, as if halachically required, at the smorgasbord of every Orthodox wedding. The outside world has seeped in even to those communities that profess to shun it. But this has always been the case. Jewish culture comes not from the whole, not from the unadulterated. Rather, it is an amalgam of intersecting worlds. Straddling several worlds, living between them, is essential to the Jewish experience.

Perhaps this is why the oft-asked question Are you a Jewish writer? is so fraught. Ask it and watch the stampede for the door. This is true even for my generation of young writers, who are supposedly comfortable writing about tradition, who are at home with Jewish texts and rituals.

This is of course the most Jewish of protests, and underlying it is, I think, a fear of being viewed as limited, as if being intimately knowledgeable about one world precludes the ability to see and know other ones. It is also a refusal to settle down firmly inside any set of borders, to live too deeply in any one place. For me, this is a familiar spot, a familiar straddle. I am happy to call myself a Jewish writer, a Southern writer, a woman writer. I am fully all of these; they are my sources of material, they are my language and my sensibility. But at the same time, I never think about such labels when I write. There isn't time, or room, for such a consideration. When I write, I don't consider myself anything. I don't live anywhere. I don't belong to anyone. I can stand in one place, in one particular shul or another, and be somewhere else at the same time. In life, there are so many restrictions, some I will hold on to, others I have and will discard. But in writing, I don't have to do either. I can move back and forth across borders. Legal categories draw lines. Writing blurs them.

DARA HORN

On the Interpretation of Dreams

I learned how to tell stories, as has been the custom in Jewish life for centuries, by being thrust on stage against my will. Traditionally this doesn't happen until the bar mitzvah, when one is sufficiently sullen, awkward, and antisocial to be more aware of who is listening than of the story one is asked to recite. But for me this rite of Jewish adulthood took place at a much younger age—when my three siblings and I were first invited, from that fateful night forward, to join our parents at the dinner table.

This was a big deal. The four of us are very close in age, and while we were still in high chairs, my mother established a strict two-seating kitchen policy: the children ate first, and she and my father ate later. No child was allowed to join the parents at the adult dinner table unless he could reasonably be expected to participate in a dining event for more than twelve minutes without inserting some type of legume into his nose. And once we finally reached this threshold, we faced severe culture shock. At the children's table, my mother had forged order from chaos by reading aloud to us during the entire meal, riveting us with stories of all kinds so as to distract us from our primary goal of inhaling our food. But now, to our astonishment, we were expected to provide the stories ourselves. Every night at the adults' table, I and my three siblings were instructed, each in turn, to "tell us about your day."

The concept baffled me. Was this what adults did? Talk about their *days?* What could possibly have happened during my boring day at school that could live up to all the stories my mother had read to us from books? But my siblings, long accustomed to fighting for attention, were not so easily squelched. At the end of the table was a bay window with a large windowsill. It was my older sister who first turned it into a stage, climbing up with an imaginary microphone in her fist and *performing* her day, complete with choreography, voice-overs, and vivid impressions of all the characters involved. I watched her "tell about her day" and was stunned by how six hours' worth of fifth grade could be transformed into a tragicomic opera that had both parents and children rolling on the floor. What actually happened in our days, I soon understood, was nothing more than report-card fodder. What mattered for the telling was what we ourselves determined the story to be, our own interpretations of our dreams. A few years later, when I found myself onstage in the synagogue to read from the Torah as a bat mitzvah, in what would later become a weekly job, the task felt strangely familiar. I was telling a story, except this time, everyone already knew how the story would end. What mattered most was how I managed to tell it.

•••

There is a passage in the Book of Genesis where Joseph, after his interpretations of dreams have driven his brothers to sell him into slavery and induced the Egyptian pharaoh to hire him as second-in-command, confronts his brothers, who have come to Egypt seeking relief from famine. For a few chapters he hides his identity, testing them until he finally breaks down and admits who he is, to his brothers' astonishment. But a few verses later, Joseph surprises not only his brothers but the reader as well. "Now don't despair or be angry at yourselves because you sold me to this place," he tells his dumbstruck brothers, "because it was to save life that God sent me ahead of you." Joseph's brothers thought they were destroying their brother's life, but in fact they were setting him in place to save them, years later, from famine. They had moved through the events of the previous years as if they were hikers at the bottom of a canyon being watched by someone at the top of the cliff: the hikers may make their own choices, turning onto one trail or another, but the lookout already knows where they are headed long before they arrive, seeing, from above, what lies at the end of each trail.

I mention this story not only because I occasionally identify with it, as many children from larger-than-average families do (sometimes as Joseph, sometimes as one of his brothers). I mention it because it is an example of what I consider the Jewish people's most important contribution to world literature: a story whose ending is preordained, but whose action unfolds precisely because of the characters' free will. It is not a blind fulfillment of prophecy like Oedipus's oracle, but something far more subtle and complex, the paradox that stands between our responsibility for what we are and our inability to know what we have the power to become.

The truth is that there is no such thing as a story in real life. It is only pure belief, a belief kept secretly by even the staunchest of atheists and rationalists, that protects us from realizing this brutal fact. Things that happen to us, if we dared to see beyond our deep faith in life's meaning, are utterly random, unrelated, no more meaningful than the movement of the continents or the rise and fall of mountains. Our lives may be a sequence of events, a series of things that happened in our "day" at school or work or wherever we may have been, but a sequence of events alone is not a story. As E. M. Forster aptly put it, the sentence "The king died, then the queen died" does not have a plot, but the sentence "The king died, then the queen died of grief" does. A sequence of events becomes a narrative only by virtue of the meaning that the storyteller interprets as connecting those events. This has been true ever since ancient people opened their mouths to describe the world they lived in, inscribing meaning onto thin air and then onto blank earth. What the Jews added to this was the belief that the world itself not only had an author, but an author who allowed his characters—as most authors ultimately do—to take the lead, even while watching where they go and knowing where their paths will end. The Mishnah advises us that "Everything is foreseen, yet freedom of choice is granted." We are assured that our lives and dreams have meaning, even if we do not always see it. What is desperately needed are storytellers, Josephs, who know how to interpret the dreams.

But there is a deeper paradox at work when Joseph reveals himself to his brothers, and which forms an even greater part of the Jewish contribution to literature. Immediately after admitting who he is, Joseph asks his brothers, "Is my father still alive?"

It's an illogical question in the story; in previous chapters, before revealing his identity, Joseph has already heard the answer. But when he asks it now, it means something more. Commentators claim that this question refers not to Joseph's father, Jacob, but to God, a question that Jews have asked for the past four thousand years—and the question, unpunctuated in the original Hebrew, is answered simply by being asked. But I believe the real reason why Joseph asks this question, and why this question matters, is far more personal. After years of separation from his family, with no one to take pride in his accomplishments or to be disappointed by his failures, Joseph is asking the question we all ask each day—not only of God, but of our own parents as well, whether living or dead. The question Is my father still alive? means: Is there someone looking over my shoulder, watching the choices I make in my thousand daily decisions between action and indifference, between honesty and vanity, between generosity and stubbornness, between good and evil? Is someone drawing the plot lines that connect my choices to their consequences, feeling proud or disappointed by the paths I choose to follow? Does someone know where all of this is going? Does someone care?

All narrative is driven by belief. Jewish narrative, at least for the past four thousand years, has been driven by the belief, no matter how denied or unacknowledged, that someone is listening, that our father, and our fathers, are still alive. As the Hasidic rebbe and storyteller Nachman of Bratslav put it, "When a person dies, he does not go from one room to another. He goes to the opposite side of the same room."

I am even luckier than Joseph; my own parents both still stand on the same side of the room as me and my siblings. But now I understand why they encouraged us to get up onstage for our stories: so that when they inevitably cross to the other side of the room, they will be able to see us better.

...

I would like to propose a new, narrow definition of Jewish literature: Jewish literature is a contemporary commentary on ancient Jewish texts. I don't suggest this in order to define a canon, or to limit what books might be called Jewish books, or even because it is something I expect to believe for longer than the time it takes me to write this essay. I suggest it, rather, to expand the possibilities for the authors who create such books, to allow them to broaden what can be an extremely narrow vision, even in the most supposedly universal works.

Jewish literature in English tends to be defined, whether consciously or not, as literature about Jewish characters. What makes these characters Jewish? Often in American Jewish literature, the answer has been anti-Semitism. The activities of these characters that make them Jewish usually involve hand-wringing over being different—and the entire question of assimilation is of course nothing more than an outgrowth of anti-Semitism, an urge to fit in simply because we have been told that we do not. But what the public really eats up, the Jewish writer knows, is when the characters' Jewish activities include something that the wider non-Jewish audience knows as the only significant thing that has ever happened to Jews—being hated, mocked, excluded, or, most marketably, murdered (preferably in the Holocaust). Being the recipients of these actions, and contending with the emotional fallout they bring with them, is what makes these characters Jewish.

I don't mean to suggest that this aspect of Jewish history doesn't deserve to be explored in fiction, and there are obviously many excellent books that explore it. But I am suggesting that this approach to Jewish literature is not only potentially limiting, but ultimately a very depressing reflection of how much American Jews, even people my age who are only now beginning to experience the rumblings of anti-Semitism, seem to have internalized the idea that what makes us Jewish is the fact that other people either secretly or explicitly hate us. For Jews writing in a non-Jewish language, and ultimately for an audience that will include non-Jewish readers, is there a way out of this trap of Jewish literature, a way to tell a story worth telling to the Jewish community and simultaneously to those outside it?

I don't pretend to know, but I know that I tried to find one. While I was writing my first novel, I was studying early modern Hebrew and Yiddish literature and became extremely jealous. The authors I was reading had written contemporary secular stories, but they would often incorporate the language of ancient religious texts into their work. To them, Jewish literature was not a question of characters but of language—not simply of writing in a Jewish language (though that too was usually a conscious choice), but of doing what Jewish literature in Jewish languages has always done, which is to create, however obliquely, a commentary on the Torah: an answer of some kind to the question, Is my father still alive? Even when they were writing against religion (which, for many of them, was almost always), these writers made their works rich and exciting not by "breaking away" from tradition, but precisely by using it, however ironically—by drawing from the Hebrew Bible and religious texts in ways that were wholly unexpected, adding layers of meaning both to their own works and to the works from which they drew. I wondered if it might be possible to create something that could honestly be called Jewish literature in English, a work that owed its life and its language less to Chaucer or Shakespeare or Cather or Faulkner or the contemporary American and Commonwealth authors who crowd today's bookstore shelves, than to Agnon and Manger and Bialik and Peretz and Berdichevsky and Mendele and Nachman and the Brody singers and the Purim players and Luzzatto and Yehudah Halevi and Shmuel Hanagid and the *paytanim* and the *amoraim* and the *tanaim* and the psalmist and the prophets and the endless others who, even with all their other influences, still consciously wrote their stories by adding their own letters to an unfinished scroll, in a continuous chain leading back to Joseph's question, "Is my father still alive?"

Without knowing in advance where the path might lead, I found myself writing a book in English that could have been written in a Jewish language, with allusions to Jewish religious sources—sometimes explicit, sometimes not—seeping in almost by accident, in the same way that one's writing absorbs any thoughts or images or sounds or feelings that take up space in one's mind. As things happened, I wound up with a story of several characters, spread across centuries and continents, who were each consumed by the question of whether their father—or their mother, or their husband, or their wife, or their friend, or their language, or their memory, or their faith— was still alive. Somewhere along the way, as I watched these characters from my perch above the page, I realized that a few of them were meandering into the Book of Job, an unfortunately popular destination for characters in both literature and life, and I failed to stop them. But I didn't realize that in the process, I was really writing a book about the country in which these characters ultimately gathered, about the freedom that America gives us—so similar to the biblical promise of free will—to determine who we are, and the burden and the blessing of having to make that choice, of deciding who we want to be without knowing who we might become.

In America, Jews have become Josephs in Egypt, former strangers who have risen to prominence through a talent for interpreting dreams—in this case, the American one. And in a world without pharaohs, we may well remain here indefinitely of our own free will. But both past and future become nothing more than a series of meaningless days unless we manage to create a story out of them, to not merely dream dreams but to interpret them, to continue asking the ancient question, Is my father still alive?

My own answer is this: He is on the other side of the room, standing behind us, breathing quietly over our shoulders as he listens to our stories, waiting to see if we will notice.

YAEL GOLDSTEIN

When God's Your Favorite Writer

I t was during the presidential election of 2000 that I finally discovered what kind of Jew I was. Asked to name his favorite political philosopher, George W. Bush thought a moment, and then replied "Jesus." An uproarious laugh erupted in my living room, as it did in living rooms across the Democratic swaths of the country. We would continue laughing for weeks, egged on by the media—but I felt my first kinship with the candidate. I thought to myself, *What's so funny about that? My favorite author is God.* That was when I first struck on the idea of a writerly Jew.

Though the term "writerly Jew" is clearly just the old familiar "Jewish writer" with the words reversed, a writerly Jew is something altogether different from a Jewish writer; "writerly Jew" is not a literary category at all. A writerly Jew is simply someone whose entire sense of herself *as* Jewish consists in stories. When a writerly Jew thinks of her Jewishness she thinks of these stories, and when she thinks of these stories she feels very Jewish. You might say that she is only Jewish when she's inside these stories, but chances are, if they mean enough to her to form her religious identity, she is, in a sense, in them always. This is certainly the case with me and my stories, the tales of the Hebrew Bible. That timeworn anthology will always saturate my thoughts, so that hardly anything passes through them without picking up a faint biblical scent, no matter how far I travel from the fold.

I was born as a writerly Jew only a few years ago. I used to be an Orthodox Jew, and had an overpowering sense of myself as Jewish, one that obviated my need to cast around for my connection to Judaism: I was a Jew because I believed that God had dictated His sacred texts to Moses in the desert; because my daily life was guided by millennia-old rituals; because half my school day was conducted in an archaic form of Hebrew that hasn't been spoken in thousands of years; because I wore long, ill-fitting jean skirts, and believed my shins and elbows to be taboo. When I arrived at college I ceased being an Orthodox Jew about as quickly as it took me to unpack, but I picked up another off-the-rack Jewish identity, becoming a social Jew. As a social Jew there wasn't much identity-mulling to be done either. I was a Jew because on Friday nights I sometimes went to the Hillel, because I understood why the word *pheh* was funny, because all the other former Jewish Day School students knew me. I could do absolutely nothing Jewish for months at a time and still be a peripheral part of the Jewish "scene," occupying a place as one of the resident heretics, an enviable position I wish I could have held on to forever.

It was only after college that I ceased to be any sort of Jew with a label. I wasn't a practicing Jew because I didn't practice, nor a social Jew because my Jewish community was gone. I wasn't even a socially conscious or political

Jew because I occupy a murky, ill-defined place between the Jewish liberal and the Jewish neoconservative. Yet I felt very Jewish, and the fact that I couldn't say quite what made me so Jewish bothered me a great deal. When friends said, "You're so un-Jewish"—I don't think this was meant as a compliment exactly, but it was only uttered by other "un-Jewish" Jews—I replied, "Are you nuts?" but I had no follow-up retort to prove their deep, deep wrongness. (Though I suspect that the desire to prove the deep, deep wrongness of people holding false positions is very Jewish.)

And then came the presidential election of 2000, and the thought that maybe what makes me so Jewish is that my favorite author is God.

I say my favorite author is God—and not the J, P, D, x, y, z biblical authorship conglomerate—and I have a good reason for putting it this way, a reason that has nothing to do with religious faith (my Orthodox upbringing notwithstanding). The interlocking jumble of myths, truths, and rules known as the Old Testament is hopelessly enmeshed in my mind with the voice of a narrator—sonorous, all-knowing, all-powerful, unpredictable, and fierce—whom I no longer believe in as a deity, but whom I still believe in as something else: as a dead grandparent, perhaps, someone who used to be around a lot, whom I used to love, and who used to enchant me with tales of my ancestors. It's not only the stories, but that narrator too—rattling around in my head, scolding or comforting from the grave—that makes me feel my Jewishness. In fact, I'd say it's the narrator—as much in his death as an object of my faith as in his lingering life as an object of my fond and intimate memory—that single-handedly makes me a writerly Jew.

I first fell in love with the voice of God and the stories it told on the juice-splattered floor of Mrs. Shlussel's nursery school classroom, between the yellow-painted cinderblock walls halfheartedly enlivened by the dancing letters of the English and Hebrew alphabets. On Friday afternoons we broke from the regular grind of learning how to count and how to share and celebrated the impending Sabbath. We would sing for a while, and then the two children chosen as that week's Mother and Father would preside over our mock Sabbath meal, handing out paper cups filled with grape juice and little bits of challah. (Due to what I must generously interpret as an oversight, I was never made the kerchief-covered Shabbos Mother, a painful slight that may or may not have had something to do with my eventual alienation from religion.) And then Mrs. Shlussel would sit us down and tell us the fabulous story that comprised that week's *parsha*, or portion, of the Torah.

I cannot possibly overstate how riveted I was by these weekly exploits of Abraham and Sarah, Isaac and Rebecca, and those star-crossed lovers Jacob and Rachel, or adequately describe the strange, loving intimacy I harbored toward the characters. All I can say is that I felt the breath of God descend around me in the stuffy room along with Mrs. Shlussel's tobacco-addled voice, and all those characters along with it. For me the Sabbath would begin then, and not hours later when my mother lit the candles and covered her eyes in prayer: time would slow and become more fluid, so that millennia lapped up against each other, and the biblical world entered into our own. Our worlds would remain fused throughout the slow and quiet hours of the Sabbath—truly a timeless time for an Orthodox Jew, when most amenities of modern life become taboo:

electricity, cars, even pen and paper—and would only separate on Saturday night when I held the twisted strands of
wax in my hand for the havdalah, and my father pronounced the magic words *hamavdil ben kodesh lichol,* "to
separate between the sacred and the profane." For a few
seconds then the air around me would feel empty and
thin: the holy had fled, and the holy, in my mind, was that
God-filled, sand-soaked era hovering near.

For the sake of honesty, I should probably mention
that the Bible wasn't the only set of stories that had this
grip on me. *D'Auliere's Book of Greek Myths* was just as holy
in my eyes, and Cinderella worship was my first religion. I
loved Abraham, Isaac, and Sarah, for much the same reason that I loved Apollo, Athena, and Cinderella: because
they were grand and larger than life, but also so rich and
alive, so full of pathos and ambiguity, that they often felt
more familiar to me than many of my classmates, whose
inner minds and characters were remote and mysterious in
contrast. (Fighting over building blocks I could not
understand; killing your sibling out of jealousy I could.) At
that point, then, I suppose, I could have just as easily
become a writerly pagan, or a writerly agnostic, or a
writerly Disney employee.

But it was only the biblical stories that were told to
me again and again, year after year; only the biblical stories that I soon began to study line by line, delving deeper
and deeper into the characters and parsing each God-
given phrase as if it held the meaning of everything. While
the boys moved on to Talmud, we girls remained right
where we had started, in Genesis and Exodus, with brief,
sketchy forays into Joshua, Judges, Samuel, and Kings.
The gendered curriculum was an affront to my feminist
mother, who wanted my mind to be challenged by the rig-

ors of Talmudic thought, but I couldn't have been happier. Why would I want to spend my days wondering who should pay for a gored ox, when I could instead explore the mystery of what it had felt like to be Leah, living in the shadow of lovely Rachel?

People tell me that it's remarkable to feel intimate with something as august as the Bible, but I can't even manage to think of those familiar pages as august. Those pages are family. I grew up *inside* of them. I measured my maturation through my understanding of them, because the more I learned about life, the deeper I could delve into the elliptical phrases of that sonorous, all-knowing, but not at all all-telling narrator; subtle tensions became apparent where none had been before, pathos turned up in unexpected places, villains suddenly aroused my sympathy and heroes my suspicion.

Home from a miserable summer at camp, having known loneliness and homesickness for the first time, shadowy Rebecca, stealing from one son to give to the other, suddenly jumped off the page at me: I sensed her deep isolation so far away from her family in Haran, living among the barbarians of Canaan. I sensed her clinging to her son Jacob, with his nice, soft ways, his civility, as the only thing in that wild land that signified home, and the painful alienation she must have felt from his twin Essau, symbol of all that had gone wrong in her life: her own flesh and blood had become a wild, barbaric man, a native of that alien land and not really her own. Was she supposed to suffer silently and in isolation forever because of just one mistake at a well? she would have wondered as she plotted her anguished betrayal.

Of course, the inverse was also true: that the more I studied the stories, the more I came to understand about life. Going over these plot lines again and again, each time with a teacher who wanted us to read them differently from the last, I began to get the sense of just how multilayered and complex even the most seemingly straightforward situation can be. The *pshat*—the simple story (as opposed to the moral lessons we were supposed to read in, or the bizarre midrashim that attempted to fill in the Bible's backstory)—was always presented as a challenge, not a given. And learning our moral lessons by putting ourselves day after day in the sandals of these ancient people and agonizing over their intentions, their choices, their sins, and their foibles meant that the moral principles my classmates and I soaked up were all deeply tinged, first and foremost, by empathy.

I think it's fair to say that even then—at a time when I believed fully in a God who cared about the state of my soul, and believed moreover that my soul's state depended heavily on following arcane and obscure rules of conduct, such as waiting six hours between meat and dairy meals— that the sacred, for me, remained synonymous with the divine narrator and His stories. The highly ritualized life felt forced and impersonal, prayer fell flat on my ears. But I loved God, and I wanted to do what was right in His eyes, because He was the narrator of the stories I lived in.

Perhaps, given that the Bible *was* my faith, it was inevitable that the Bible would ultimately be the thing to challenge it. In fact, this happened very early on. In third grade we added a new subject to our mornings. In addition to studying Humash (the five books of Moses) we began to study Navi (the latter Deuteronomic histories, plus the prophecies). We began at the beginning, which meant with the book of Joshua and the brutal conquest of Canaan by the Israelites. Reading Joshua was much like learning that the beloved grandparent who bounced you on his knee stuck that same knee in thousands of unsuspecting groins. Gone was God the protector, the teacher, the vanquisher of evil, the occasionally peevish. In his place was God the bloodthirsty. As the warrior Jews made their way through their promised land, God had one simple rule for them: kill every living thing. Every man, woman, and child. Every animal. I thought at first that this was a test, much like God's test of Abraham at Moriah: just as God didn't really want Abraham to kill his son Isaac, He didn't really want the Jews to kill newborn babies. But it was no test. Failure to fully comply brought on His wrath.

I was devastated by the account, naturally, and asked my teacher how this mayhem could be God's desire. My teacher was a bewigged eighteen-year-old in her ninth month of pregnancy who had no time for moral subtleties. (The boys were taught by rabbis, and we were taught by their young wives. Sometimes these young wives were very intelligent and effective teachers, but this one was not.) With a sigh of impatience she explained that every single person inhabiting Canaan when the Israelites invaded was evil. Even the newborn babies were evil. They were born evil. Something struck me as odd about this, but being in third grade I couldn't quite put my finger on the problem of free will and moral determinism. Instead of an objection, I found an image that wouldn't leave me alone: I saw myself standing in ill-fated Jericho, watching in awestruck horror as Joshua's army lifted up their voices in a shout and brought the walls down with the sound of God's name. I'd love to say that it was because of this moral revulsion that I began to feel alienated from my faith, but it wasn't really. I was angry at God for His surprisingly inhumane ways, and I was ashamed. But I still loved Him.

It was because of an altogether amoral slip-up that I
began to doubt the reliability of my favorite narrator. In
my freshman year of high school we studied Deuteron-
omy for the second or third time. As we read through
Moses's final blessings of the twelve tribes before his
death, a line suddenly struck me: "Of Reuben he said, May
Reuben live and not die out, but may he be few in number." What kind of crazy blessing was this, I wondered? I
wondered for days before it began to dawn on me that this
was not a deathbed blessing at all, but a politicohistorical
piece of writing, composed at a time when the tribe of
Reuben seemed poised to vanish (a time considerably
later, necessarily, than the portrayed scene suggested). I
was devastated by this realization because until then I had
believed that the Bible was dictated by God to Moses in
the desert and had remained unaltered since that time.
Perhaps if I had been raised as a Conservative Jew or a
Reform Jew or any sort of Jew other than Orthodox, my
faith would not have been rocked by the discovery of this
blatantly late and blatantly political piece of writing within
a sacred text. But I was raised Orthodox and had no idea
that one could believe in Judaism without believing that
God had written the Torah through Moses. I had been
raised thinking that these books were so sacred that you
had to kiss them every time you closed them, that you
could never place another object on top of them (there
was even an order in which they had to be placed on top of
each other), that if you dropped one on the ground you
had to do penance. I was in no position, therefore, to
calmly accept that they were anything other than infallible
and perfectly honest.

And yet once I suspected they weren't, I needed to
know. Painful as this was, I began to gather the evidence to
prove that my hunch was right: that the entire Hebrew

Bible was nothing but a motley collection of an ancient people's writings. I went to the library and read about the naturalized theories of biblical authorship, about how Israel had sprung up from the Canaanite tribes and how their practices (still my practices) reflected their pagan origin; how the politically motivated rules of a struggling new people (don't eat pig because the seductive Philistines love it; don't eat milk and meat together because a kid cooked in its mother's milk is the ritual food of a certain cultic practice) had become the supposedly God-given rules I'd been living by.

On a Sabbath afternoon not long after I began these treacherous researches, I decided to confide in my mother, who had always been (and still is) my chief sounding board and adviser. As we strolled through the local park, I poured out my doubts to her, but rather than greet them with a stricken look, her face was calm and encouraging, as if she'd been waiting a long time to hear me voice these thoughts. As it turned out, she had been, having come to them herself decades earlier. I think a part of me knew this all along. In fact, during my first crisis of faith, the one in the third grade, when I asked my mother what she made of God's immoral dicta, and she looked at me quite seriously and said, "Do you really want to know what I think?" I must have already suspected strongly, because my response then was a hasty "Not yet." As I seem to have understood even back then, tacitly knowing and explicitly hearing are worlds apart, and that Sabbath afternoon, learning that my mother only went through the motions of belief for my sake and the sake of her other Orthodox family members, I felt the last vestiges of belief slip away from me.

Being an adolescent, there must have been a brief period when I felt angry and resentful to be so brusquely defaithed, but what I remember feeling is emptied and abandoned. The worst of it was that I began to feel alienated from the stories I loved. I bided my time until I could escape to college and leave the unsacred texts behind.

The only problem was that I couldn't leave them behind. I tried very hard to create a new mental family for myself at college, one based on rational, objective choice rather than blind faith and the accidents of my birth. (Although I've often wondered, with a physicist father and a philosopher mother, were these purely intellectual affiliations any less the accidents of my birth?) My new Adam was supposed to be Thales, the world's first scientist, my Abraham Socrates, my Moses Descartes. But when I read Plato, I found my thoughts wandering eastward, wondering what was going on in Judaea while Plato contemplated the Forms; when I read Hobbes I thought of the anarchy that had reigned in Israel in the years before kingship. Each time my mind presented me with one of these old familiar stories I welcomed it with an acute sense of loss: *that one was mine too,* I'd think, and rather than pursue whatever thought I'd meant to think (what *was* happening in Judaea at the time of Plato?) I pushed it away.

At the beginning of this essay I made a point of distinguishing between the writerly Jew and the Jewish writer, and I still want to hold that distinction firmly in place. But these very distinct qualities can easily come together in one person—in fact, I'd be willing to bet the confluence is common—and, in my case, I think the worst thing about losing my writerly Jewish faith was the way it affected me as a Jewish writer. As my favorite works of literature, the stories of the Bible had always functioned as the standard of depth and largeness I longed to reach when I wrote. They were my Platonic Form of narrative excellence, and they hovered in the back of my mind from the moment I struck on an idea until the moment I tweaked the final word. Now, since I was dead set on avoiding any thoughts about the Bible, I had to avoid writing fiction as well. Not writing fiction wasn't nearly as big a sacrifice then as it would be now, when it's pretty much all I do with my time, but it was not exactly pleasant to stifle my ideas. Eventually I started to do something even worse than not write at all: I started to write *wrong*. I seized on plots and themes and settings that could not possibly use the Bible as their archetype: small stories of modern, everyday life, heavy on close observations of manner, light on heady, tangled drama. For a girl whose great young passions were the Bible, the Olympians, and Cinderella, this was not a fruitful genre. My stories were consistently terrible, and writing them was never satisfying. I was aching to do something grander, messier, and more *me*, but the pain of my loss always threatened from the sidelines.

I think it's fair to say that I would have had to choose another career path if my alienation from the Bible had persisted. (Whether this inevitability would have been entirely bad remains to be seen.) As it happened, though, my irreligiosity slowly ceased to function as a positive part of my identity, and became a simple absence, and somewhere in this transformation my favorite stories were given back to me. Surely, this all must have happened gradually, but I became aware of the change quite suddenly. One day in lecture a professor made a passing reference to the prophecies of Jeremiah. Warily and wearily, I went through the mental translation in my head—*Who is that? What would that sound like in Hebrew or Aramaic? Oh yes, Yirmiyahu.* I was certain that once I'd hit on the old familiar name in the old familiar language hovering in the

Godless air, I'd feel the typical sadness, desolation, vulnerability. But I didn't. In fact, I felt happy to roll the sounds
over in my mind: Yir-mi-ya-hu. It was like catching the
whiff of home cooking after years abroad.

Afterward I rushed back to my dorm room and
straight to the bookshelf, where all the old, sacred books
languished, unopened, between well-thumbed Homer
and Hume. (I always kept them between Homer and
Hume from room change to room change, my old
favorites surrounded by my new ones.) I opened them one
after the other, looking lovingly at their weathered, geo-
metrically fascinating pages—the archaic Hebrew swal-
lowing the archaic English hovering above the pithy
commentary of the medieval exegete Rashi. I became lost
in Jeremiah's prophecies of doom, then in Absalom's
treachery against his father, David, then in Leah living in
the shadow of the lovely Rachel. I hopped from favorite to
favorite all afternoon, and when I finally emerged it was
with the realization that I had never been abandoned. I
found myself kissing the leather covers, the way I'd done
back when I believed that they were alive with the spirit of
divine authorship, and that night I scribbled out a convo-
luted, biblical sort of story that was not particularly good
but was absolutely mine.

With or without divine inspiration, I learned that
afternoon Jeremiah was still calling out his dire predic-
tions. David was still forging a kingdom out of an unruly
confederation, Jonathan still torn between his father and
his dearest friend, Saul still driven mad by insecurity,
and Abraham still following an idea into the unknown.
And there was a God, a sonorous, all-knowing, fierce and
unpredictable old grandfather narrating the stories I
loved.

ABOUT THE CONTRIBUTORS

Pearl Abraham was born in Jerusalem in 1960. She is the author of three novels, *The Romance Reader* (1995), *Giving Up America* (1998), and *The Seventh Beggar* (2005). Recent stories and essays have appeared in the *Michigan Quarterly*, the *Forward*, *Dog Culture: Writers on the Character of Canines*, and *Brooklyn Noir*. She lives in New York City.

Max Apple was born in Grand Rapids, Michigan, in 1941. He is the author of two novels, *Zip* (1978) and *Propheteers* (1987); two short-story collections, *The Oranging of America* (1976) and *Free Agents* (1984); and the memoirs *Roommates* (1994) and *I Love Gootie* (1998). He has been awarded fellowships from the National Endowment for the Arts, the National Endowment for the Humanities, and the Guggenheim Foundation. His stories and essays have been published in *Esquire*, *The Atlantic Monthly*, *The New York Times*, and elsewhere. He lives near Philadelphia and teaches at the University of Pennsylvania.

Saul Bellow was born in Lachine, Quebec, in 1915 and moved with his family to the United States when he was nine years old. He is the author of fourteen novels and numerous novellas and stories. He is the only novelist to receive three National Book Awards, for *The Adventures of Augie March*, *Herzog*, and *Mr. Sammler's Planet*. In 1975 he won the Pulitzer Prize for his novel *Humboldt's Gift*. He was awarded the Nobel Prize for Literature in 1976 "for the human understanding and subtle analysis of contemporary culture that are combined in his work." He lives in New England.

Melvin Jules Bukiet was born in New York City in 1953. He is the author of seven books, most recently *Strange Fire* and *A Faker's*

Dozen, and the editor of two anthologies, most recently *Nothing Makes You Free*. His work has been frequently anthologized and translated into nine languages. He still lives in and will never live anyplace other than New York, where bad things never happen.

Robert Cohen was born in New York in 1957. He is the author of three novels, *Inspired Sleep*, *The Here and Now*, and *The Organ Builder*, as well as a collection of short stories, *The Varieties of Romantic Experience*. His literary honors include a Guggenheim Fellowship, a Whiting Writer's Award, and a Lila Wallace–Reader's Digest Writer's Award. He teaches at Middlebury College in Vermont, where he lives with his wife and children.

E. L. Doctorow was born in New York in 1931. His novels include *Welcome to Hard Times*, *The Book of Daniel*, *Ragtime*, *Loon Lake*, *World's Fair*, *Billy Bathgate*, *The Waterworks*, and *City of God*. He has published two collections of short fiction, *Lives of the Poets* and, in 2004, *Sweet Land Stories*. His selected essays are published under the title *Jack London, Hemingway, and the Constitution*. His play, *Drinks Before Dinner*, was produced by the New York Shakespeare Festival. Among Mr. Doctorow's honors are the National Book Award, two National Book Critics Circle Awards, the PEN/Faulkner Award, the William Dean Howells Medal of the American Academy of Arts and Letters, and the presidentially conferred National Humanities Medal.

Leslie Epstein was born into a film family (his father and uncle wrote, among fifty others, *Arsenic and Old Lace*, *Yankee Doodle Dandy*, and *Casablanca*) in Los Angeles in 1938. He is the author of nine novels, including *King of the Jews*, *Goldkorn Tales*, *Pinto and Sons*, *Pandaemonium*, and *San Remo Drive*. He has received a Rhodes Scholarship and Guggenheim and Fulbright Fellowships, as well as an Award for Distinction in Literature from the American Academy and Institute of Arts and Letters. For the many years that he has directed the Creative Writing Program at Boston University, he has lived with his wife, Ilene, in Brookline, Massachusetts. His children are Paul, Anya, and Theo.

Rebecca Goldstein was born in White Plains, New York, in 1950. She has a Ph.D. in philosophy from Princeton, and has taught at Barnard, Rutgers, and Columbia. She is currently professor of philosophy at Trinity College. She is the author of five novels (*The Mind-Body Problem, The Late-Summer Passion of a Woman of Mind, The Dark Sister, Mazel,* and *Properties of Light*) and a collection of stories (*Strange Attractors*). She is also the author of *Incompleteness: The Proof and Paradox of Kurt Gödel* and is currently working on a book entitled *Betraying Spinoza: The Philosopher and the Jews.* Among her honors are two Whiting Foundation Awards (one in philosophy, one in writing), two National Jewish Book Awards, the Edward Lewis Wallant Award, and the Prairie Schooner Best Short Story Award. In 1996 she was named a MacArthur Foundation Fellow.

Yael Goldstein was born in New Brunswick, New Jersey, in 1978. Her stories and essays have appeared in *Commentary, Sh'Ma,* and *Beginning Anew: A Woman's Guide to the High Holy Days,* among other places. She lives in Princeton, New Jersey.

Allegra Goodman was born in Brooklyn in 1967. She is the author of two collections of stories, *Total Immersion* and *The Family Markowitz;* and two novels, *Kaaterskill Falls,* which was a finalist for the National Book Award, and *Paradise Park.* Her work has appeared in *The New Yorker, The American Scholar, Commentary,* and in many other magazines and anthologies. She is the recipient of the Award for Achievement in Literary Arts from the National Foundation for Jewish Culture, and has been named by *The New Yorker* as one of America's "Best Writers Under Forty." Her new novel, *Intuition,* will be published in 2006. She lives with her family in Cambridge, Massachusetts.

Dara Horn was born in New Jersey in 1977. She is the author of the novel *In the Image* (2002), which received a 2003 National Jewish Book Award, the 2003 Reform Judaism Prize for Jewish Fiction, and the 2002 Edward Lewis Wallant Award. Her second novel, *The World to Come,* will be published by W. W. Norton in September of

2005. A doctoral candidate at Harvard University in Hebrew and Yiddish literature, she lives with her husband in New York City.

Erica Mann Jong was born in New York in 1942 and is both a poet and a novelist. Her first novel, *Fear of Flying* (1973), sold twenty million copies around the world. Despite that, she went on to write seven more novels, six books of poetry, and many works of nonfiction. She has been awarded the Woodhull Institute Prize for Ethical Leadership, the United Nations Award for Excellence in Literature, the Hokin Prize from *Poetry* magazine, and many other awards. She currently lives in New York City and Weston, Connecticut.

Rachel Kadish was born in the Bronx in 1969. She is the author of the novel *From a Sealed Room* and the forthcoming novel *Love* [*sic*]. Her short stories and essays have appeared in *Zoetrope*, *Story*, *Bomb*, and *Tin House*, and have been reprinted in the *Pushcart Prize Anthology* and elsewhere. Her awards include fellowships from the National Endowment for the Arts, the Bunting Institute, and the Koret Foundation. She lives outside Boston with her husband and daughter.

Johanna Kaplan was born in New York in 1942. She is the author of *Other People's Lives* (1975), a collection of stories, and *O My America!* (1980), a novel. Her books were finalists for the National Book Award, the American Book Award, and the Hemingway Foundation/PEN Award, and she has twice received the National Jewish Book Award for Fiction, as well as the Edward Lewis Wallant Award and the Kenneth B. Smilen–Present Tense Literary Award. Her stories, essays, and reviews have appeared in *Commentary*, *Harper's*, *Moment*, *The New York Times Book Review*, and *The City Journal*, and her stories have been widely anthologized. She lives in Manhattan, where for more than three decades she worked as a teacher of emotionally disturbed children at Mt. Sinai Hospital.

Binnie Kirshenbaum was born in Yonkers, New York, in 1959. She is the author of five novels, including *A Disturbance in One Place*, *Hester Among the Ruins*, and *An Almost Perfect Moment*, and two story collections, *Married Life* and *History on a Personal Note*. Among other distinctions, she has twice received the Critics' Choice Award and has been nominated for the National Jewish Book Award. A professor at Columbia University Graduate School of the Arts, she lives with her husband in New York City.

Alan Lelchuk was born in Brooklyn in 1938. He is the author of *American Mischief* (1973), *Miriam at Thirty-Four* (1974), *Shrinking* (1978), *Miriam in Her Forties* (1985), *Brooklyn Boy* (1990), *Playing the Game* (1995), and *Ziff: A Life?* (2003). He has also written *On Home Ground* (1987) for young adults and is the editor of *8 Great Short Hebrew Novels.* He has received Guggenheim and Fulbright Fellowships at Haifa University in Israel and International University in Moscow, and has also been the Otto Salgo Professor of American Writing and Letters at Eötvös Loránd University in Budapest, Hungary. He teaches at Dartmouth College and lives in Canaan, New Hampshire, with his wife and two sons.

Tova Mirvis was born in Bethesda, Maryland, in 1972, and grew up in Memphis, Tennessee. She is the author of two novels, *The Ladies Auxiliary*, published by Norton in 1999, and *The Outside World*, published by Knopf in 2004. She now lives in Newton, Massachusetts, with her husband and two sons.

Cynthia Ozick was born in New York City in 1928. A novelist, essayist, and playwright, she has won, among other awards, four O. Henry First Prizes for her short stories and a Lannan Foundation Award for her fiction. Her most recent essay collection, *Quarrel & Quandary*, won the 2001 National Book Critics Circle Award, and her novel *The Puttermesser Papers* was named one of the top ten books of 1997 and was a National Book Award finalist. Her work has been published in thirteen languages. Her most recent novel, *Heir to the Glimmering World*, was published in 2004. She lives in Westchester County, New York.

Grace Paley was born to Russian-Jewish immigrant parents in the Bronx in 1922. She has published three collections of short stories, *The Little Disturbances of Man*, *Great Changes at the Last Minute*, and *Later the Same Day*, which together form *The Collected Stories*. Other

About the Contributors

books by her are *New and Collected Poems, Begin Again: Collected Poems, Just as I Thought* (essays and reports), and *Long Walks and Intimate Talks*, with paintings by Vera B. Williams. She lives with her husband, Robert Nichols, in Thetford Hill, Vermont.

Chaim Potok was born in New York City in 1929. He began to write fiction at the age of sixteen, graduated summa cum laude with a B.A. in English literature from Yeshiva University, and earned a Ph.D. in philosophy from the University of Pennsylvania. An ordained rabbi, he served as an army chaplain in Korea for sixteen months, with, successively, a frontline medical battalion and an engineer combat battalion. His first novel, *The Chosen*, was nominated for the National Book Award and received the Edward Lewis Wallant Award. His other novels include *My Name Is Asher Lev, The Gift of Asher Lev* (winner of the National Jewish Book Award), *I Am the Clay*, and a collection of stories about young adults entitled *Zebra*. Potok died in 2002.

Lev Raphael was born in New York City in 1954. He is the author of *Dancing on Tisha B'Av, Winter Eyes, The German Money*, and twelve other books. His award-winning, widely anthologized fiction and essays are taught in universities around the world. He lives in Okemos, Michigan, with his partner of twenty years and two West Highland White Terriers.

Nessa Rapoport was born in Toronto, Canada, in 1953. She moved to New York City in 1974. She is the author of a novel, *Preparing for Sabbath;* a collection of prose poems, *A Woman's Book of Grieving;* and a memoir of family and place, *House on the River: A Summer Journey*, which was awarded a grant by the Canada Council for the Arts. With Ted Solotaroff she edited *The Schocken Book of Contemporary Jewish Fiction*. "Body of Love" draws on essays published in the *Los Angeles Times Book Review, Re://collections*, and *The Jewish Week;* and on writing in *House on the River, Objects of the Spirit, The Schocken Book of Contemporary Jewish Fiction*, and *The Writer in the Jewish Community*.

Jonathan Rosen was born in New York City in 1963. He is the author of the novel *Eve's Apple* and the nonfiction book *The Talmud and the Internet: A Journey Between Worlds*, which was a *New York Times* Notable Book of the Year. His most recent novel is *Joy Comes in the Morning*. His essays have appeared in *The New Yorker*, *The New York Times Magazine*, *The American Scholar*, and several anthologies. He lives in New York City with his wife and two daughters.

Thane Rosenbaum was born in New York City in 1960. He is a novelist, essayist, and law professor. His novels include *The Golems of Gotham* (2002) (*San Francisco Chronicle* Top 100 Book); *Second Hand Smoke*, which was a finalist for the National Jewish Book Award in 1999; and the novel-in-stories *Elijah Visible*, which received the Edward Lewis Wallant Award in 1996 for the best book of Jewish American fiction. His articles, reviews, and essays appear frequently in *The New York Times*, *Los Angeles Times*, *The Wall Street Journal*, and *The Washington Post*, among other national publications. He teaches human rights, legal humanities, and law and literature at Fordham Law School. He is also the author of *The Myth of Moral Justice: Why Our Legal System Fails to Do What's Right*. He lives in New York City with his daughter, Basia Tess.

Philip Roth was born in Newark, New Jersey, in 1933. He has published more than twenty-five books, beginning with *Goodbye, Columbus* in 1959. In 1997 he won the Pulitzer Prize for *American Pastoral*. In 1998 he received the National Medal of Arts at the White House, and in 2002 received the highest award of the American Academy of Arts and Letters, the Gold Medal in Fiction, previously awarded to John Dos Passos, William Faulkner, and Saul Bellow, among others. He has twice won the National Book Award, the PEN/Faulkner Award, and the National Book Critics Circle Award. In 2005 Philip Roth will become the third living American writer to have his work published in a comprehensive, definitive edition by the Library of America. The last of the eight volumes is scheduled for publication in 2013.

Art Spiegelman was born in Stockholm, Sweden, in 1948. His family moved to the United States when he was three years old. He began cartooning professionally at age sixteen. In 1980 he founded *RAW,* the acclaimed avant-garde comics magazine, with his wife Françoise Mouly. His work has since been published in many periodicals, including *The New Yorker,* where he was a staff artist and writer from 1993 to 2003. He is the author of *Maus* (1986) and *Maus II* (1991), for which he was awarded a Special Pulitzer Prize. His most recent work is *In the Shadow of No Towers* (2004). He lives in Lower Manhattan with his wife and their two children, Nadja and Dashiell.

Steve Stern was born in Memphis, Tennessee, in 1947. He is the author of several works of fiction, including *Lazar Malkin Enters Heaven,* which won the Edward Lewis Wallant Award for Jewish American Fiction in 1988, and *The Wedding Jester,* which received the National Jewish Book Award in 2000. He lives in Saratoga Springs, New York, where he is a professor of literature and creative writing at Skidmore College.

Lara Vapnyar was born in Moscow in 1971. She emigrated to the United States in 1994. She is the author of the story collection *There Are Jews in My House,* which received the National Foundation of Jewish Culture Award. Her short stories have appeared in *The New Yorker* and *Zoetrope.* She lives in Staten Island, New York, with her husband and two children.

Jonathan Wilson was born in London in 1950. He has lived in the United States since 1976 with a four-year interlude in Jerusalem. He is the author of two novels, *The Hiding Room* and *A Palestine Affair;* two books of stories, *Schoom* and *An Ambulance Is on the Way: Stories of Men in Trouble;* and two critical works on the novels of Saul Bellow. His short fiction, essays, and articles have appeared in *The New Yorker, The New York Times Magazine, Ploughshares, Tikkun,* the *Forward,* and numerous journals and anthologies including *Best American Short Stories.* In 1994 he was awarded a Guggenheim Foundation fellowship in fiction. He lives in Newton, Massachusetts, with his wife and two sons.

ACKNOWLEDGMENTS

An anthology like this can come about only with the help and cooperation of many people. I consider myself truly lucky to have been blessed with the generosity and kindness of colleagues, friends, family, and others who helped at every step of the way not only to make this book possible but also to make working on it a joyous and gratifying experience. There are so many people I am indebted to that I hope I'll be forgiven for mentioning only those most directly involved.

My heartfelt thanks to the writers whose essays appear in this anthology; without them this book would simply not have existed. I remain deeply moved by their willingness to embark on this journey with me. I am particularly indebted to Melvin Jules Bukiet and Thane Rosenbaum, who from the beginning of this project helped in more ways than I can list here.

The people I worked with on this anthology at Schocken Books and Random House were wonderful: always helpful and friendly, and eminently efficient and reliable. I am especially grateful to Altie Karper, editorial director of Schocken Books, for making this book happen and for putting up with my greenhorn ways in what to me was the New World of commercial publishing. I am equally grateful to Ilana Kurshan, my editor at Schocken Books. With wisdom and knowledge way beyond her years, Ilana tirelessly worked to turn this anthology into a coherent book, one far better than I would ever have dreamed it could become. Many thanks also to Rahel Lerner, who took over from Ilana Kurshan late in the day and so skillfully helped to oversee the final stages of publication.

The Research Institute for Culture and History at Utrecht University supported this project generously by enabling me to take time off from teaching during the final, time-consuming stages of completing the editorial work for this book. I consider it a privilege to be part of an institute that takes such a broad-minded view of what constitutes scholarly work. It is also a true pleasure to work with Jaap Verheul in the American Studies Program at Utrecht University; I am particularly thankful for his support while I was working on this book.

Very special thanks go to my lifelong friend Shimon Schocken, who made the *shidduch* between Schocken Books and me at an early stage of this project. Thanks also to Beth and David Tabatznik and to Helen Nissenbaum and Peter Sarnak for the terrific places to stay in Manhattan; their hospitality enabled me to do important work on this book. I am greatly indebted to Willem-Jan Goudsblom, who repeatedly prevented this project from coming to a standstill by magically fixing my computer whenever something went wrong.

I am eternally thankful to my brother Alan, who for almost thirty years has helped me to bridge the distance between the United States and the Netherlands by responding with enthusiasm to my passion for Jewish American literature and supplying me with an endless flow of books, articles, and reviews from the *Goldene Medine*.

And, finally, thanks beyond words to my wife, Marijke—for everything.

D.R.

PERMISSIONS
ACKNOWLEDGMENTS

Grateful acknowledgment is made to the following for permission
to reprint previously published material:

Max Apple: "Max and Mottele" by Max Apple from *Pakn
Treger.* Copyright © by Max Apple. Reprinted by permission of the
author.

Farrar, Straus and Giroux, LLC.: "Writing About Jews" from
Reading Myself and Others by Philip Roth. Copyright © 1969, 1975
by Philip Roth. Reprinted by permission of Farrar, Straus and
Giroux, LLC.

Rebecca Goldstein: "Against Logic" by Rebecca Gold-
stein. Originally appeared in slightly different form in *Tikkun*
(November–December 1997). Copyright © by Rebecca Goldstein.
Reprinted by permission of the author.

Allegra Goodman: "Writing with a Return Address" by Allegra Goodman. Copyright © by Allegra Goodman. Originally
appeared as "Writing Jewish Fiction In and Out of the Multicultural Context" in *Daughters of Valor: Contemporary Jewish American
Women Writers* edited by Jay L. Halio and Ben Siegel (1997).
Reprinted by permission of the author.

International Creative Management, Inc.: "Deism" from
Reporting the Universe by E. L. Doctorow. Copyright © 2003 by
E. L. Doctorow. Reprinted by permission of International Creative
Management, Inc.

Erica Jong: "How I Got to Be Jewish" by Erica Jong, copyright © by Erica Jong, from *American Identities: Contemporary Multicultural Voices* edited by Robert Pack and Jay Parini (1994).
Reprinted by permission of the author.

Johanna Kaplan: "Tales of My Great-Grandfathers" by
Johanna Kaplan. Originally appeared in slightly different form in
Commentary (July–August 2000). Copyright © by Johanna Kaplan.
Reprinted by permission of the author.

ABOUT THE EDITOR

DEREK RUBIN was born in South Africa in 1954, grew up in Israel, and has lived in the Netherlands since 1976. He teaches in the American Studies Program at Utrecht University, and from 2001 to 2004 he was coordinator of Scenarios for the Humanities, a program in the Research Institute for Culture and History of the Faculty of Arts at Utrecht University. He has taught American literature at various universities in the Netherlands and, as a Fulbright scholar, at the State University of New York at New Paltz. Rubin has lectured widely in the Netherlands and in the United States, at Princeton, UCLA, and the University of New Hampshire, among other universities. He has published articles about Saul Bellow, Philip Roth, Paul Auster, and the younger generation of Jewish American fiction writers. He is also the coeditor of a collection of essays entitled *Religion in America: European and American Perspectives* (2004).

A NOTE ON THE TYPE

This book was set in Janson, a typeface long thought to have been
made by the Dutchman Anton Janson, who was a practicing typefounder in Leipzig during the years 1668–1687. However, it has
been conclusively demonstrated that these types are actually the
work of Nicholas Kis (1650–1702), a Hungarian, who most probably learned his trade from the master Dutch typefounder Kirk
Voskens. The type is an excellent example of the influential and
sturdy Dutch types that prevailed in England up to the time William
Caslon (1692–1766) developed his own incomparable designs from
them.

Composed by North Market Street Graphics
Lancaster, Pennsylvania

Printed and bound by Berryville Graphics
Berryville, Virginia

Book design by Pamela G. Parker